APPLYING PSYCHOLOGY

to the environment

SUSAN CAVE

Series Editor: **ROB McILVEEN**

Hodder & Stoughton

A MEMBER OF THE HODDER HEADLINE GROUP

DEDICATION

To Leigh. Don't ever doubt it.

Order: please contact Bookpoint Ltd, 39 Milton Park, Abingdon, Oxon OX14 4TD.
Telephone: (44) 01235 400414, Fax: (44) 01235 400454. Lines are open from 9.00 - 6.00, Monday to
Saturday, with a 24 hour message answering service. Email address: orders@bookpoint.co.uk

British Library Cataloguing in Publication Data
A catalogue record for this title is available from The British Library

ISBN 0 340 647574

First published 1998
Impression number   10 9 8 7 6 5 4 3 2
Year   2004 2003 2002 2001 2000

Typeset by Transet Ltd, Coventry, England.
Printed in Great Britain for Hodder & Stoughton Educational, a division of Hodder Headline Plc,
338 Euston Road, London NW1 3BH by Redwood Books, Trowbridge, Wiltshire

CONTENTS

Preface   v

Acknowledgements   vi

Chapter One: What is Environmental Psychology   1

What does environmental psychology deal with? The development of
environmental psychology; major areas of research; methods used by
environmental psychologists; characteristics and assumptions of
environmental psychology; people and the environment: a general model

Chapter Two: Environmental Cognition   18

Environmental perception; spatial cognition; environmental appraisal
Focus on application ... cognitive maps

Chapter Three: The Physical Environment   44

Noise; temperature; light; air quality; environmental toxins;
environmental load
Focus on application ... sick building syndrome

Chapter Four: The Social Environment   67

Personal space; territory; privacy; crowding and density
Focus on application ... institutions and crime

Chapter Five: The Built Environment   92

Implications for designers; design of rooms; residential environments; work
environments; institutions; neighbourhoods and communities; cities
Focus on application ... high-rise flats

Chapter Six: The Natural Environment   115

Attitudes to nature and their determinants; environmental preferences and
their origins; applications to outdoor recreation; applications to travel
Focus on application ... greenlock

Chapter Seven: The Environment and Stress   137

The nature of stress; types of environmental stressor; measurement of
stressor and stress response; ambient stressors and their effects; practical
applications; cataclysmic stressors; extreme environments; theories of
stress
Focus on application ... post-traumatic stress disorder

Chapter Eight: How People Affect the Environment 170

Environmental problems; role of environmental psychology; perception of environmental damage; the commons and the social trap; strategies for intervention; practical applications; implications
Focus on application ... increasing recycling behaviours

Chapter Nine: Future Applications 203

References 206

Index 235

Picture Credits 247

PREFACE

It has always been a great source of concern to me personally that so few links have been made between psychology and the environment. In America, there has been a great deal of research and some major text books have resulted, but in the UK it has proved difficult to arouse much interest. Now that the area is finally being recognised by being incorporated into some 'A' level and GCSE syllabuses, it is to be hoped that interest will finally be kindled in a subject which most urgently requires our attention. This statement can be justified on a number of levels. First, we cannot exist without the environment and all that it provides; second, we need to make use of it in more carefully considered ways if we are not to damage it further and third, as the effects of our behaviour begin to feed back to us, it is becoming clear that we must also change the way that we operate for our own safety. We are inseparably interlinked with the environment, and therefore we need to consider and control our behaviour carefully if we are to avoid repercussions. This is not just an exhortation to be 'green' – it is a plea to incorporate our psychological knowledge into the way that we approach such issues; to use psychology to think, research, plan, intervene and, hopefully, to enjoy the environment more fully.

The book is divided into nine chapters. As this will be a new subject to many readers, the first chapter is an introduction to the field. Chapters 2–7 focus on the effects that the environment has on people and Chapter 8 emphasises the feedback process mentioned above by looking at the effects that people have on the environment. Chapter 9 concludes by considering key areas that may warrant the attention of psychologists in the future.

There is plenty of material here for both introductory and intermediate readers to pursue; and hopefully what is provided will stimulate further interest in this crucial area of psychology and, even more importantly, in its application. The book has developed out of my passion for psychology and for the environment; I sincerely hope that it provokes the same feelings in others. I can think of no other area of application where psychology has more to offer or more to lose.

ACKNOWLEDGEMENTS

Many thanks to all those people who have spurred me into action and without whom this would still be a fantasy, particularly to Rob for his unquenchable enthusiasm; to Tim at Hodder for his gentle prompts and to Phil Banyard for his apt and insightful suggestions. Thanks also to those who have endured my absorption and made space and time for me to work; to my parents, to Leigh, Bob and Beryl and of course, the ever-supportive Charlie. I couldn't have done it without you all!

chapter one

CHAPTER OVERVIEW

In this chapter we will start by defining the subject matter of environmental psychology and look at the way that it has developed from both mainstream psychology and other disciplines. The major areas of research will be outlined, together with the methods used by environmental psychologists. Finally, the characteristics and assumptions of environmental psychology and a general model of the interaction between people and their environment will be presented.

WHAT DOES ENVIRONMENTAL PSYCHOLOGY DEAL WITH?

Wherever we are and whatever we are doing, our behaviour is influenced by some aspect of the environment that we are in at the time, whether it is the buildings, the scenery or the people we are with. These influences can be so powerful that they can completely change the way we behave. Consider, for example, the dramatic changes that may occur when people move to a different environment, such as going away on holiday; people who are normally very active may choose to lie on the beach all day and others who are usually quiet and withdrawn may become nightclub addicts! This may be one reason why holiday romances rarely succeed. Changes are also initiated when the normal environment is disrupted by a major disaster, such as the outbreak of war or an earthquake. People who are normally in charge may 'go to pieces' and control may be assumed by others who are not usually assertive in nature. The other side of the coin is the way that we can affect our environment and it is this that is the concern of the current environmental movement. We can significantly improve our environment by creating conservation areas or buildings that are efficient and beautiful or we can cause massive destruction, through pollution, for example, or technological catastrophes such as Chernobyl.

As a distinct area of applied psychology, environmental psychology has been slow to gain recognition but it has grown in popularity recently because of the growth of the environmental or 'green' movement in society. It is still difficult to define because the term 'environment' refers to so many different things, including the natural environment, the built environment and the other people who inhabit these alongside us. As a guideline, we will take the definition of Stokols and Altman (1987), which states that it is 'the study of human behaviour and well-being in relation to the socio-physical environment'. This emphasises the fact that what we are dealing with here is a *relationship*, so that we influence the environment as well as the environment influencing us. An example of this relationship can be seen in areas of outstanding natural beauty which may attract so many visitors that they begin to deteriorate.

THE DEVELOPMENT OF ENVIRONMENTAL PSYCHOLOGY

Concern with environmental issues within psychology can be seen to have developed from research in two main areas, perception and social psychology, which we will discuss in turn.

Perception is the study of how we interpret stimulation received from the environment; in other words, it is how we make sense of the input received. How do we go about grouping visual input into distinct objects, so that we can identify them, for example? Even before the establishment of the first psychology laboratory by Wundt in 1879, the study of *psychophysics*, the relationship between physical stimuli and our experience of them, was under way. In 1834 Weber, a physiologist, was looking at our ability to notice changes in stimuli and he found that the more intense the stimulus is to begin with, the bigger the change must be before we will notice it. In a very quiet room, we may hear a pin drop, but we certainly will not notice the same increase in noise level at a rock concert! This tells us that what is taking place in the environment does not necessarily correspond with our experience of it. This is sometimes known as the 'inside–outside problem' (Allport, 1955).

When the Gestalt school (e.g. Koffka, 1935) became influential in the study of perception, the emphasis was shifted away from the environment to the study of internal mechanisms in the brain which help us to make sense of our sensations. It wasn't until Brunswik (1956) that the importance of the environment, or 'ecology' as he termed it, became recognised again as providing us with cues in the form of information which we can use to create more or less accurate representations of our environment. This idea was extended by Gibson (1960), who is well known to modern students of perception for his *ecological theory*, which emphasises the function of perception in enabling us to operate in an adaptive way in our environment. He makes the point that 'Stimuli must specify something beyond them, and they cannot be empty of meaning'. Another group of psychologists, called the transactionalists, argued that perception is an active process which is based on past experience, so our experience of particular environments will affect the way that we perceive what is presented to our senses. For example, Ames (1952) demonstrated that because people expect rooms to be rectangular, they will make incorrect judgements about the height of people who they see in distorted rooms, even to the extent of seeing twin sisters as being dramatically different in size (Figure 1.1(a)). Other researchers such as Segall et al. (1966) showed that people from different cultural backgrounds perceived visual illusion figures, such as the Müller–Lyer (Figure 1.1(b)), in different ways.

(a)

(b)

FIGURE 1.1 (a) *The Ames room. People generally assume that these two people differ in height, rather than seeing the room as distorted.* (b) *The Müller–Lyer illusion. The line with the outgoing fins appears to be longer*

As well as the study of perception, environmental psychology has grown out of work on social psychology, which is the study of the way that other people influence our behaviour. Lewin (1951) proposed that behaviour was a result of the interaction between the person and the environment, particularly the social environment. This can be seen in his famous statement 'In principle it is everywhere accepted that behaviour (B) is a function of the person (P) and the environment (E)'. He took this idea, called *psychological ecology*, to America, where it inspired several different groups of researchers to look at these issues. Hall (1959) explored the concept of personal space, which is the distance that we like to keep from others, and the way that this varies with culture, situation and the relationship between people; this was expanded by Sommer (1969) in his studies of the effects of invasion of personal space, and Calhoun (1962) developed research on the importance of space by looking at the effects of crowding on rats. The built environment also received much attention: Festinger et al. (1950) focused on the effects of housing design on the formation of friendships while Ittelson et al. (1970) carried out research into how the design of psychiatric wards could affect behaviour. An important development was the work done by Barker and Wright (1955), who set up 'field stations' in small towns in America and England for the purpose of understanding, through their observations, how the environment they live in influences the behaviour of children. They coined the term *ecological psychology* to describe their approach and carried out some influential work on the behavioural differences between children who attend large and small schools. In 1964 this was superseded by the term *environmental psychology*, which was introduced by Ittelson.

Influences outside psychology must also be mentioned. In the field of architecture, the work of Ittelson and Sommer had prompted the realisation that design had to take into account more than just the aesthetic qualities of the building; the needs and comfort of the users were also important. Town planners similarly came to realise that the layout of a town significantly affects the way that it is used by its occupants and the extent that it will attract people to live in it. In Britain, this led to the establishment of the Building Research Unit and the Building Performance Research Unit in 1967; the aim of these groups was to devise systems for evaluating the performance of buildings. In 1972 David Canter produced a manual on psychology specifically for architects.

Another discipline which has been influential is, not surprisingly, geography. Interest in the images that people have in their minds to represent their environments began in the 1940s and developed into the field of *behavioural geography*. This looks at the way that people not only influence, but are also influenced by their environment, as they perceive it. The final influence that we will mention here is the UNESCO Man and Biosphere programme (MAB) which was set up in the 1970s as a result of the increasing pressures on governments to deal with environmental problems. It is defined as an 'international programme of applied research on the interactions between man and his environment; source of scientific knowledge needed by decision-makers for managing natural resources' (UNESCO-MAB, 1988). This has emphasised the fact that planners and experts need detailed information about the way that the users of the environment function and in turn, the users need feedback about the effects of their behaviour.

Any proposals for solving environmental problems need to be firmly based, then, on psychological research if they are to be effective. It is to this research that we turn next.

MAJOR AREAS OF RESEARCH

We have already emphasised that the relationship between people and the environment is two-way; the environment affects our behaviour and our behaviour in turn affects the environment. The research that has been carried out can be divided into two groups, according to which of these processes it emphasises.

Effects of environments on behaviour

A wide range of different behaviours, emotions and moods can be influenced by a change of environment, whether that change is in the natural environment, the built environment or the social environment. Research has been carried out into the effects of physical aspects of the environment, such as noise, temperature, wind, light and air pollution, and their effects on task performance and mood. This will be discussed in Chapter 3. Consider, for example, how you feel on a hot, sunny day in summer, compared with a grey, drizzly day in autumn when the wind is blowing fallen leaves around. You are unlikely to want to do the same things, you will dress differently and possibly have a very different outlook on life. Changes in natural scenery will also affect you in various ways; just think about the difference between walking or climbing on a mountain range and crawling or scrambling along in an underground cave or a pothole.

Other researchers have investigated the effects of the built environment on behaviour, looking at the effects of settings such as cities, high-rise developments, hospital wards, prisons, schools, open-plan offices and parks and other man-made leisure facilities. Compare, for example, your response to the idea of living in the two different developments pictured in Figure 1.2. This will be discussed further in Chapter 5.

The physical environment (both natural and built) also affects our cognition – how we perceive it and think about it, and our feelings towards it. This in turn affects our use of the environment. Chapter 2 deals with psychologists research into environmental cognition.

■ First, there is our *aesthetic* response to the environment we are in. Do we find it attractive or ugly? What does it suggest to us? Palaces and prisons are both large impressive buildings for example, but visually they convey very different impressions regarding their purpose.

■ Second, there is the extent to which we can easily find our way around our environment; to do this we use mental images (referred to as *cognitive maps*) and research here has focused on how easy it is to form such maps for different environments. You can probably identify, from your own experiences, a city that you have a clear cognitive map of and could easily

FIGURE 1.2 *Which of these two would you prefer to live in and why?*

find your way around and another that you have been to just as many times but have not been able to form a clear map of.

■ This often links in with the third important aspect of cognition, which is *perception of risk*; people will not want to venture out into their environment if they consider that they are at risk, from crime or from pollution, for example.

■ Finally, *response to disasters*, whether natural disasters such as earthquakes or manmade disasters such as oil slicks or nuclear accidents, has also attracted some research interest.

The social environment has been a major interest from the early days of environmental psychology. Our need for personal space and the variation in this with culture, relationship and surroundings has already been mentioned. The extension of this, inspired by ethological studies of animal behaviour, is the study of territorial behaviour in humans – how do we indicate to others that certain areas are 'ours'? Lastly, there are studies of crowding and population density, inspired by the attribution of many of the problems experienced by inner cities to their ever-increasing population. This is the topic that we will look at in Chapter 4.

Much of this work has pointed to the environment as a major source of stress in our lives and has led to the demonstration that such influences as the urban environment provides can be linked with an increase in mental illness and crime rates, as we shall see in Chapter 7. This has provided the impetus for a more careful approach to the design of housing, offices, schools, prisons, hospitals and residential homes, as well as urban planning, that takes into account the characteristics of the people who will be using the environment and how their behaviour will be affected.

Effects of behaviour on the environment

The ability of humans to construct tools and to manipulate the environment has led society to increase its level of industrialisation and this in turn has led to increases in urbanisation. Our success as a species can be seen in the ever-increasing population of the world. Inevitably, all these things have had a profound effect on the environment in which we live. To sustain the population, the environment's resources, such as farmland, forests, fisheries and drinking water, have been depleted severely; industrialisation has produced acid rain, ozone depletion and pollution and has consumed vast amounts of energy. At the same time, in many countries, people also want areas of countryside in which they can spend their leisure time and this has led to the construction of golf courses and other sports facilities, as well as to the designation of certain areas as nature reserves. All these changes need to be monitored in terms of both the way that people behave and their attitudes towards the environment; only then will it be possible to develop policies designed to preserve and sustain the environment and influence the behaviour of the people who are 'consuming' it. Research along these lines looks at population issues, recycling, energy consumption, littering, vandalism and the effects of leisure activities and wars. These topics will be discussed in Chapters 6 and 8.

METHODS USED BY ENVIRONMENTAL PSYCHOLOGISTS

The nature of the topic under investigation means that the bulk of the research carried out by environmental psychologists is done in the field, rather than in the laboratory. This in turn means that certain methods will be more appropriate than others, along with particular data collection techniques, and also that specific ethical problems will be created that must be dealt with carefully.

Experimental method

As in other areas of psychology, this is regarded by many as the most scientific of the methods available because, through the manipulation of variables, it is possible to establish cause and effect relationships. Provided that all the other variables which could affect behaviour (*confounding variables*) are controlled, it is possible to manipulate a variable such as temperature (*independent variable*), and demonstrate that this has an effect on performance of a task, or on mood (*dependent variable*). So, for example, Glass and Singer (1972) were able to show that the effects of noise on performance were greater if the noise was unpredictable and if subjects felt that they had no control over it. One criticism of such approaches is that they cannot do justice to the complexity of behaviour in the natural setting. It is difficult, for example, to equate noisy neighbours with an experimenter delivering a burst of noise or a tone in a laboratory.

Experiments can also be carried out in real-life or 'field' settings, in which case they should have greater ecological validity, or applicability to everyday life, because subjects will behave in more natural ways. As an example of this, Page (1977) manipulated the levels of noise that subjects were exposed to in the field by dropping items in front of them when noisy machinery was or was not being operated in the background; their levels of altruism were significantly lower in the noisy condition, as shown by the reduced amount of help they gave. The difficulty with such field studies is that it is more difficult to control the variables (e.g. the level of noise to which subjects are exposed) than it is in the laboratory.

Another possibility, which represents a compromise between laboratory and field studies, is to use a simulation technique to represent the real environment in the laboratory. A simple method for doing this is to use slides to present different scenes to subjects. This method was used by Kaplan and Kaplan (1989) in their research into environmental preferences and it is claimed by Pitt and Zube (1987) that the method is reliable. In 1977 McKechnie used models to create interactive film simulations; modern computer technology is presently being applied to the development of virtual reality simulations that will enable subjects to be 'driven around' different environments.

Correlational studies

In some cases, it is not possible to interfere with subjects and manipulate variables that could affect their behaviour, so the experimental method is not an appropriate choice. In that case, the correlational method, which simply looks for a relationship between an environmental variable and an aspect of behaviour, can be used. For example, Abey-Wickrama et al. (1969) compared the rate of admission to psychiatric hospital of people living in noisier and quieter areas around Heathrow airport, again demonstrating the adverse effects of noise on well-being. Another possibility here is to use written records, such as meteorological records or crime statistics; for example, Goransen and King (1970) correlated average daily mean temperatures with rioting and found that outbreaks of rioting were associated with heat-wave conditions.

One major problem with the correlational method is that it is difficult to establish which variable is the cause and which the effect. Instead of rundown urban areas leading to psychiatric problems in residents, it may instead be the case that people predisposed to psychiatric problems are more likely to move into rundown urban areas. Aggression studies have also shown some inconsistent findings, indicating that rioting and aggression may be related to other variables such as humidity or alcohol consumption, which vary along with temperature in many cases.

Descriptive research

Because environmental psychology is in its infancy, this type of research is still quite necessary, compared with other areas of psychology. Instead of looking for causes, the aim of this type of study is to describe the way that people use their environment, how they feel about it and how satisfied they are with it. For example, Flin et al. (1996) investigated perception of risks in workers on offshore oil rigs, showing which environmental hazards they were most worried about.

Data collection techniques

'The bottom line in doing research in environmental psychology is to apply measurement techniques that address the questions you are asking, that disturb the setting as little as possible, and that allow you to study people in real environments.' (Bell et al., 1996).

This statement summarises the important requirements for any approaches to research and also makes it clear that in some cases there will not be one ideal technique and therefore several may need to be used together to give a comprehensive picture. Here, we will look at self-reports, observations, task performance, trace techniques and archival research.

Self-report techniques

These rely mainly on the use of questionnaires and rating scales to obtain information about behaviour, feelings and attitudes; the materials may be sent out in survey form or they may be administered in an interview situation. For example, Craik and Zube (1976) produced a self-report scale which gives a Perceived Environmental Quality Index (PEQI) for air, water and noise pollution, scenery, landscapes, leisure facilities, transport, work and home environments. This indicates the presence of particular qualities in the environment and then emotional responses can be measured using an Environmental Emotional Reaction Index (EERI) developed by Russell and Lanius (1984) which looks at how pleasant and how arousing the individual concerned finds the environment. For example, the perceived level of noise could be measured by a PEQI and emotional response to it by an EERI. As with self-report techniques in other areas of psychology, there are advantages in that data can be obtained rapidly and subjects are able to report directly on their experiences. The disadvantages are that they are open to bias by the subject, who may not be entirely truthful if they think that it would not be in their interests, and by the researcher, whose expectations may bias the way that they ask the questions, or even the questions which they ask.

Another form of self-report technique that has been developed by researchers in this field is the technique of cognitive mapping. This requires subjects to either produce a sketch map of the area of interest or estimate distances between key points, which the researcher can then use to build up a map representing their image of the area. This technique was used, for example, by Moar (1978) to show that housewives in Glasgow and in Cambridge had very different mental maps of the British Isles (Figure 1.3). Glasgow housewives tended to exaggerate the size of their own part of the country compared to areas to the north and south; Cambridge housewives increased the size of the south of England and reduced the size of the north, as well as distorting the shape.

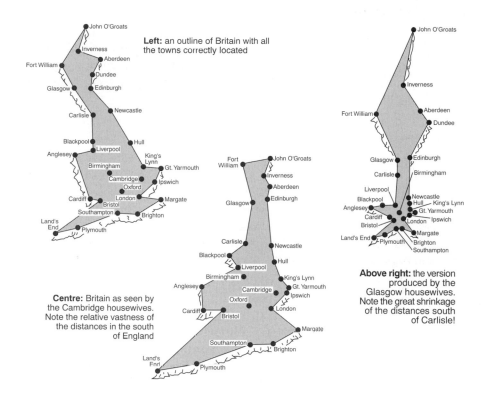

Left: an outline of Britain with all the towns correctly located

Centre: Britain as seen by the Cambridge housewives. Note the relative vastness of the distances in the south of England

Above right: the version produced by the Glasgow housewives. Note the great shrinkage of the distances south of Carlisle!

FIGURE 1.3 *Moar's research into cognitive maps*

Observational techniques

Here people are watched and their behaviour recorded in the form of written notes, observation checklists or audiovisual recordings. These can be used to sample behaviour and give information about the frequency of occurrence of particular behaviours or to look for patterns in behaviour. For example, Thrower (1987) used observational techniques to investigate how well elderly people were able to manage in their purpose-built accommodation in Dundee and was able to reveal a number of inadequacies such as shelves that were difficult to reach. Where it is important that observers are not visible, mechanical recording devices such as the hodometer, which records movement in a room by means of pressure-sensitive pads, may be employed.

Apart from mechanical devices like the hodometer, observational techniques are susceptible to various flaws: researchers can bias the findings if they allow their own expectations to influence what they see; subjects may behave differently if they are aware of being observed; observation is limited to relatively frequent, overt behaviours; mental processes cannot be observed. The advantage is that they should give a realistic account of behaviour, if done properly.

Task performance

Sometimes it is important to find out if people's cognitive abilities have been affected by environmental conditions, in which case cognitive tasks may be given. For example, Cohen et al. (1973) recorded problem-solving and reading ability in children attending schools in noisy and quiet neighbourhoods and found that the former were poorer.

Trace measures

Looking at the traces that people leave behind them in the environment can give a great deal of information about patterns of use, for example, wear patterns in carpets (known as an *erosion measure* because it is shown by something being taken away) or the presence of litter, territorial markers or graffiti (known as an *accretion measure* because something is left behind). Sommer and Becker (1969) employed this technique when they looked at the items, such as coats and bags, used to signal that seats in libraries and refectories were taken.

Archival research

This makes use of written records, usually produced originally for other purposes, as a source of data to test hypotheses. Examples include meteorological records such as temperature, wind and rainfall, census data, crime statistics and medical statistics such as rates of admission to psychiatric hospitals. Whilst these are useful indices, it is well known that biases occur when such data are being collected. For example, the rate of admission to psychiatric hospital is only a weak indicator of the rate of occurrence of psychiatric problems because not all sufferers will seek help and admissions will depend on the facilities available and the admission policy prevailing at the time.

Ethical problems

All psychological research has to face the issue of ethics in some form and follow the guidelines set by bodies such as the British Psychological Society. These specify that participants should not be maltreated, stressed, deceived or made to continue participating if they do not wish to do so and that data obtained must remain confidential. The extent to which environmental psychology uses field studies means that two issues in particular need special consideration: informed consent and invasion of privacy.

The principle of informed consent means that participants in psychological research should first be informed about what the study involves and then asked, on the basis of this, if they wish to participate. Full information about the study can rarely be given to participants because it is likely to influence their behaviour and thereby invalidate the research (for example, they may choose to behave in accordance with the researcher's expectations or to do the opposite), but it is expected that they should be told everything that is likely to influence their willingness to participate. Problems arise when field studies are carried out without the knowledge or consent of those who take part in them. Do such participants still have the right to be informed afterwards that they have been involved in research or is it better to leave them in the dark, so that the public in general are not expecting to find themselves involved in such studies?

The related issue, invasion of privacy, is also raised when people are studied without their knowledge. Even when this is done in public places, it can be argued that the rights of subjects are being infringed. A good example of the difficulties in distinguishing between public and private space is the study carried out by Middlemist et al. (1976) on the effects of invasion of personal space in a men's lavatory. Use of closed-circuit television in many city centres in the UK as a method of deterring and solving crime raises the same issue in a different context.

Many psychologists regard such guidelines as the bare minimum and this is perhaps particularly the case in environmental psychology, where concern for participants goes hand in hand with concern for the environment. To protect the interests of the environment, it would not be unreasonable to suggest a further set of guidelines, such as not conducting research that causes long or short-term damage to the environment.

CHARACTERISTICS AND ASSUMPTIONS OF ENVIRONMENTAL PSYCHOLOGY

The description given so far of environmental psychology enables us to identify some key characteristics of this area of psychology and some additional assumptions that it can be seen to make about the relationship between people and their environment.

The main characteristics that have been identified are as follows.

1 It takes a *holistic* approach to both people and the environment. This means that neither is broken down into small parts for analysis; what is of interest is how we respond in general to a whole setting for our behaviour.

2 It looks at the relationship between *systems* which are all inter-related, so that change in one will lead to change in another. This can be seen in the environment, where ozone depletion has led to global warming, for example, and in the relationship between people and the environment, where use of CFCs in refrigeration units has contributed to global warming and excessive ultraviolet radiation, which has led in turn to increased danger in exposing the skin to the sun's rays and hence to changes in our

patterns of use of the environment. Thus the approach is one that emphasises interactions between systems.

3 Free will is at the core of this approach. We are not at the mercy of our environment, but have the freedom to change it, and the way that we behave in it if we wish to (within certain limits).

4 Use of *eclectic field research*. As we saw in the section on methods and techniques used by environmental psychologists, most of their research is done in natural surroundings and will draw upon a range of different approaches as required.

5 Research tends to be *problem oriented*. This means that practical issues, such as noise control, generate research which is then used as the basis for theoretical approaches.

6 Environmental psychology is an *interdisciplinary* effort. As the history of the area demonstrates, it is derived from and of interest to a range of subjects both within and outside psychology itself.

To these characteristics we can add the following assumptions, to further clarify the nature of the subject we are concerned with.

1 Different social groups will be affected by the environment in different ways. For example, the countryside at night may be frightening for a city dweller, but it is unlikely to be for a farmer.

2 Different behaviours will be affected to a greater or lesser extent by the environment. Mood may be affected quite easily, for example, but deep-seated beliefs are unlikely to be, unless we have a profound spiritual experience as a result of contact with a particular environment.

3 Many environmental influences are unconscious. Sometimes we may feel uncomfortable in a particular place but cannot put our finger on the reason; sometimes we may feel slightly depressed but are not aware until we go somewhere else that our environment was partly responsible.

4 Our perceptions of the environment may differ from reality. Cognitive maps are a good example of this; Moar's housewives produced maps that were very different from the official map of the British Isles, as shown in Figure 1.3 (see page 11).

5 Mental images are used to represent the environment. Again, cognitive maps demonstrate how common this is and illustrate the fact that different people may have very different images of an area and how best to travel from one place to another.

6 The environment is often symbolic, in the way that it has meaning for us. A skyscraper (Figure 1.4) could be considered to symbolise man's attempts to 'reach for the sky'. Others may see it as an example of human excess and folly.

FIGURE 1.4 *Reaching for the sky — buildings as symbols*

PEOPLE AND THE ENVIRONMENT:
A GENERAL MODEL

In the remainder of the book, we will be looking at the research carried out by environmental psychologists and at the theories and models that have resulted. To provide a framework for this, a model is given in Figure 1.5 as a summary. The model indicates that environmental variables, both natural and manmade, and the social situation that the individual experiences have an impact on the individual that is moderated by the nature of that person and their past experiences. The impact of the environment is further modified by the way that the person thinks and feels, so cognitive and emotional factors are also important. Resulting behaviour will then depend on how suitable or otherwise that environment is for that individual; if an unsuitable environment is not dealt with effectively, behaviour may be severely disrupted. This behaviour then itself has an impact on the environment, which feeds back into the process at several points, as shown at the bottom of Figure 1.5. In future chapters, we will be exploring a wide spectrum of these issues: environmental factors (such as noise, design and natural features) will be explored in Chapters 3, 5 and 6; social influences (such as population density) will be examined in Chapter 4; cognitive influences (such as differences in perception and affective responses) are the subject matter of Chapter 2; the maladaptive nature of behaviour that can result when the environment is too stressful is dealt with in Chapter 7; and the variety of effects that people can, in turn, have on the environment are described in Chapter 8. Chapter 9 tackles the issues raised by looking at prospects for the future.

MODEL OF PERSON–ENVIRONMENT INTERACTION

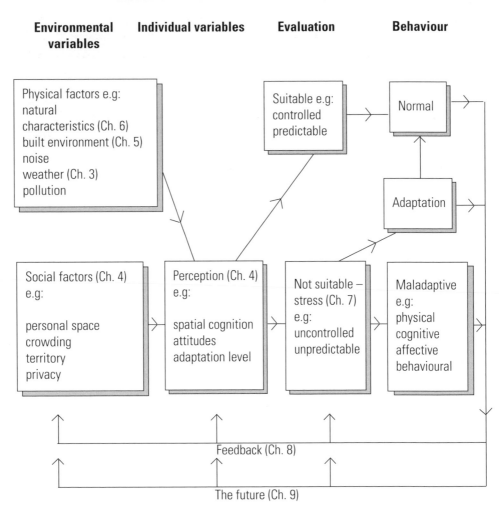

FIGURE 1.5 *A general model of person–environment interaction*

CHAPTER SUMMARY

The general approach of environmental psychology is to look at the two-way relationship between people and their environment, including its natural, manmade and social aspects. The area has developed from research into perception and social behaviour, with influences from other disciplines, such as architecture and behavioural geography, and organisations such as UNESCO. The main focus of research is on both the effects of the environment on behaviour and the effects of behaviour on the environment. Methods used include experiments, correlational studies and descriptive research; data collection techniques vary from observation and self-report to task performance, trace and archival measures. The emphasis on field studies raises ethical issues of informed consent and invasion of privacy. Environmental psychology has some key characteristics and assumptions and a general model of the person–environment interaction has been proposed as a framework for subsequent chapters.

chapter two

ENVIRONMENTAL COGNITION

CHAPTER OVERVIEW

Cognition refers to the processes we use to think about our experiences. Psychologists use this term to refer to such aspects of thinking as attention, perception, memory, problem-solving and the development of attitudes. In this chapter we will be exploring how we think about our environment, in terms of *perception* (how we see the environment), *spatial cognition* (or 'mapping') and environmental *appraisal* (attitudes towards the environment). This type of thinking produces images of what the environment is like, tells us whether it is like other environments that we are familiar with, what we can do in it and whether or not we like it. Therefore, our cognition is at the root of many of the behaviours that we will be considering in later chapters, such as responding to stress (Chapter 7) and consumer behaviour (Chapter 8).

ENVIRONMENTAL PERCEPTION

Perception is the process of interpreting and making sense of the information which we receive via our senses. It includes detecting, or becoming aware of information, processing and adding meaning to it, and using it to make decisions about how to behave or respond.

Environments typically provide us, via our sense organs, with far more information than we can possibly process in the time available, so perception is based on a selection from this information. This selection is made according to what is most likely to be relevant at the time (Treisman, 1964). It can then be used to plan behaviour and as a result, we receive feedback from the environment about the consequences of that behaviour. Will we be able to cross a busy road safely, for example? Environments also have symbolic meanings, which tell us about their purposes and what kinds of behaviours are expected in them. For example, a doctor's surgery and a church have quite different associations and expectations; a farm tells us about a way of life, a range of activities and makes us think about seasonal changes. Perception, then, involves selecting and summarising sensory inputs, labelling them, attaching meaning to them, and using them in planning behaviour.

Perception begins with the process of stimulus *detection*. Early work on psychophysics (Fechner, 1860) studied the extent to which our senses are capable of detecting stimuli – how dim could a light be made before we would fail to notice it, for example? This led to the concept of the threshold, which is the minimum level of stimulation required for us to notice it. For example, the minimum visual stimulus that we can detect is a candle flame 30 miles away on a clear night (Galanter, 1962)! Psychophysicists also explored the way that we respond to changes in stimuli. The minimum amount of change needed in a stimulus before we will notice it was termed a *just noticeable difference* (j.n.d.); the size of this change was found to vary according to the strength of the original stimulus (Weber's Law). So you would notice if a candle was lit in a dark room, but not on a bright, sunny day.

In environmental perception, this type of research has important implications when considering the issue of stress (see Chapter 7). What is regarded as stressful depends on how intense the stimulus is perceived to be, rather than on its objective intensity. This means, for example, that a noise that will be tolerated by one person will be intolerable to another; the context in which it is heard (e.g. at home or in a nightclub) and changes in intensity may also influence the way that it is perceived, and whether or not it proves to be stressful.

Stimulus detection is followed by the process of *recognition* – what is it that has been detected? This is particularly affected by our expectations and previous experience and has lead to an important distinction being made in the study of perception between top-down and bottom-up processing. Bottom-up (or data-driven) processing refers to the analysis of information received from the senses, without interference from our expectations and previous experience. This occurs primarily when we are confronted with new experiences. Top-down (or concept-driven)processing refers to the influence of expectations and past experience. If we are expecting to see a certain person, for example, we may mistake someone else for them; on the other hand, we may fail to recognise people if we are not expecting to see them. In most situations, both processes operate, with expectations (top-down processes) being checked against sensory input (bottom-up processes). This can be seen in Neisser's (1976) cyclical model of perception, shown in Figure 2.1.

Theories of environmental perception

Three theories about the nature of environmental perception will be considered here, to illustrate the variety of different approaches that exist in this area: Gestalt theory; Gibson's theory of ecological perception; and Brunswik's lens model.

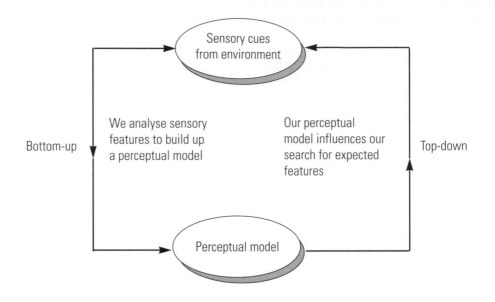

FIGURE 2.1 *Neisser's (1976) cyclical model of perception demonstrates the interaction between top-down and bottom-up processing*

Gestalt

Gestalt theory was developed by a group of German psychologists, including Koffka, Kohler and Wertheimer. They argued that the brain is organised in such a way that we make 'good forms' (which is what the word *Gestalt* means) out of the information we receive. This process was thought to be automatic and to require very little learning. An example of this can be seen in the Kanizsa figure (Figure 2.2(a)), where we do this to such an extent that we see things which are not there. Another important premise of this

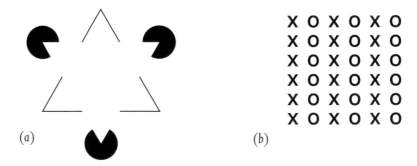

FIGURE 2.2 (a) *The Kanisza figure. Filling in the gaps to make whole figures makes us see things that aren't there. This is the principle of closure in some instances.* (b) *The Gestalt principle of similarity means that the circles and crosses are seen as separate groups*

approach is that 'the whole is greater than the sum of the parts', meaning that we group things together to make wholes which have meaning for us. The principle of similarity, for example, indicates that the circles and crosses in Figure 2.2(b) will be seen as separate groups; we group them according to shape, which is a meaningful category. In the same way, buildings are more than just combinations of bricks and mortar; the way that they are combined to make a whole is an important determinant of their meaning and their aesthetic quality. Another example is a wall, which again is not just a collection of bricks and mortar, it is also an indicator of territorial boundaries, even if it is too low to keep anyone out. Some of the other laws of perceptual organisation that have been derived from Gestalt principles are illustrated in Box 2.1.

Box 2.1   Gestalt laws of perception

Proximity
Objects which are close together will tend to be grouped together to make a whole. Thus in (a) the dots will be perceived as being grouped into vertical columns and in (b) they appear as horizontal rows.

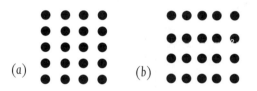

Good continuation
Existing lines tend to be seen as continuous, and as part of one item, even when crossed over by other lines. In the example shown the pattern is more likely to be described as a wavy line and a straight line, than as a row of alternating semi-circles.

Part-whole relations
A collection of identical parts can be assembled to make wholes which will be perceived in very different ways, as shown in the example below.

Ecological perception

Gibson's (1966) ecological perception differs in that it does not see perception as the result (as above) of organising features into meaningful patterns, but as the result of our senses being 'wired' so that they 'tune in' to the meaning that already exists. This means that things which have a *functional* value in terms of assisting survival will be perceived automatically. Babies, for example, seem to have an innate tendency to respond to human faces more than any other stimulus (Fantz, 1961). Gibson describes the visual information available to us as the *optic array*, and argues that it provides a lot of information that is useful for survival and is detected automatically without the need for higher level processing by the brain. Distance of objects, for example, is indicated by such cues as texture and superimposition, as shown in Figure 2.3. The importance of taking the whole scene into account is emphasised in this approach too and can be seen in the phenomenon of size constancy. If we see a small human figure, we use information from the surroundings to decide if it is a child or dwarf who is close to us or an adult who is further away. The retinal image can change as a result of changes in distance or changes in the size of the person seen.

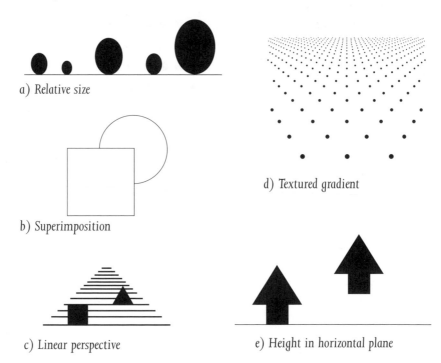

a) Relative size

b) Superimposition

c) Linear perspective

d) Textured gradient

e) Height in horizontal plane

FIGURE 2.3 *Some of the cues we can use to tell us how far away objects are*

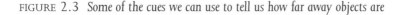

Another concept introduced by Gibson is that of *affordances* or uses. This refers to the idea that objects encountered, or even environments as a whole, have *invariant functional properties*, which indicate what they can be used for. These properties are discovered by exploration, for example, babies will put a variety of objects in their mouths until they discover what is good to eat and what isn't. Similarly, animals will look for places to sleep that are likely to afford food and shelter. Perceiving these affordances then, tells us what the environment can be used for – to build a house, to grow vegetables, etc. An ecological niche refers to a set of affordances, as in the case of animals instinctively seeking out an environment that gives them the best chance of survival. Here humans differ; not only can we do this but we can also alter the environment's affordances for us and for other animals by, for example, building industrial zones or clearing forests. These alterations are not, of course, always beneficial to all users, as Chapter 8 will make clear.

Lens model

Brunswik's (1956, 1969) *lens model* is a probabilistic functional theory of perception. It sees perception as being more dependent on learning and experience than the theories previously discussed and is illustrated in Figure 2.4. Environments scatter stimuli, which are sampled and then recombined and focused by the individual (the 'lens' in the model). The result of focusing is perception, and this is tested for accuracy by carrying out actions in the environment. For example, you may decide to go out without a coat because it looks warm outside. Perception may not always be accurate, because the environment can only be sampled. In the example given above, it may not be as warm as you think, because you failed to notice the wind. It is possible to work out through experience how useful particular cues are (the fact that the sun is shining is not sufficient to guarantee that it is warm) and decide which ones are reliable in the sense of leading to accurate perception (and the right choice of clothes!). These will be regarded as having *ecological validity*. Perception, then, is based on probabilities in this approach.

This implies that different environmental stimuli may differ in their objective usefulness as cues and also that different individuals may regard them differently as a result of past experience, personality or other individual differences. This latter is known as *cue utilisation*. For example, although the weather can be measured objectively (e.g. temperature, wind speed), individuals will differ in their subjective estimates (what one person finds warm, another will find cool) and in the relative importance of different aspects in determining whether they think it is a nice day; a holidaymaker may want sunshine, while a farmer may want rain, for example.

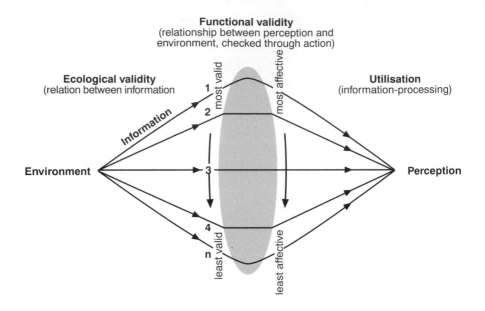

FIGURE 2.4 *Brunswik's probabilistic theory illustrates one way of relating the information available from the environment to the way the individual perceives that environment*

An experimental example of cue utilisation is the Ames room (1952), shown in Chapter 1. People who stand in the opposite corners of this distorted room appear very different in size to the viewer, who has to decide whether they are different, using apparent size as a cue, or whether the room is distorted in shape, using a different set of cues. The probability of the room being out of square seems low, based on past experience, so most people will report that the individuals are different in size. A real-life example is the study by Stewart (1987) of perceptions of air quality in Colorado. This research found that the level of smog was commonly regarded as a good indicator (or cue) for pollution, although in fact it has less ecological validity than the number of cars in the area in predicting actual pollution levels. In Box 2.2 there is an example of how Brunswik has applied his model.

One important consequence of these theories is that not only will a given environment carry with it particular expectations and meanings, so that different environments lead to different perceptions, but also that perception of the same environment will vary according to individual and cultural differences. This has been vividly demonstrated by Segall et al. (1966), who found that Zulus were less susceptible to the Müller–Lyer illusion (see page 000) and by Deregowski (1980), who showed that some Africans (e.g. Zambians) find it more difficult than Europeans to see depth in Western-style pictures. The different art forms used in different cultures may make it necessary to

Box 2.2 An application of Brunswick's lens model

Brunswick put his model to the test by obtaining three measurements from participants in his study as they went about their daily routines.

1 Participants' perceptions of the environment were measured by stopping them at random and obtaining their judgements about the size and distance of objects visible at the time. This provided a record of the nature of the environments they encountered as well as their judgements of the size and distance of a variety of objects, ranging from food to mountains.

2 The real physical dimensions of the surroundings were also noted to give actual sizes and distances.

3 Photographs were taken from which he was able to analyse the visual information or cues available to his participants.

His research showed that the relationship between the real physical measurements (2) and the visual cues available (3) was actually quite low in most cases, i.e. the cues had low ecological validity. Despite this, the participants' perceptions (1) were highly accurate when compared with reality (2). Therefore, as a result of utilising an information-processing system which combined a great many pieces of information (each of which may be low in ecological validity), participants were able to arrive at perceptions which were both valid and functionally useful.

learn to 'read' pictures, at least to some extent. Occupational differences have also been found; for example, artists are also less affected by the Müller–Lyer illusion. These findings have been explained by the *carpentered world hypothesis*, which suggests that people who live in a geometric, 'carpentered' environment, with a lot of sharp angles and parallel lines, become more sensitive to stimuli in that form. Zulus, coming from a culture where the traditional way of life involves living in round huts in a natural environment, would be less affected; artists would be less affected because they are trained to be objective and to represent things as they really are.

Differences in perceptual ability are also found. For example, men judge distances to visible buildings to be less than to hidden buildings, but females show no such differences. It has also been shown that more familiar buildings will be judged as closer than unfamiliar ones. A study by Edney (1972) showed that observers who had been in a room for 30 minutes judged it to be smaller than those who had just entered it. An everyday example is that of a journey; a familiar journey usually seems shorter than an unfamiliar one unless, of course, you are very tired and eager to get to your destination, in which case it can seem interminable! So differences in perception can be seen both between individuals and at different times within individuals.

Perception of change and constancy

So far, we have looked at perception of the environment as if the environment were constant, but what happens when it changes? Or conversely, stays the same for long periods?

If it stays the same, there is a process called habituation or *adaptation*, whereby the individual responds less and less. An example of this would be people who live next to busy roads or railway lines and don't even notice traffic or trains going past. This has been explained physiologically in terms of the nervous system itself firing off nerve impulses less frequently (a bit like changing the setting on a thermostat so that a heater doesn't operate). In terms of cognitive adaptation, stimuli are considered to be less worthy of attention, because they are less of a threat or less interesting; the sound of traffic, for example would not necessarily be an indicator of the arrival of visitors. Adaptation may involve some degree of effort, especially if the stimulus is annoying (e.g. a dripping tap) or irregular (e.g. a pneumatic drill). This means that it can be stressful, as we shall see in Chapter 7.

Perception of change is governed by Weber's Law, mentioned earlier, which states that the amount of change required for it to be noticeable depends on the original strength of the stimulus. This can also be applied to environmental characteristics such as pollution and littering (Sommer, 1972). Litter, for example, is more obvious in an area that is normally free of it. The principle can be put to positive use to improve behaviour, in that small changes (e.g. using non-biological washing powder) are less likely to be noticed than larger ones (e.g. not using cars) and people may therefore be more willing to accept them. A negative aspect is that slow change, such as that resulting from acid rain or low-level radiation, is less likely to be noticed than rapid change such as forest clearances.

When we are confronted with a novel environment, as in a move to a new house, responses can take six forms, according to Ittelson et al. (1974).

1 *Affect*. There is likely to be an increased awareness of the environment and increase in arousal, together with a need to feel secure and in control. The nature of the environment will also affect how we feel, because it may make us want to do different things. A city centre suggests different activities to a countryside retreat, for example.

2 *Orientation*. We need to locate our particular 'niche' in relation to important elements in the environment. Where are the shops, sports facilities, etc.? This is the cognitive equivalent of 'You are here' on a town plan for tourists.

3 *Categorisation*. The environment is evaluated in terms of our own concerns. Which is the best pub? Which restaurant does the best food?

4 *Systemisation*. This relates to the best way to use the environment; for example, we soon learn when and where there are likely to be traffic hold-ups and how to get round them by using 'rat-runs' or travelling at different times.

5 *Manipulation*. We develop the ability to control the environment to meet our own needs; for example, we may order fuel from one company rather than another because they come at more convenient times.

6 *Encoding*. This involves separating and labelling the different parts of our environment in such a way that we can communicate with others about it and think about it effectively ourselves (e.g. by working out the best route to take to travel around it). Different areas, roads and landmarks will be labelled and organised into a 'cognitive map' or mental representation of the area. This is an important research topic in environmental psychology and is the subject of the next section.

SPATIAL COGNITION

Psychologists consider that all individuals have an organised mental representation of their environment, called a cognitive schemata or *cognitive map*. These maps are rather different from the maps that we are used to, being typically incomplete, sketchy and distorted. According to Garling et al. (1984), they consist primarily of places (rooms, buildings, towns), spatial relationships between places (indicating both distance and direction) and travel plans (how to get from one place to another).

Cognitive maps were described as early as 1913, by Trowbridge, but the term was coined by Tolman (1948), who found that rats trained to run a maze learnt maps of the maze. When the route that they had been trained on was blocked, they were able to find an alternative route, suggesting that they had a general map of the location of the goal box.

In 1960 Lynch, an urban planner, first applied cognitive maps to the way that people make sense of their environment. In studies carried out in Boston, Los Angeles and Jersey City, he asked participants to draw sketch maps of the city, showing the routes they used most commonly and the landmarks they could remember. The drawings showed that the maps of all three cities shared certain features:

1 *Paths*. Shared traffic routes (including roads, rivers, etc.) through the city, such as the River Thames in London.

2 *Edges*. Natural or manmade boundary lines that edge the city or areas within it, e.g. the old city walls of Berwick-on-Tweed, rivers, railway lines, etc.

3 *Districts*. Large areas of the city that have an identity, e.g. the old town, the industrial zone, the East End of London.

4 *Nodes*. Intersections between major paths, e.g. the market square in a town like King's Lynn, traffic lights.

5 *Landmarks*. Distinctive architectural features that are used for reference and visible for some distance, e.g. a cathedral such as that in Canterbury. Sometimes these are so distinctive that they have become symbols for the city or even the country. Thus, Downs and Stea (1977) have shown that people link Big Ben with London, the Eiffel Tower with Paris and the Taj Mahal with India.

This work was followed up by Appleyard (1970), whose research in a city in Venezuela showed that residents produced maps of two kinds. Sequential maps were the most common and were made up primarily of paths and nodes. Spatial maps represented a bird's eye view, known as 'survey knowledge', and focussed more on landmarks and districts. Examples of these are shown in Figure 2.5.

Maps of larger environments include information about distance, direction and travel times (Downs and Stea, 1973), all of which may be used when giving directions to others. Cognitive maps of familiar places tend to be fairly accurate, as shown by Appleyard (1970). When asked to draw larger areas, people place familiar areas in the centre; Saarinen (1973) found that people asked to draw a map of the world put their own country in the centre, indicating that they were using it as an anchor point. They are also likely to expand the

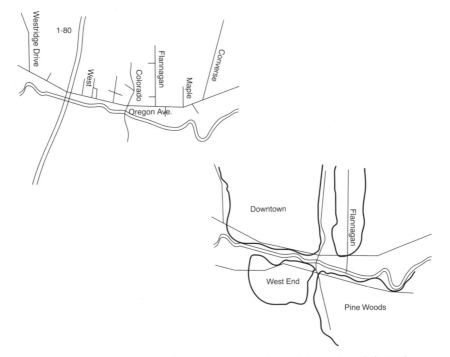

FIGURE 2.5 *Examples of sequential and spatial maps obtained by Appleyard (1970)*

relative size and detail of familiar areas, as was the case with Moar's house-wives described in Chapter 1.

The sketch map technique established by Lynch remains the most popular method of gathering information on cognitive maps. The method has been criticised, however, since many individuals may lack the drawing skills or experience with maps to put down accurately what they have in their heads. It is also difficult for the researcher wishing to compare maps to find a satis-factory way of measuring the differences between them.

An alternative approach is to use a recognition task. Lynch pioneered this by giving his Boston participants photographs of landmarks embedded in a set of unfamiliar photographs, and asking them to identify any that they recog-nised. This obviously does not provide information about locations and distances, nor does it enable the researcher to decide if that landmark is important to the participant. You may not include a particular house on your own map, but you may still be able to recognise it, for example. Another way to avoid drawing is to ask participants to estimate distances between locations such as towns or landmarks. These can then be plotted by a computer to give a map that links all the paired places. This technique, called *mental triangulation*, was used by Moar in his study of housewives from different parts of Britain and has the advantage that it is easily quantified. One problem with this tech-nique is that estimates are not reversible, so an estimate of the distance from London to Cambridge is likely to differ from that given for Cambridge to London, for example. It also fails to show paths and landmarks.

Cognitive maps, then, enable us to communicate with others about the environment, in situations such as giving directions, and they provide us with symbols that we can use to communicate, such as landmarks. Their primary purpose, however, is *wayfinding*, a term used to describe the process of navigating our way around the environment. Many species of animals, fish and migratory birds particularly, travel thousands of miles to breed, finding their way with the use of cues from water temperature, position of the sun and stars and the pull of magnetic fields (Emlen, 1975). Humans find their way by using their extremely good memory for visual material (Nickerson (1968) found 95% accuracy for facial recognition, for example) to form cognitive maps. This means that the maps have an adaptive function, allow-ing us to locate food and shelter and arrange meetings with others in an effi-cient way. They also enable us to draw up an action plan prior to a journey that will take us where we want to go (Garling et al., 1984) and to visualise and follow instructions given to us when we are lost.

According to Garling et al. (1984), wayfinding can be divided into four stages:

- a destination, such as a shop, will be decided on;

- the location of the destination is established (e.g. a particular street in a particular town);

■ a route will be chosen to get us there, based on official or cognitive maps;

■ a choice will be made about how to get there, e.g. whether to walk or take the car.

After the trip, information will be fed back into the system to improve its efficiency next time, e.g. avoiding traffic jams and one-way streets.

Other writers, such as Passini (1990), prefer to see wayfinding as a sequence of decisions based on recognising the correct choice at each point along the route – for example, turning left out of the house and right at the junction.

Factors affecting cognitive maps

Cognitive maps can be affected by a variety of factors, which have been grouped here into environmental, individual and developmental influences.

Environmental influences

Environments differ in how easily they can be mapped. Lynch (1960) introduced the term *legibility* to describe the ease with which a clear image of the environment can be produced. A legible environment will have features which are easy to recognise, organise into a pattern and remember. For example, cities which have a definite centre are easier to map than those which do not. When the environment has structures that stand out and when it is passed through frequently it will be easier to form a map. This is known as the *anchor point hypothesis*, which suggests that clear physical reference points make it easier to organise space cognitively.

These ideas have been extended by Garling et al. (1984), who proposed that there are three main characteristics of environments that affect wayfinding.

1 *Differentiation*. This refers to the extent to which different parts of the environment look the same (low differentiation) or are distinctive (high differentiation). Buildings that stand alone or are an unusual shape will be better remembered (Evans et al., 1982a).

2 *Degree of visual access*. Can the setting be seen from different angles? If it can, it is more easily incorporated into a cognitive map.

3 *Complexity of the spatial layout*. This refers to the amount of information that needs to be dealt with in order to get around effectively; is the floor plan, for example, simple or complex?

It is possible to add *transition* to this list (Evans et al., 1982a), which refers to the presence of direct access from the building to the street. This also makes orientation easier.

Individual factors

As more time is spent in a particular environment, so our spatial cognitions about it will change. Research has shown that students who had spent a year on campus produced more detailed and accurate maps than those who had arrived more recently. Time is not the only factor; the nature of our activity is also influential. Pearce (1981), for example, found that drivers will acquire better organised information than passengers. Urban and rural dwellers, and people from different social classes, will acquire different information (Orleans, 1973). Poorer people have different activity patterns and will come to know different areas from those who have more money (Karan et al., 1980). Most of these differences are due to different mobility patterns rather than anything else.

Differences in spatial ability also exist and have been shown by Pearson and Ialongo (1986) to account for 14% of differences in environmental knowledge. In terms of gender, Appleyard (1970) found that the cognitive maps of males are more accurate than those of females. Pearce (1977) found that males emphasise routes, whereas females focus on districts and landmarks; when giving directions, males are more likely to give distances and refer to points of the compass and they make fewer errors. According to Orleans and Schmidt (1972), this may reflect differences in mobility, with females being more home centred than males. This is supported by their finding that women's maps are more detailed for their home and neighbourhood areas, while men's are better for the larger surrounding area. Males also learn more quickly when driven around a new area than females do, although females learn equally quickly when they both walk (Garling et al., 1981). This may be partly attributable to motivational factors, since a 'good sense of direction' is more important to the self-esteem of men than of women (Bryant, 1982).

Some interesting research on blind people by Passini et al. (1990) compared their performance on a wayfinding task with that of sighted individuals. Their performance was comparable, indicating that the spatial cognitive abilities of blind people may be normal. Their cognitive maps appear to rely on sequences of actions rather than visual images (Downs and Stea, 1977) and they prepare in advance for journeys more than sighted subjects. Tactile cues, such as handrails and textures in the building, are also utilised to a greater degree.

Developmental factors

Younger children are generally poorer at estimating distances (Anooshian and Wilson, 1977), so it can be seen that spatial cognition changes during the course of development. Most of the work in this area has been based on Piaget's theory, which argues that there are four broad stages in the development of cognition. At each of these stages, representations of the environment will

Table 2.1   Piaget's Development Stages and Environmental Cognition

Developmental stage	Spatial ability
Sensorimotor period (birth to age 2)	Completely egocentric; defines space and the location of objects only in relation to own body
Period of intuitive or preoperational thought (age 2 to age 7)	Still egocentric, but begins to build crude symbolic representations of immediate environment
Concrete operations period (age 7 to age 12)	Can conceive of objects and places as existing apart from the self; becomes more sophisticated at using landmarks to locate objects and places
Formal operations period (age 12 to adult)	Can use symbols and abstractions to represent space; can form larger and more unified cognitive maps

Source: McAndrew (1993)

differ, as outlined in Table 2.1, becoming more abstract and less based on the body and immediate surroundings as the child gets older. Research generally supports the theory (Evans, 1980), although there are indications that, as with other aspects of Piaget's work, the artificial nature of laboratory studies has lead to the underestimation of children's abilities. Six-year-olds, for example, have been shown to be able to use aerial maps (Spencer and Darvizeh, 1981). Hart and Moore (1973) have argued that the child uses three frames of reference in coming to understand the spatial world: egocentric, fixed and co-ordinated. Like Piaget, they consider that egocentric impressions come first, then maps are developed around specific, fixed places. These are then integrated into the co-ordinated survey-type maps of the adult.

Siegel and White (1975) have extended this work by looking at actual spatial behaviour rather than cognitive mapping. Again, four stages have been observed. At first, the child can only use landmarks to mark the beginning and end of a journey and to gauge progress. In the second stage, routes between places are learnt gradually, as landmarks become more familiar and knowledge is derived from movement through the environment. In the third stage, landmarks and paths are organised into clusters and in the fourth stage, clusters and other features are co-ordinated into an overall framework.

Heft and Wohlwill (1987) point out that the function of the environment is important to the child, so affordances will be learnt first, such as where to buy sweets and how to get to friends' houses. These then become landmarks and form the basis of cognitive maps. Development can be speeded up by giving plenty of opportunity to explore (Acredolo, 1982).

Research generally supports the idea of stages in development and the importance of landmarks early on, but children appear to be better at survey wayfinding than theories would predict (Acredolo et al., 1975). Much of the research relies on drawing ability, which is generally poor, so this too indicates that the ability of children may be being underestimated (Matthews, 1985).

Adults may also show similar development from landmark to routes to survey knowledge (McDonald and Pellegrino, 1993), although they have the advantage of being able to learn from maps as well. McDonald and Pellegrino distinguish primary and secondary spatial learning: primary spatial learning involves direct experience of movement through the environment; secondary spatial learning comes from studying maps or written descriptions of the environment. Learning probably occurs in different ways in the two cases. For example, cartographic maps are presented in a particular orientation (generally they have north at the top of the page) and this may affect the memory they produce (Warren and Scott 1993), so that you have to reverse left and right if you travel from north to south instead of south to north. Cognitive maps do not suffer from this problem.

How is information represented in cognitive maps?

One view is that the information is in the form of a picture – an *analogue representation* – rather like a series of photographs stored in the brain. Another view is that there is *propositional storage* – the environment is represented by words, referring to concepts or ideas (propositions) which are interconnected (Neisser, 1976; Pylyshyn, 1981). The most likely answer is that both are involved (Tye, 1991), e.g. the propositional network may be used to reconstruct an image. Estimating distances, for example, would require both. The more images and information scanned, the longer it takes to give an estimate of distance and the greater the distance is in reality (Baum and Jonides, 1977). Memories may also be clustered or 'chunked' in order to organise them. This may be applied to landmarks (Allen, 1981). Each cluster may in turn be represented by a reference point or outstanding landmark (Figure 2.6) (Couclelis et al., 1987), which may then be organised in memory in an orderly way. This is supported by evidence that landmarks within clusters are judged to be closer together than those which are in different clusters, even if the objective distance is the same (Holding, 1992).

In physiological terms, O'Keefe and Nadel (1978) have proposed that the cognitive maps are located in the hippocampus, part of the limbic system in the brain. Some neurons in the hippocampus are thought to be coded for place; the part in the left hemisphere of the brain houses the semantic, word-based map and the part in the right hemisphere houses the pictorial map. There are two systems for spatial cognition according to this view:

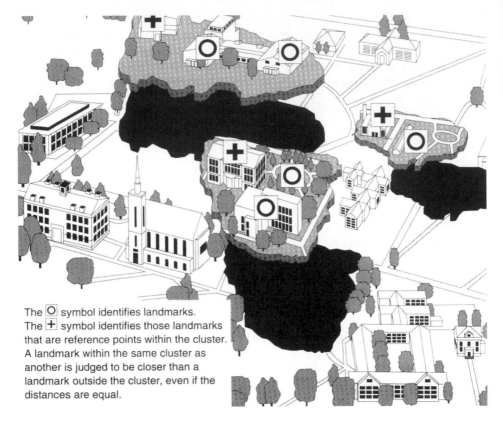

The ☐O☐ symbol identifies landmarks.
The ☐+☐ symbol identifies those landmarks
that are reference points within the cluster.
A landmark within the same cluster as
another is judged to be closer than a
landmark outside the cluster, even if the
distances are equal.

FIGURE 2.6 *An illustration of the clustering of landmarks*

1 the *taxon* system represents routes and is based on objects and orientations;

2 the *locale* system represents knowledge about places, such as what they are useful for.

As with most other abilities, other areas of the brain are probably involved as well. For example, damage to the parietal lobe of the cortex leads to loss of the ability to draw maps and loss of knowledge about how places are arranged geographically.

Errors in cognitive maps

Cognitive maps are only rough representations of the environment, so errors are inevitable. What is interesting is that they tend to fall into particular patterns. Downs and Stea (1973) have categorised these errors into incompleteness, distortion and augmentation and we will consider each of these in turn.

Incompleteness involves leaving things out; usually these are minor paths and details but sometimes complete districts and landmarks will be omitted.

Distortion includes such errors as placing things too far apart, or too close together or aligning them incorrectly. So lines may be made parallel or road junctions drawn as right angles, when they are not. An example is given in the maps produced by Moar (see Chapter 1). De Jonge (1962) pointed out that, like the Gestalt principle of good form, people appear to remember right angles better than any others and straight lines better than curved ones. This may be important in urban planning. For example, Lee (1978) found that Wolverhampton housewives preferred to use town centre stores rather than closer out-of-town ones; one explanation of this would be that they overestimated the distance when going out of town and underestimated the distance when going in (perhaps because the journey in was more interesting). This was termed Brennan's Law.

Augmentation is the addition of non-existent features to a map, such as a rail link between towns that doesn't exist.

Another example is the *superordinate scale bias* (Tversky, 1981) whereby our memory for larger places, such as countries, can distort our memory for smaller ones, such as towns. Are you aware, for example, that Edinburgh is further west than Bristol? In general, we make more mistakes with east–west judgements than with north–south judgements (Russell and Ward, 1982).

FOCUS ON APPLICATION ...
cognitive maps

One important use is in city planning, where Evans et al. (1982a) have made the following four suggestions.

1 Place landmarks at major decision points in the road system.

2 Make them highly visible (tall) and distinctive (unique in style).

3 Make roads into district boundaries.

4 Preserve buildings that make good landmarks and construct landmarks in areas that lack them.

Another important development has been the use of you-are-here maps in places such as shopping centres. Key features of these (Levine, 1982) are that they should be placed in the correct orientation for the observer's position, include an arrow to indicate the observer's position and have labels that match those in the environment.

Colour-coding and numbering systems have also been introduced to improve the legibility of the environment. For example, colour coding the floors in large buildings such as museums helps people to find their way around (Evans et al., 1980). The clarity of the numbering system in streets and large buildings has also been shown to have a considerable influence on the number of people getting lost (Carpman et al., 1984). Similarly, transit maps showing bus or train systems have been shown to work best when they represent the journey in a schematic way and use colour coding, as in the map of the London underground system.

The *planfulness* of behaviour can be used to develop action plans for travel, to identify potential problem areas in cities and to predict the routes that may be used by criminals, leading to more effective law enforcement (Smith and Patterson 1980). It can also help to predict the paths which may be taken by lost people; as these are not random, searchers may be assisted by this information. For example, lost children under the age of six are generally found in open spaces, while 6–12-year-olds tend to seek enclosed spaces (Cornell and Hay, 1984).

ENVIRONMENTAL APPRAISAL

We like some places more than others; they may also make us feel different. This kind of appraisal of the environment is an important part of our cognitive response. McAndrew (1993) has used the term to refer to six different impressions that we can form: descriptions, evaluations, aesthetic judgements, emotional responses, meanings and attitudes. In the following section we will look at each of these in turn.

Descriptions

Descriptions of the environment have been found to employ a wide variety of terms and concepts, depending on the nature of the environment and the individuals concerned. One of the best-known attempts to categorise these is that of Cass and Hershberger (1973), whose results are given in Figure 2.7.

Evaluations

Evaluation is the process of deciding whether or not the environment is a good one and if it is preferred over another. Physical aspects of the environment, such as pollution, can be measured objectively using the Environmental Quality Index (EQI); to measure subjective responses to the environment, a self-report scale called the Perception of Environmental Quality Scale (PEQI), devised by Craik and Zube (1976), can be used. Currently, scales exist to measure air, water and noise pollution, residential quality, landscapes, scenery, outdoor recreational facilities, transport systems and work environments.

Another way to find out about evaluations is to ask people to express their preferences for different scenes. For example, Sonnenfeld (1966) found that people prefer familiar scenery, although this has not always been confirmed.

Factors or concepts	Primary and alternate scale	
1 General evaluative	good–bad	pleasing–annoying
2 Utility evaluative	useful–useless	friendly–hostile
3 Aesthetic evaluative	unique–common	interesting–boring
4 Activity	active–passive	complex–simple
5 Space	cosy–roomy	private–public
6 Potency	rugged–delicate	rough–smooth
7 Tidiness	clean–dirty	tidy–messy
8 Organisation	ordered–chaotic	formal–casual
9 Temperature	warm–cool	hot–cold
10 Lighting	light–dark	bright–dull

Secondary scales might include old–new, expensive–inexpensive, large–small, exciting–calming, clear–ambiguous, colourful–subdued, safe–dangerous, quiet–noisy, stuffy–draughty

FIGURE 2.7 *Cass and Hershberger's (1973) scales for describing the environment*

One important factor here is individual differences; females, for example, prefer warmer, lusher scenes and younger people prefer more exotic scenes. Some settings do seem to be generally preferred to others: Nasar (1981) has shown that square rooms are preferred to rectangular ones; while Kaye and Murray (1982) found that rooms with windows are preferable to those without.

These preferences have been related by Kaplan and Kaplan (1982) to the adaptive value of the setting. Based on Gibson's concept of affordances, they propose that we prefer settings that allow us to find food and shelter and feel safe. We also need to be able to make sense of the environment and get involved with it. Four factors are suggested as being important here.

1 *Coherence*, which is the ease with which we can organise and make sense of the environment.

2 *Complexity*, which is the degree to which it keeps us occupied, without being either bored or overstimulated.

3 *Legibility* is whether we think that the environment could be explored without getting lost.

4 *Mystery* is whether we think that we could get more out of that environment if we got involved with it.

Aesthetics

Is it a beautiful environment? Research here has concentrated on identifying the features which influence our judgements. Despite individual differences, some consensus is possible; most people are impressed by the Grand Canyon, for instance. Natural landscapes tend to be preferred to urban scenes (Kaplan et al., 1972) and these also produce more positive physiological effects (Ulrich, 1981). Placement of vegetation in the centre, either in the middle of a scene or in the background, makes it more attractive (Patsfall et al., 1984).

Berlyne (1960, 1974) identified four basic *collative properties* of environments. These are characteristics that lead us to pay attention and can be used to compare that environment with others. *Complexity* is determined by the variety of different elements in the scene, *novelty* by how new it is to the observer, *incongruity* by the extent to which something appears out of place and *surprisingness* by the presence of elements that the observer does not expect to find there. Aesthetic judgements should be most positive for environments at intermediate levels of each of these elements. Wohlwill (1976) found that this is only true for complexity; increases in novelty and surprisingness led to straightforward increases in judgements of beauty, while increases in incongruity led to a decrease in perceived beauty. This was also found to apply only to the built environment, not to landscapes.

Berlyne argued further that these collative properties would influence aesthetic judgements and the desire to explore through their effects on hedonic tone (beauty and pleasure) and uncertainty arousal. Pleasantness is greatest at intermediate levels of uncertainty: at low levels of uncertainty there is diversive exploration, seeking stimulation to avoid boredom; at high levels, there is specific exploration to identify the source of the arousal, to see if it is dangerous, for example. We will return to this in Chapter 6.

Emotional responses

Affective (emotional) responses deal with how the environment makes you feel. Mehrabian and Russell (1974) produced a *three-factor theory* which identified three primary emotional responses to the environment, consisting of pleasure, arousal and dominance. These are influenced by both the setting and the personality of the individual and in turn, influence how the individual behaves in that environment. Studies which gave descriptions of scenes to individuals of measured personality tested their *pleasure–arousal hypothesis*. This states that we appreciate more stimulating surroundings as the pleasantness of the setting increases. Research by Russell and Mehrabian (1978) showed some support for this idea: pleasant settings were liked more if they were also more stimulating; and neutral settings were most popular at moderate levels of stimulation. Unpleasant settings, however, did not conform to prediction, both low and high levels of stimulation being preferable to moderate levels.

The affective appraisal of settings can be measured using Environmental Emotional Reaction Indices (EERIs), devised by Russell and Lanius (1984). These researchers have produced a list of 40 descriptors of places, which can

FIGURE 2.8 *According to the Russell and Lanius model of the affective quality of places, emotional reactions to environments can be described by their relative position on unpleasant–pleasant and arousing–not arousing continua. Note that we have few words for emotional neutrality (adapted from Russell and Lanius, 1984)*

be ordered along the dimensions of pleasant–unpleasant and arousing–not arousing, as in Figure 2.8. Notice that dominance is no longer regarded as important.

The concept of affective appraisal has led to the introduction of *adaptation level theory* (Helson, 1964) into this area of research by Wohlwill (1966). Adaptation level refers to the level of stimulation that we are used to and therefore prefer; for example, some people prefer quieter environments than others. Wohlwill proposes that our affective responses to the environment are determined by the degree of discrepancy between our adaptation level and the present level of stimulation we are receiving. The *butterfly curve hypothesis* predicts that moderate changes in either direction from the adaptation level will be viewed as pleasant, while bigger changes will be perceived as unpleasant. This could explain why places will be evaluated differently by different observers or at different times.

Meanings

Meaning is used to refer to three processes in environmental psychology (Gifford, 1987).

1 *Attachment* to or feeling part of a place. Place attachment (Gold and Burgess, 1982) refers to the way that people feel rooted in a particular place and are reluctant to leave, even in the face of disasters such as floods, famine and war. This comes with familiarity and may involve feelings of ownership (e.g. of a home) and special experiences in that place (such as the birth of a child). Some people, known as 'place people', may be more likely to develop such attachments (Mitchell et al., 1991) and it is often an important part of the self-concept, e.g. the Fenmen of East Anglia, who were traditionally part of an isolated rural community and became proud of their reputation for repelling outsiders.

2 *Communication* is the way that a place can signify a concept; for example, Hitler employed architects to build in a style that was intended to convey the Nazi image (Espe, 1981), as shown in Figure 2.9.

FIGURE 2.9 *An example of Nazi architecture*

3 *Purpose* refers to the way that the appearance of a place can signify its purpose, e.g. a church is instantly recognisable for what it is. Architects need to be able to convey a building's purpose to potential users. Prak and Van Wegen (1975) found that pictures of buildings would be judged very differently by research participants according to the function ascribed to them, e.g. if they were labelled as a college or a railway station.

Attitudes

Attitudes are defined in psychology as a 'learned predisposition to respond to an object or class of objects in a consistently favourable or unfavourable way' (Allport and Odbert, 1935). They consist of three components: cognitions (thoughts and beliefs); the affective component (feelings); and the behavioural component (actions or action tendencies). For example, attitudes towards London will incorporate thoughts about its size, buildings and pollution levels, feelings of excitement or fear and possible things to do if you go there. Attitudes to the environment can be measured using the Ecological Attitude Scale (Maloney and Ward, 1973). This has four subscales: knowledge; affect; verbal commitment (what people say they will do, for example to conserve the environment); and actual commitment (what they have actually done). This has been validated by testing pro-ecology groups to check that they obtain different scores from those who are not ecologically minded. Gifford et al. (1982) used it to show that females said that they were more upset about such issues than males and intended to do more (verbal commitment), but they reported doing less (actual commitment) and knew less about environmental problems (knowledge).

Attitude formation rests on two important cognitive foundations – beliefs and values. According to Bem (1970), beliefs can be divided into two kinds: primitive and higher order. Primitive beliefs are those which we are not conscious of and do not question, such as the belief that smoking makes you cough. They are based either on our own experiences or on external authority figures such as parents. Higher-order beliefs are derived through thought processes, so they may be rational, although this is not necessarily the case. For example, on the basis of information from scientific reports, we may believe that smoking is bad for the health; we may not necessarily have checked those reports for inaccuracies and logical flaws.

Values represent preferences for certain end states and they give attitudes a purpose. For example, if we value clean air we will support campaigns to control pollution.

The affective component of attitudes is learnt through a process of association, known as *classical conditioning*. According to ·the *reinforcement affect model* (Byrne and Clore, 1970), what happens is that a neutral stimulus is associated with a stimulus that already elicits an affective response, and therefore comes to elicit the same response itself, as shown in Figure 2.10. This means that an environment may come to be disliked if something unpleasant or frightening happens there.

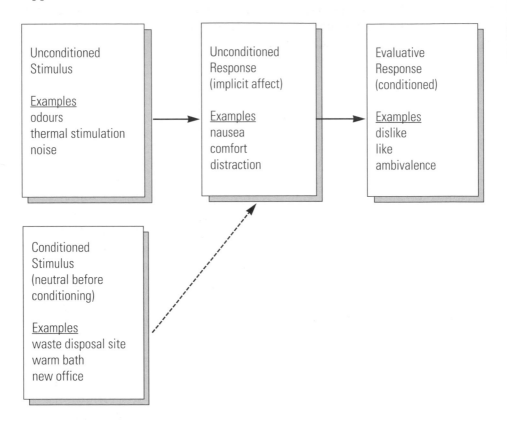

FIGURE 2.10 *Conditioning of the affective component of environmental attitudes*

Learning can also occur through a process of reward and punishment, known as *operant conditioning* (Skinner, 1938). If a behaviour is followed by a pleasant consequence (positive reinforcement) it is likely to be repeated. So if an attitude towards the environment is likely to have pleasant personal consequences or be supported by friends, it is likely to be maintained. Thus hikers have been found to be more pro-environment than motorsport enthusiasts.

Observation is another important source of attitudes. Social learning often occurs through a process of observation and imitation, as shown by Bandura (1969) in his studies of children's aggression. Observation of the consequences of other people's behaviour, known as *vicarious learning*, is an important part of this process. Social influences are another key element; many people will adopt similar attitudes to their friends in order to be accepted as part of the group.

A final consideration in this section is the relationship between attitudes and behaviour. Consistency theories of attitude change (e.g. Festinger, 1957) suggest that people generally try to behave in ways that are consistent with their attitudes. Despite this, a large body of research indicates that they do not always do so, and it is important to consider why this is. We will return to this in Chapter 6.

CHAPTER SUMMARY

To summarise this chapter, it has been shown that cognition about the environment is a complex process. It involves firstly perception or interpretation of information received by the senses (bottom-up processing), which is influenced by past experience (top-down processing). This leads to individual and cultural differences in perception. Theories of what perception involves and how it operates include the Gestalt principle of the 'good form', Gibson's theory of ecological perception and affordances and Brunswik's lens model. As well as constancy, environmental changes are monitored and responded to.

Research on the second cognitive process, spatial cognition, has focused on cognitive maps (Lynch, 1960; Appleyard, 1970) and their use in wayfinding (Garling et al., 1984) and has shown them to be affected by a range of environmental, individual and developmental factors. This research has been applied to planning, colour coding and map making.

Third, research on environmental appraisal explores the ways in which we describe and evaluate our environment, our aesthetic judgements and affective responses and the development of attitudes towards the environment. These issues will be followed up in Chapter 6, which deals with the natural environment, and Chapter 7, on stress and the perception of risk.

In the next two chapters we will continue our examination of the effects of the environment by considering the influence of the physical and social aspects of our surroundings.

chapter three

THE PHYSICAL ENVIRONMENT

CHAPTER OVERVIEW

The environment in which we live bombards all our senses with a massive amount of information, often referred to as 'ambient stimulation', most of which we do not attend to because it is unimportant to us at the time. Whether we attend to it or not, however, it has important effects on our physical health, psychological well-being and ability to perform the tasks that are part of our daily lives. Stimulation, for example in the form of visual, auditory and tactile information, is essential to make us function well (as studies of sensory deprivation have shown), but it can also have adverse effects. In addition, we can also be affected by the weather, the altitude, air pollution and other aspects of the environment of which we may be less aware. In this chapter we will be exploring a range of these factors and their effects on behaviour.

NOISE

Noise is the first of these. It can be defined as *unwanted sound*, a definition which makes the point that what one person considers to be noise, another may judge to be desirable sound – rock music blasting from a car stereo being a good example. Sound, then, is a physical change in air pressure that creates sound waves. These can be measured in decibels and detected by the ears. Examples of decibel levels associated with a range of common sounds are given in Figure 3.1. Noise, on the other hand, is a psychological concept. Noise can come from anything that makes a sound but whereas the sound may be constant, its effect on the hearer may vary, so a sound that we find acceptable at one time may be considered a noise at another. For example, a dripping tap may not be noticeable during the day but could be infuriating when we are trying to sleep. The environment in which we hear the sound is also important, so that the sound of a racing car may be thrilling on the circuit but a major disruption on the road outside your home.

Despite these variations in response, there are two good examples of environments where noise is almost always a problem. First of all, there is the noise

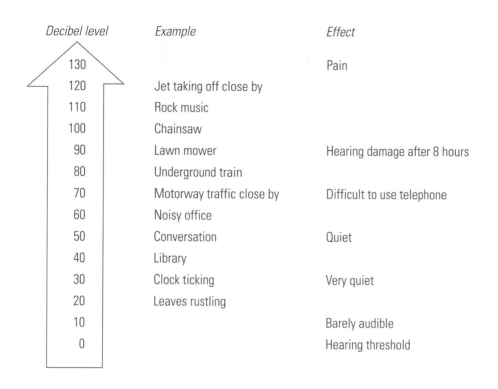

FIGURE 3.1 *Decibel levels associated with common sounds*

caused by *transportation* – cars, lorries, trains, planes, etc. – which is the most frequently mentioned source of urban noise (Lawson and Walters 1974). It has been estimated that over 11 million Americans are exposed to vehicular noise at levels that could cause hearing loss (Bolt et al., 1982) and research has shown that people living near airports, railways or motorways report increased levels of annoyance, blood pressure and ear problems (Ising et al., 1990).

The second example is *occupational* noise. Some jobs are associated with high sound levels, for example, construction workers may be exposed to 100 dB sound, despite the legal limit being set at 90 dB (Raloff, 1982). Even when sound levels are not high, as with the sound produced by air conditioners, there may be effects on psychological well-being and reports of annoyance (Bradley 1992).

In general, there are three aspects of noise that have been shown by Glass and Singer (1972) to influence how annoying it is. These are described in Box 3.1.

Box 3.1   What makes noise annoying?

The first factor is *volume*: above 90 dB noise is psychologically disturbing; if regularly exposed to such levels for eight hours or more (as might happen at home or at work), hearing loss is likely. The second factor is *predictability*; if noise is unpredictable, it is more annoying than if it is constant or predictable. So people who live near railway lines may habituate to the sound of trains because it is predictable, but intermittent bursts from a pneumatic drill are more difficult to deal with. The third factor is *perceived control*; if we think that we can control the noise, e.g. by closing a window, it will not bother us so much. Our own vacuum cleaner, for example, will not bother us as much as our neighbour's. Note that we may not actually be able to control it – what matters is that we think we can.

Thus research has indicated that loud, unpredictable noise over which we think we have little control is the most damaging. Other factors which influence our response have been identified by Borsky (1969) and include the following.

■ *Necessity*. Annoyance will be increased if we think that the noise is unnecessary, e.g. a lawn mower may be more acceptable than a stereo if we think that a neatly trimmed lawn is important.

■ *Concern*. Annoyance is increased if we think that those making it have no interest in the well-being of others. So if we generally dislike our neighbours, we are more likely to be upset by their noise.

■ *Perceived health risks*. Fear of damage to health will increase our annoyance (which in turn increases the health risks!). If we have already suffered hearing loss, for example, we may feel more vulnerable in future.

■ *Satisfaction*. If we are generally dissatisfied with our environment (e.g. if we want to move from the neighbourhood) our annoyance is likely to be greater.

Effects of noise

What, then, are the effects of noise? These can be considered in terms of health, task performance and social behaviour.

Noise affects *health* in three ways. First, it can cause hearing loss by damaging the receptor cells in the ear; this may be temporary or permanent (Kryter, 1970). Health and safety regulations cover exposure at work, but in many cases of transport noise little action is taken. Cohen et al. (1973) found that children living on the lower floors of apartment blocks above a busy road in New York City had poorer hearing discrimination than those who lived on the upper floors. Leisure activities can also be hazardous; rock groups can produce up to 120 dB, exposure to which should only be permitted for 30 minutes per day, according to the regulations.

Noise can also lead to increases in physiological arousal and stress-related diseases. Effects have been observed on the endocrine, nervous, digestive and cardiovascular systems. Rosen (1970) found increased production of adrenaline, Jerkova and Kremorova (1970) found an increase in stomach ulcers and Ponomarenko (1966) found increases in blood pressure. The immune system may also be affected, leaving us more vulnerable to infection (McCarthy et al., 1992). Increased cigarette smoking and alcohol consumption is also likely, which in turn will affect health (Cherek, 1985).

Noise can also affect mental health. Studies in industry have shown that exposure is associated with increased irritability, anxiety, mood changes, instability and sexual impotence (Cohen et al., 1977). Increased rates of psychiatric admissions have been associated with living in noisier areas near Heathrow airport (Abey-Wickrama et al., 1969), although this has not always been confirmed. Stansfield et al., (1993) for example, found that traffic noise led to increases in reported annoyance, but not to psychological disorders.

Noise also affects *performance*, as has been demonstrated in studies in the laboratory, at school and at work. Laboratory studies (Stansfield et al., 1992) show mixed results, depending on the task type, characteristics of the individual (such as tolerance) and characteristics of the noise (such as intensity, predictability and control). Intermittent noise will affect performance on divided attention, vigilance and memory tasks, for example, but only if there is a lack of control over the noise source (Glass and Singer, 1972).

School performance was studied by Cohen et al. (1973) in their New York study mentioned earlier. Findings are given in Box 3.2.

Box 3.2   The effects of noise on school performance

Children who lived on the noisier lower floors of an apartment block were found to have poorer reading ability, which was thought to be the result of poor sound discrimination resulting from their hearing loss. Cohen et al. (1986) found that even when the researchers controlled for levels of hearing, children living near an airport had more difficulties with solving complex problems. A study of the area around Munich airport by Evans et al. (1993) confirmed this finding and found the children to be less motivated and less tolerant of frustration, leading them to give up more easily.

At work, although there are no clear effects on productivity (Kryter, 1970), effects have been found on morale, fatigue and the effectiveness of communication. Sundstrom et al. (1994) found, for example, that after offices had been renovated the increase in noise was responsible for a decline in job satisfaction. The major problem was that of 'masking', in which important sounds (such as what someone is asking us to do) are 'covered up' by other sounds.

Finally, noise can also affect *social behaviour*, such as attraction to others, aggression and helpfulness. In areas where traffic noise is high, for example, there is less informal interaction between neighbours (Appleyard and Lintell 1972). We may like other people less in noisy environments (Bull et al. 1972), but this may be complicated by gender differences; females may want to be with others more if they are afraid of the noise.

Probably because it increases levels of arousal, noise also increases aggression; this is especially likely if the situation suggests aggression, e.g. if provoked or if watching a violent film (Geen and O'Neil, 1969). Lack of control over the noise increases the likelihood of aggression as well. Given this, it might be predicted that helping behaviour (or altruism) would be decreased. This was confirmed by Mathews and Canon (1975), who found that researchers were given less help to pick up dropped books in noisy situations.

To conclude, if sound is perceived as noise, it can have detrimental effects on physical and mental health, on performance in the laboratory, at school and at work and on both pro- and antisocial behaviour. These effects will differ according to the characteristics of the noise and the perceiver.

TEMPERATURE

Temperature is another physical feature where a distinction can be made between the physical temperature of the environment (as measured in degrees Centigrade or Fahrenheit) and the perceived or psychological temperature. The latter depends on two things: first, deep body (or core) temperature, which is the internal temperature of the body, maintained close to 98.6° by homoeostatic mechanisms; and second, skin temperature, as registered by the receptors in the skin.

Perception of temperature depends on the difference between the body and the ambient temperature. We may think that a room is warm, for example, if we have just come in from the cold but the same room may feel cool when we have been sitting in the sun. It also depends on what we have acclimatised to. We become used to a particular climate and it can take up to 14 days to adapt to change (Tromp, 1980).

Temperature perception also depends on humidity and wind. If the humidity is high and there is little air movement, we cannot lose excess heat by sweating and perceive the environment as being hotter. Therefore it is normal practice to measure the effective temperature by using an index that takes this into account as well (Tromp 1980).

Another important factor is our own activity level and the amount of clothing worn. Thus, the Tuareg of the Sahara wear loose clothes and avoid activity in the middle of the day (Sloan 1979). Figure 3.2 demonstrates the effect of clothing on temperature.

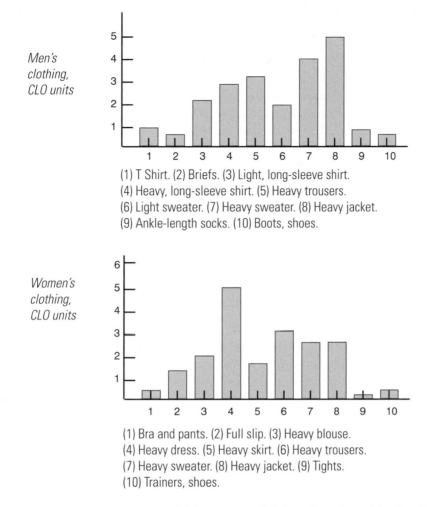

(1) T Shirt. (2) Briefs. (3) Light, long-sleeve shirt.
(4) Heavy, long-sleeve shirt. (5) Heavy trousers.
(6) Light sweater. (7) Heavy sweater. (8) Heavy jacket.
(9) Ankle-length socks. (10) Boots, shoes.

(1) Bra and pants. (2) Full slip. (3) Heavy blouse.
(4) Heavy dress. (5) Heavy skirt. (6) Heavy trousers.
(7) Heavy sweater. (8) Heavy jacket. (9) Tights.
(10) Trainers, shoes.

FIGURE 3.2 *The insulating properties of different items of clothing for males and females (from Kantowitz, B.H. and Sorkin, R.D. Human Factors: Understanding People System Relationships. Copyright © 1983 John Wiley & Sons, Inc. Reprinted by permission)*

Putting all the above research together has made it possible to identify 'comfort envelopes', which specify the temperature ranges found to be acceptable for different levels of humidity, air speed, activity and clothing (Gifford, 1987).

Effects of temperature

As with noise, the effects of temperature on health, performance and social behaviour have been researched. Heat and cold can be looked at separately. The effects on *health* of high temperatures show up when the body core temperature rises to 101.8°F. This leads to heat exhaustion and deterioration in function. Heart rate increases, as does perspiration; as a result of increased perspiration, blood volume decreases and blood pressure falls. Fainting occurs because the brain is starved of oxygen, leading eventually to coma and death. At low temperatures, discomfort is experienced when the skin temperature falls to 68°F. If it falls further to 41°F it becomes painful and if this is prolonged chilblains (inflammation and swellings) and frostbite (ulcerations) develop. Shivering leads to piloerection (the hairs on the skin stand on end to trap heat) and blood flow to the surface of the skin is decreased, leading eventually to muscle rigidity. If the core temperature falls to 90°F heart irregularities occur, blood pressure falls and there is a loss of consciousness. At a core temperature of 75°F heart failure is likely (Kazantizis 1967).

Studies of general health show that there are more respiratory problems in the winter and more intestinal and insect-transmitted diseases in the summer. It is not certain whether this is due to differences in vulnerability or to the activity levels of bacteria and insects, however. Coronary heart disease is increased in both hot and cold conditions, while diabetes and arthritis are aggravated by cold (Burch and De Pasquale, 1962). Temperature changes are more likely to affect the elderly and young children, whose own temperature regulation mechanisms are less adequate.

Effects on *task performance* have also been investigated. Temperature increase impairs visual acuity, as well as performance on tasks of vigilance, attention, reaction time, memory and mathematics (e.g. Provins and Bell, 1970). This is especially true of people who are unskilled at the task (Hancock, 1986). In general, temperatures in excess of 90°F will impair mental task performance after two hours exposure in unacclimatised individuals. Moderate physical work will be affected after just one hour. These effects have been found in occupational and school environments as well as in the laboratory, e.g. Link and Pepler (1970) found reduced productivity in the clothing manufacturing industry as temperature increased. At the opposite extreme, Poulton (1970) found reduced performance on tasks of reaction time and muscle dexterity at temperatures below 55°F (13°C).

As regards *social behaviour*, the popular belief is that aggression and riots are more common in the summer when temperatures are high. Research into this is summarised in Box 3.3.

Extreme temperatures also seem to affect how much we like others. Thus, Cunningham (1979) has shown that people are less likely to agree to be interviewed in the winter and in the heat of summer; a warm day in winter led to more co-operation. Exposure to hot conditions reduces the likelihood of offers to help (Page, 1978) and reduces our liking for strangers (Griffitt, 1970). Research in cold weather may be confounded by the 'cold weather helping norm', suggested by the finding that in harsh winters there is increased helping and reduced levels of crime. The fact that general crime rates in different countries do not vary according to climate (Alaska is no

Box 3.3   Do high temperatures increase aggression?

The US Riot Commission (1968) reported that all but one of the riots that occurred in 1967 began on days when the temperature was at least in the 80s (27°C or above). This is illustrated in Figure 3.3, taken from the study by Goransen and King (1970), which showed that riot years were associated with heat wave conditions. Anderson and Anderson (1984) found an increase in the number of aggressive crimes (such as rape and murder) as the temperature rises during the year. This may be partly the result of increased opportunities, since people are more likely to be outside or to leave doors and windows open in warm weather. Baron (1976) noted that there is more horn honking in car drivers when the temperature rises above 85°F (29°C). In the laboratory, Bell and Baron (1977) found that moderate cold led to an increase in aggression. It has been suggested that at extremely high or low temperatures there may be a decrease in aggression due to the amount of discomfort experienced.

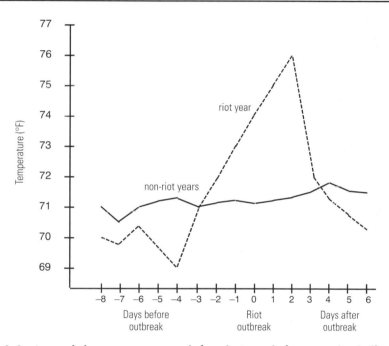

FIGURE 3.3 *Average daily mean temperatures before, during and after riot outbreak (from Goransen and King, 1970)*

better in this respect than Saudia Arabia, for example) suggests that what is important here is the perception of change, not the actual recorded temperature.

To conclude, perception of temperature is dependent on acclimatisation, differences between body and ambient temperature, humidity, wind speed, activity and clothing. Deviation from the ideal in either direction has a detrimental effect on physical health, task performance aggression and helping behaviour.

LIGHT

Light needs to be looked at in two ways: the effects of natural light and the effects of artificial light. One of the major effects of *natural light* appears to be on the mood of some individuals, as described in Box 3.4.

Box 3.4   Seasonal affective disorder

As the seasons change, so does the amount of available sunlight. It has been shown (Rosenthal and Blehar, 1989) that in some people this produces a depressive state in winter, known as seasonal affective disorder (SAD). The other symptoms are overeating, leading to weight gain, oversleeping, lack of energy and social withdrawal. They also have a preference for brightly lit rooms (Heerwagen, 1990). A summer version has also been found, which is associated with weight loss and insomnia. The disorder may result from disruption of the production of melatonin by the pineal gland in the brain. Melatonin is known to affect mood and how energetic people feel. It is produced in the dark but suppressed in light conditions so it may be that in winter sufferers are producing too much. Summer SAD may be associated with producing too little. Winter SAD can be treated by using phototherapy, where sufferers are exposed to artificial sunlight for a couple of hours a day. After 2–4 days, improvement should occur (Jacobsen et al., 1989), possibly because melatonin production is suppressed.

The effects of jet lag and shift work can also be considered here. In both cases, our circadian rhythm, the daily changes in activity levels that we experience, is disrupted. Although this is not entirely the result of the daily changes in light and darkness, as studies of people living in constant light have shown, light is one of the cues (or *Zeitgebers*) that our internal clock responds to. In the case of jet lag, we may experience headaches, digestive disorders and sleep disturbances for anything up to two weeks after the journey. Exposure to properly timed bright light can help with this too. Shift work is an illustration of what happens when our body clock and the absence of light are telling us to go to sleep, but we need to stay awake in order to work. One important consequence of this is an increase in accident rates. It takes about three days to adjust to a 12-hour shift in time, which can be assisted by exposure to bright light for four hours on the first night of the shift.

In more general terms, there are seasonal rhythms in birth and death rates, suicide, growth, weight (which increases in the autumn and is lost in the spring and summer; Attarzadeh (1983)) and food preferences (for starch in autumn and winter and protein in the summer; Zifferblatt et al. (1980)). Some of these are likely to be light related.

Artificial light is not generally liked as much as natural light. The preferred level of illumination depends very much on the activity we are engaged in. Compare, for example, a romantic candlelit dinner with the light level required when doing needlework. There are different types of artificial light and some are preferred to others. Full-spectrum fluorescent light, which is more like natural light, is preferred to cool white fluorescent light, but is under-utilised because it is expensive. Children have been found to be less overactive, less fidgety, pay more attention and perform better under full-spectrum light (Colman et al., 1976). However, Veitch et al. (1991) claim that such findings may be the result of demand characteristics – children changing as a result of the researchers' expectations – and argue that any effects that do exist are likely to be small. Brightly lit rooms are generally more arousing (Mehrabian, 1976b) but dark ones help to release social inhibitions, making people more likely to behave in intimate, aggressive or impulsive ways (Gergen et al., 1973), as detailed in Box 3.5.

Box 3.5   Deviance in the dark

Gergen et al. (1973) conducted an interesting demonstration of how darkness leads to disinhibiton of social behaviours. Subjects (mostly college students) volunteered for the experiment entitled Environmental Psychology. Each person was escorted alone to a completely darkened chamber. They removed their shoes, emptied their pockets and were left in the pitch-black room with the other subjects in that session. In each group there were four males and four females. They were told that they would be left in the chamber for no more than an hour, that they would be escorted from the chamber alone and that they would never meet the other participants. Control groups had the same experience in the same chamber with one important difference: in the control groups, the lights were left on. The question was, would the subjects in the totally dark room with people they would never meet feel freer to 'let down their guard' and be less encumbered by the rules that regulate interactions between strangers?

The difference between the behaviours of the people in the lighted and darkened rooms was marked. People in the lighted room kept a continuous stream of conversation going for the whole session and they tended to sit in one spot throughout the experiment. On the other hand, people in the dark room talked much less and moved around much more. There was also more touching in the darkened room. All dark-room subjects touched one another accidently and over 90% of them purposely touched someone else. In the lighted room, accidental touches were rare and intentional touching was almost non-existent. About 50% of the subjects in the dark room hugged someone else and almost 80% reported feeling some sexual excitement. Many of the dark-room subjects even engaged in kissing. Interestingly, these intimate behaviours decreased dramatically in dark-room groups where the participants thought that they would meet each other after the session.

Clearly, the deindividuation and anonymity encouraged by the darkness left the participants feeling freer to deviate from the usual societal restraints about interacting with strangers. Perhaps the 'dark side' of human nature is not so dark after all!

Source: McAndrew (1993)

In health terms, there are no clear effects of artificial light. Where problems such as eyestrain, headaches and nausea have been reported (Ponte 1981), these have generally been attributed to incorrect installations leading to too much glare (Fletcher, 1983). Adding ultraviolet light to fluorescent, producing full spectrum, has been found in Russian studies to increase height and weight in children but the accuracy of this research has been queried.

Light, then, can affect both mood and activity levels, probably through its effects on our circadian rhythm. Natural light is preferred to artificial, but there is no clear evidence that they have different effects.

Colour and its effects have been the subject of a great deal of speculation but little research. Colour has three dimensions — brightness (intensity), hue (wavelength) and saturation (the amount of white it contains). Mehrabian and Russell (1974) have found that both brightness and saturation are associated with liking. People prefer light colours and those from the green/blue end of the spectrum ('cool') to those from the orange/red ('warm') end. Malandro et al. (1989) found that putting blue granules into washing powder resulted in favourable reports; with yellow, it was alleged that clothes did not come up as clean, while red was reputed to be rough on the hands.

Room colour also affects physiological reactions, such as blood pressure and respiration rate (Acking and Küller, 1972), but does not affect perception of room temperature (Greene and Bell, 1980). Thus arousal is increased by red, but not by green/blue (Wilson, 1966). It has been suggested that red may induce aggression and pink relaxation (Schauss, 1979) and pink rooms do seem to reduce anxiety more than red ones do (Profusek and Rainey, 1987).

When overt behaviour is considered, red/orange hallways lead people to walk faster (Seaton, 1968). More hand tremor is shown on tracing tasks carried out in red compared with grey surroundings (Nakshian, 1964) and male students have stronger grips when exposed to red than to green (O'Connell et al., 1985). Greater strength is exerted with the hands and the legs when staring at blue than at pink (Pellegrini et al., 1980), although it has been suggested that this may be the result of associating colours with masculinity and femininity.

Cognitive task performance is also affected; when sitting under a red light, people overestimate the passage of time and the heaviness of weights; when sitting under a green/blue light, they underestimate them (Goldstein 1942). Other studies have reported effects of room colour on IQ (an increase of 26 points in bright blue, orange and red rooms, compared to drab white, brown and black rooms) and on friendliness (increased by 53% in orange rooms), but this research needs to be checked for reliability (Gifford, 1987).

In general, light rooms are perceived as being bigger and more spacious while dark rooms appear richer and more expensive (Acking and Küller, 1972). In a study of activity levels in an art gallery, Srivastava and Peel (1968) observed that people move around more but spend less time in a chocolate brown room compared with a beige room. Many colours are associated with moods, which means that they could affect response to the environment indirectly. Thus Wexner (1954) found that blue was associated with calmness and security, red with excitement and defiance, orange with being distressed and upset, black with power and despondency, purple with dignity and yellow with cheerfulness.

The effects of colour, then, are complex and subject to a variety of interpretations. In particular, the learned associations that they have for us may be more influential than the physical quality of the light itself.

AIR QUALITY

Air quality is determined by five main factors: wind; ionisation; electromagnetic fields; pressure and altitude; pollution levels. We will consider each of these in turn.

Wind, or air movement, is a natural variation that includes changes in speed and turbulence (gustiness). As well as natural variations, winds can be created or exaggerated by tall buildings, such as those in city centres, which create a wind tunnel effect. By channelling winds into narrow passageways, the force of the wind is increased to such an extent that people can be sucked along by it.

Table 3.1 Beaufort wind scale and related effects*

Beaufort number	Wind speed (mph)	Atmospheric and behavioural effects
0,1	0–3	Calm, no noticeable wind.
2	4–7	Wind felt on face.
3	8–12	Wind extends light flag; hair is disturbed; clothing flaps.
4	13–18	Dust, dry soil, loose paper raised; hair disarranged.
5	19–24	Force of wind felt on body; drifting snow becomes airborne; limit of agreeable wind on land.
6	25–31	Umbrellas used with difficulty, hair blown straight; walking becomes unsteady; wind noise on ears unpleasant; windborne snow above head height (blizzard).
7	32–38	Inconvenience felt when walking.
8	39–46	Generally impedes progress; great difficulty with balance in gusts.
9	47–54	People blown over by gusts.

The Beaufort Wind Scale contains three additional levels that involve damage to property.
Source: Bell et al. (1996)

Wind is not perceived by any specific sense organs. It is detected by pressure receptors in the skin; its temperature and humidity are registered by temperature detectors in the skin; the sound it creates is picked up by the ears; there is also feedback from the muscles about the amount of work they are having to do to resist its pressure. Measurement of perceptions of wind was introduced by Admiral Sir Francis Beaufort in 1806 and his scale is shown in Table 3.1. More recent scales (Penwarden, 1973) take into account such additional factors as angle of lean and body heat loss (wind chill).

When it comes to behavioural effects, little research has been carried out, although there are plenty of anecdotal allegations, e.g. reports from teachers that children are more restless, quarrelsome and careless on windy days. Sommers and Moos (1976) carried out correlational studies on the behavioural effects of winds in different parts of the world, e.g. the Mistral in Europe, the Chinook in America. The latter, which is a warm, dry wind, was found to be associated with depression, nervousness, irritability and an increase in traffic accidents in the residents of affected areas. Rim (1975) found that IQ scores were lower and neuroticism and extraversion higher when testing people during periods of hot desert wind than during calmer periods. Banzinger and Owens (1978) obtained a relationship between wind speed and crime, delinquency and mortality rates. Cohn (1993) found that wind speed was correlated with domestic violence, such that there was less domestic violence when the wind speed was increased. This study also controlled for the effects of other changes, such as temperature and humidity. In the Near East, some governments excuse criminal behaviour that occurs during windy periods and surgeons prefer not to operate on such days (Leiber, 1978).

Ionisation refers to the splitting of air molecules into positively and negatively charged particles or ions. Generally, there are slightly more positive than negative ions. This bias is increased inside buildings and other enclosed spaces and where pollution is higher. An increase in negative ions is associated with moving water, e.g. after a storm or beside rivers and fountains (Hansell, 1961). As an example, clean rural air contains about 1200 positive and 1000 negative ions per cubic centimetre, while an air-conditioned office contains 150 positive and 50 negative ions per cc (Hawkins, 1981). Commercially produced ionisers are now available which aim to generate negative ions and redress this balance. Although their claims of beneficial effects have been disputed and in the 1950s their sale was prohibited in America, there is research evidence that they do affect behaviour (Figure 3.4). For example, they have been found to improve learning in rats (Falkenberg and Kirk, 1977), slow brain waves (Assael et al., 1974), speed up reaction times (Hawkins and Barker, 1978), enhance positive moods (DeSanctis et al., 1981) and intensify interpersonal attraction (Baron, 1987). Positive ions are associated with worse performance and mental outlook, irritability, depression, insomnia, tension, and migraines (Assael et al., 1974),

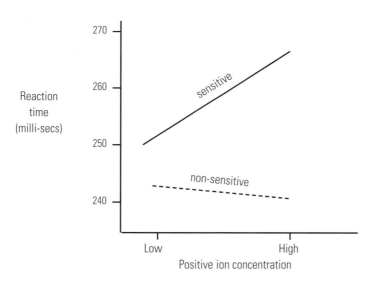

FIGURE 3.4 *The performance of a single behaviour (reaction time) that is important in many tasks such as driving and operating equipment is harmed by high concentrations of positive air ions for those who are ion sensitive (i.e. have low autonomic lability) but not for those who are not ion sensitive (adapted from Charry and Hawkinshire, 1981)*

and impaired memory in rats (Lambert and Olivereau, 1980). There are, however, individual differences in sensitivity (as shown in Figure 3.4) (Charry and Hawkinshire, 1981) and some inconsistencies in research findings.

Baron et al. (1985) found that negative ions may act as arousers and therefore exaggerate natural tendencies, which would explain the contradictory findings in the research. In a study of aggression, they found that increase in positive ions increased aggression levels in people who naturally tend to be aggressive (type A personalities). They argue that negative ions operate to increase arousal level, which in turn increases the likelihood of making dominant, well-learned responses (Zajonc, 1980). This would fit in with some British double-blind studies which have shown improved feelings when negative ions are increased. Hawkins (1981) reported that office workers felt warmer and more alert and judged the environment as fresher. Buckalew and Rizzuto (1982) found that after six hours exposure, students reported feeling more relaxed and stimulated and less irritable and depressed.

Another explanation could be that positive ions increase the level of serotonin in the brain. This is an inhibitory neurotransmitter which could have the effect of slowing down or reducing behaviour (Ray, 1978). This explanation is supported by case studies reported by Giannini et al. (1983) of the *serotonin irritation syndrome*, an anxiety state associated with environments rich in positive ions and increased serotonin levels.

Pressure and altitude have an inverse relationship: at high altitudes, air pressure is reduced, which in turn reduces the amount of available oxygen (as well as being associated with increased wind and solar radiation and lower temperatures). Below sea level, on the other hand, there is an increase in pressure and reduction in temperature. Normal atmospheric pressure, measured at sea level, is 14.7 lb/sq. inch.

The most immediate effect of low air pressure (Frisancho, 1979) is hypoxia (reduction in the available oxygen), which is compensated for by more rapid, deeper breathing. The heart rate increases and eventually the heart itself may enlarge. The retina of the eye becomes less light sensitive and there are cravings for sugar, although hunger in general is reduced, leading to weight loss. Hormone production is also affected: testosterone, sperm counts and thyroid activity are reduced; menstrual complaints and discomfort and adrenal activity are increased. Acclimatisation occurs after about six months and symptoms are reduced but long-term changes include increased lung capacity, enlargement of some areas of the heart, lower birth weights, slower growth and sexual maturation in children. Behaviour may also be affected; McFarland (1972) found that strenuous work was more difficult and the learning of new tasks was impaired.

High pressure effects, which may cause problems for divers, include difficulties with breathing, oxygen poisoning (due to excessive intake), nitrogen poisoning (leading to light-headedness and mental instability) and decompression effects ('the bends'), including permanent bone damage and development of nitrogen bubbles in the bodily tissues, if the pressure is reduced too quickly.

Changes in the weather involve changes in barometric pressure on a smaller scale, e.g. tropical storms involve low pressure and sunny days high pressure. Although there are often other changes as well, such as temperature, making the effect of these pressure changes difficult to research, some effects have been reported. First, there is an increase in medical complaints such as arthritis (Hollander and Yeostros, 1963); second, there is an increase in suicide rates and mental hospital admissions (Kevan, 1980), although these may also be affected by the time of year and changes in patterns of social contact (increases being found in the spring and summer); third, there is an increase in disruptive behaviour, such that classroom behaviour deteriorates when barometric pressure is low (Dexter, 1904) and there are more accidents and complaints to the police (Sells and Will, 1971).

Air pollution levels are the final area to consider. The atmosphere normally consists of 78% nitrogen, 21% oxygen, 0.9% argon and 0.03% carbon dioxide. Minute traces of ozone, hydrogen sulphide, methane, carbon monoxide and other particles may also be found. It is when the levels of these other substances change dramatically that the air can be considered to be polluted. This can occur in many ways, for example, exhaust gases from vehicles, smoke from fires and cigarettes, aerosol sprays and refrigeration equipment (releasing chlorofluorocarbons or CFCs), factory emissions, etc. Problems can be caused by the sheer volume of these emissions or by the lack of any wind to move them around and distribute them more thinly. The most common air pollutants are carbon monoxide, carbon dioxide, sulphur dioxide, nitrogen dioxide, formaldehyde, hydrocarbons and particulate matter. Many other chemical pollutants are waterborne and will therefore be considered in the next section.

Pollution may be detected by visible signs such as dust and smog or smell, but many pollutants are not easy to detect. As with other aspects of the physical environment, perceptions of pollution do not necessarily correspond to objective levels. For example, airtight double-glazed homes may have high levels of pollution, but their occupants are unlikely to be aware of this. Research has also shown that emissions from a chocolate factory lead to fewer complaints than comparable emissions from an oil refinery! (Winneke and Kastka, 1987).

Perception of pollution is also affected by other factors: people from lower socioeconomic groups are less aware (Swan, 1970); more anxious people are more aware (Navarro et al., 1987); familiarity may either lead to people becoming less bothered (Evans et al., 1979) or more concerned (Medalia, 1964). De Groot (1967) found that only 50% of people interviewed considered air pollution to be a problem and even those who did were unlikely to complain. Many report that they are satisfied with their neighbourhood, even if it smells awful and there is visible damage to house paint.

As well as the occasional disaster, such as the London smog of 1952 which killed 3500 people as a result of sulphur dioxide poisoning (Goldsmith, 1968), general lower level pollution can have serious health effects, some of which are summarised in Box 3.6. A general condition called *air pollution syndrome* (APS) has been identified, whereby a combination of pollutants results in headaches, fatigue, insomnia, irritability, depression, sore eyes, back pain, impaired judgement and gastrointestinal problems; there may also be a link with some cancers. There are in addition a wide range of specific effects.

Carbon monoxide, the most common pollutant, comes from vehicles, furnaces and steel mills and leads to hypoxia (deprivation of oxygen). Exposure to less than 0.1% in the air over several hours will lead to death. Lesser exposures produce impairment of hearing and vision, epilepsy, headaches, heart disease, fatigue, memory disturbances, mental retardation and psychotic symptoms.

Carbon dioxide results from the combustion of fossil fuels and it acts like a layer of glass in the atmosphere, trapping heat and giving rise to what is called the greenhouse effect. There is a projected increase of 8°C in the mean global air temperature over the next 40–50 years as a result of this. Little research has been carried out into the effects this would have on humans, although a decrease in visual acuity and sensitivity to the colour green have been reported.

Box 3.6 What you can't see in the air can hurt you: the major components of air pollution have a variety of health effects

Respiratory symptoms: Ozone, formed in sunlight when nitrogen oxides and hydrocarbons combine, aggravates respiratory problems by damaging epithelial cells in the trachea.

Skin problems: Arsenic, produced by furnaces, can cause skin cancer. Depletion of the ozone layer of the atmosphere may also contributed to skin cancer.

Nervous system diseases: Arsenic and lead can disrupt development in children or cause central nervous system problems.

Liver: Lead can cause liver disease.

Reproductive difficulties: Cadmium can retard development of the foetus.

Eyes: Hydrogen chloride causes irritation; carbon monoxide and ozone affect eye–hand co-ordination.

Heart: Carbon monoxide can reduce blood's ability to carry oxygen and cause symptoms of heart disease.

Lungs: Almost all particulates and metals accumulate in lungs and can contribute to cancer.

Source: Bell et al. (1996)

Sulphur and nitrogen dioxides are generated by the combustion of fossil fuels, smelting and transport. These combine with water in the atmosphere to produce acid rain, which has caused severe environmental problems in Europe and North America. It affects freshwater lakes and forests, leaches nutrients from soils and affects their productivity and damages buildings (especially those made from marble and limestone) and paintwork.

Ozone in the upper levels of the atmosphere absorbs ultraviolet rays from the sun and has a protective function. When it is destroyed by CFCs used in refrigeration and aerosol sprays, holes are created in the ozone layer. At present the holes are above the North and South Poles and have led to an increase in the levels of skin cancer as a result of the increasing ultraviolet radiation penetrating the atmosphere. At lower levels of the atmosphere, ozone is a pollutant, derived indirectly from nitrogen dioxide released in car exhaust fumes. It leads to nose and throat irritation, fatigue and lack of co-ordination, affects enzyme production and may accelerate the ageing process. Breathing excessive amounts for several hours leads to deterioration of lung tissue, haemorrhaging and death in rats and mice.

Formaldehyde (HCOH) is used in manufacturing particle board, paper, plywood, home insulation, leather, preservatives, drugs and cosmetics, so it will be found in all homes in many forms. It can be inhaled, ingested and absorbed through the skin, is toxic to all cells of the body and causes DNA damage. The general effects include eye, nose and throat irritation, sneezing, shortness of breath, sleeplessness, nausea, excess phlegm and genetic abnormalities. It is also linked to asthma, pharyngitis, reproductive disorders, bronchitis and cancer. Morticians, who use it as a preservative, have a high mortality rate from these disorders. Its psychological effects are unknown.

Particulates (dust) from vehicle emissions and combustion of fossil fuels, as well as natural sources such as volcanic eruptions and soil erosion, can become lodged in the lungs and interfere with respiration. Asbestos is a good example; others are mercury, arsenic, cadmium and lead. They exacerbate the effects of asthma and lower the resistance to disease, leading to cancer, anaemia, respiratory and nervous system problems.

Tobacco smoke, which is often cited as the major indoor pollutant, contains a cocktail of pollutants; in all there are 4720 compounds, including tar (a particulate), carbon monoxide and formaldehyde. It is linked with cancers (e.g. mouth, lung and bladder), lung diseases (such as bronchitis) and cardiovascular disease. These effects are produced by both mainstream and sidestream (passive) smoking; for example, the Report of the Surgeon General (1984) found an increase in the prevalence of bronchitis and pneumonia in the children of smokers.

As well as the specific effects on health documented above, which all have psychological implications, there are some general reactions to pollution that are worth noting. Bad-smelling air pollution, for example, has been found to impair performance of a relatively complex task (proofreading) but not a simple one (arithmetic), according to Rotton (1983). It reduces liking for paintings and photographs but increases attraction to other people if interaction with them is expected (Rotton et al., 1978). Moderately unpleasant smells also increase aggression (Rotton et al., 1979).

Carbon monoxide impairs performance on a time judgement task (Beard and Wertheim, 1967) and reaction time, manual dexterity and attention (Breisacher, 1971) Given the high levels of carbon monoxide where there is a lot of traffic, this suggests that there will be impaired information processing, leading to reduction in driving ability when it is most needed.

High ozone levels have been found to be associated with an increase in complaints about household disturbances (including child abuse) according to Rotton and Frey (1985). People who are experiencing high levels of stress from life events are more vulnerable to the effects of ozone exposure (Evans et al., 1987). In general, high levels of pollution are associated with reduced participation in outdoor activities (Evans et al., 1982b), reduction in helping behaviours (Cunningham, 1979) and an increase in anxiety, irritability and depression (Weiss, 1983) and psychiatric admissions (Briere et al., 1983). In some cases this may be because people who live in more polluted areas are likely to be poorer as well. The above behaviours may then be the consequence of poverty rather than (or as well as) pollution.

Air quality, then, has a significant effect on mental and physical functioning. Wind appears to be detrimental, as is a reduction in negative ions; changes in altitude and pressure have negative effects, as does any increase in the levels of pollution.

ENVIRONMENTAL TOXINS

Environmental toxins can be encountered at work or at home and include radiation, radon gas, asbestos, agrochemicals such as dioxin and organophosphates and a wide range of toxic chemical wastes. Many have the drawback, like much air pollution, of being undetectable by the senses – they cannot be seen, heard, smelt, touched or tasted, making them difficult to avoid or even be aware of.

Asbestos, for example, may be found in many old buildings, homes, schools and occupational settings. Inhalation of particles, which lodge in the lungs and form obstructions, can lead to cancer and lung disease. Despite being aware of the risks, Lebovits et al. (1986) found that their exposed sample did not show any more mental health problems than average and many continued to aggravate lung problems by smoking. *Lead* exposure has been linked to neurophysiological disorders and anxiety. Spivey et al. (1979) found that it may increase aggression and hostility; supporting this, Bromet et al. (1986) found that exposed workers were more likely than controls to report conflict in interpersonal relationships. Exposure during childhood leads to poorer school performance and lower IQ scores (Needleman et al., 1982).

Agrochemicals such as organophosphates (OPs) (found in sheepdip) have recently been linked with physical and mental health problems. Farmers exposed to polybrominated biphenyls in contaminated feed have been found to show increased guilt, depression, anxiety and withdrawal (Brown and Nixon, 1979). Toxic landfill sites can contaminate the water supplies and lead to increased depression, anger and mistrust (Gibbs, 1986). Some researchers have suggested that for many people, the effects are exaggerated by the stress and worry associated with living in close proximity to such known toxins, e.g. people living close to the Three Mile Island nuclear power plant.

A more recent cause for concern is *radon* gas, which leaks from natural uranium deposits in the ground and has the effect of increasing the ambient radiation levels in that area. In some areas (Figure 3.5), the concentration is higher than normal and homes are regularly tested. Some homes, however, are more easily infiltrated and others seem to trap the gas because they are well insulated and not ventilated, so levels within a street can vary considerably. Many people underestimate the possible problems that can result from the increased exposure to radiation (Sandman et al., 1987). We will return to the issue of radon and the effects of OPs in Chapter 8, when we consider the effects that people have on the environment.

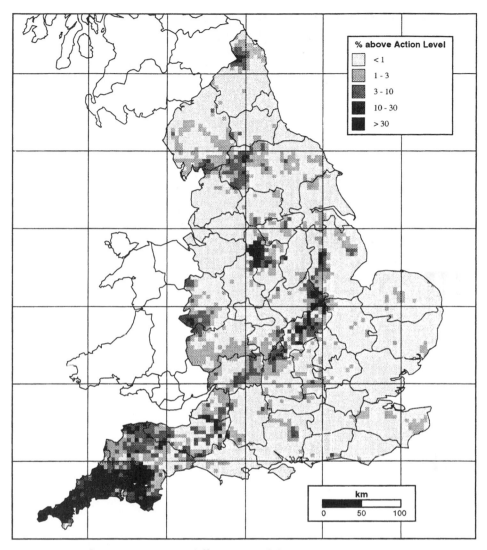

FIGURE 3.5 *Radon concentrations in different parts of the UK*

FOCUS ON APPLICATION ...
sick building syndrome

A recent development here is the concept of sick building syndrome. This should be distinguished from *building-related illness*, where illness and disease are related to toxic exposure or other aspects of the indoor environment (Woods, 1988). In sick building syndrome, on the other hand, there may be discomfort or symptoms, but no clear disease, leading to the implication of psychological factors. Symptoms disappear in the evenings and at weekends, for example and their nature—headaches, eye and nose irritation-makes it feasible that they could be due to either environmental conditions or to stress and fatigue. In some cases, up to 80% of the occupants of a building have been affected.

It appears to be more common in air-conditioned offices than in those with natural ventilation, so it may be due to the nature of the heating and ventilation systems and design of the building (Mendell and Smith, 1990). Poor air quality has often been blamed (Hedge, 1984), but research has been unable to confirm this (Hedge et al., 1993). The stress explanation also lacks support, as there is no link between susceptibility and personality (Eysenck, 1975). Generally, it is accepted to be environmentally caused, but the mechanism is unknown, and some writers (e.g. Pilkington, 1995) consider that it could equally well be termed 'sick management syndrome'. Higher status within the company is associated with better environmental conditions; it may be the status differentials that are the cause of illness and not the environmental differences.

The major symptoms are eye, nose and throat irritations, skin irritations, headaches, nausea and fatigue and allergic reactions such as asthma and runny nose and eyes. Complaints tend to be associated with gender, job stress and use of VDUs; complaints increase with temperature increases, number of hours worked per week, decreased job satisfaction and amount of photocopying carried out (Hedge et al., 1993). The largest study to date, by Hedge et al. (1989, 1993), covered 64 buildings in the U. K. and found that the best predictors of symptoms were job stress, environmental comfort ratings and perception of conditions, VDU use and job satisfaction. Hedge's model is shown in Figure 3.6.

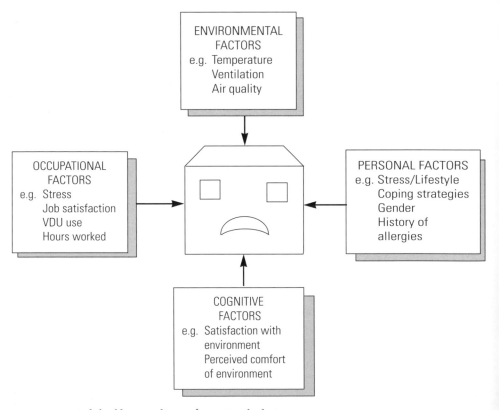

FIGURE 3.6 *Sick building syndrome: factors involved*

ENVIRONMENTAL LOAD

As well as considering the effects of specific elements of the environment that surrounds us, the section above on sick building syndrome illustrates the importance of the *holistic* approach. We can therefore conclude this chapter by exploring ways in which the general impact of the environment can be considered. Mehrabian (1976b) refers to this as *environmental load*, a highly loaded environment being one that delivers a lot of information and a low-load environment being one that is less stimulating. As well as being more stimulating, a highly loaded environment is more arousing and will in general lead to higher activity levels. Compare, for example, Alton Towers with a deserted beach.

Mehrabian argues that environmental load is a function of three aspects of the environment:

1   *intensity*, which refers to how much sensory stimulation there is (e.g. how loud the noise is);

2   *novelty*, referring to how familiar it is (e.g. how many times you have been there before);

3   *complexity*, which depends on how many different stimuli are present (compare holidays based on a single activity with those that offer a wide range, for example).

In general, intense, novel, complex stimuli lead to more load. This could be explained in evolutionary terms (Tooby and Cosmides, 1990) since intensity and novelty could be signs of danger and complexity could indicate that further exploration could be useful. Therefore individuals who respond to these kinds of things would be favoured in the course of natural selection.

This implies that not everyone will respond in the same way and that environmental overload or underload could occur, producing changes in arousal level which could be stressful. We will return to this topic again in Chapter 7.

CHAPTER SUMMARY

To conclude this chapter, the physical environment stimulates us in a variety of ways; changes in noise levels, temperature and humidity, light and colour, air quality (incorporating wind, ionisation, pressure and altitude) have all been shown to affect us physically and to alter psychological functioning in terms of task performance and social relationships. The effects of air pollution and environmental toxins have also been considered; although in many cases research has yet to be carried out into their psychological consequences, the effects on health can be severe and this awareness alone can have psychological implications. Research into sick building syndrome illustrates the importance of taking a holistic view, in that some buildings seem to have effects on their occupants that cannot be attributed to one particular variable. The general level and type of stimulation, or environmental load, must also be considered in terms of intensity, novelty and complexity, as this too must be at an optimum level for effective functioning. One major issue that has not yet been considered is the way in which the other occupants of the environment affect our behaviour and it is to this that we turn in the next chapter.

chapter four

THE SOCIAL ENVIRONMENT

CHAPTER OVERVIEW

The way that people use space in social interaction and the effects that this has on behaviour is defined as the study of *proxemics* (Hall, 1959). In this chapter we will be looking at four aspects of this topic – personal space, territory, privacy and crowding and density.

PERSONAL SPACE

Personal space is a term coined by Katz in 1937, subsequently defined by Sommer (1969) as 'an area with invisible boundaries, surrounding a person's body, into which intruders may not come'. It is often described as being like a bubble which we carry around with us, which can expand and contract according to the situation (Figure 4.1). It can be divided into alpha personal space, which is objectively measured distance and beta personal space, which is a subjective estimate of distance (Gifford & Price, 1979).

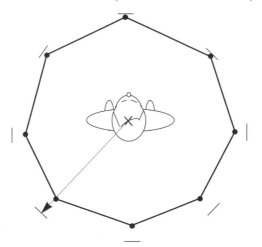

FIGURE 4.1 *The shape of personal space. The lines represent average distances around the bodies of students when approached by a young male researcher until they told him they felt uncomfortable about his closeness (based on Gifford, 1987)*

Measurement

There are three ways of measuring alpha personal space: simulation (or projective) measures; laboratory stop-distance methods; and naturalistic observation. *Simulations*, where real people do not actually interact during the measurement process, have been popular in the past because they are easy to use. Silhouette figures are employed instead and participants are asked to imagine that they are interacting and place them in appropriate positions (Kuethe, 1962). Another example is the Comfortable Interpersonal Distance Scale or CID (Duke and Nowicki, 1972), illustrated in Figure 4.2. This is a projective technique, where people are asked to mark on a line where they would like a person to stop when approaching them from different angles. The obvious problem with such measures is that they may not be valid or reliable indicators of behaviour in real situations.

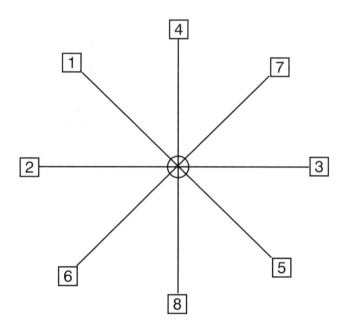

FIGURE 4.2 *The Comfortable Interpersonal Distance (CID) scale is a projective method of studying personal space. Respondents are instructed to imagine they are in the centre of a room and someone is approaching them from one of the eight directions. They are to mark the line at the point they would begin to feel uncomfortable (from Duke and Nowicki, 1972)*

Laboratory stop-distance methods differ in that a real person is asked to approach the individual concerned, who indicates for them to stop when they reach a comfortable distance (e.g. Hayduk, 1985). This method is reliable but because its purpose is obvious and participants are made to focus on their distance preferences to an unusual extent, it is unlikely to be valid.

Naturalistic observation has the advantage of being a disguised method and is therefore more natural as participants are unaware of being observed. This can be done by the use of recording devices to film, photograph or video people in natural settings; distance can be measured by counting floor tiles of known size or by making grids out of tape. This has been used in a wide range of situations, e.g. schools, beaches, zoos, shopping centres and amusement parks (e.g. Dabbs and Stokes, 1975). There are, however, still problems with the technique. First, obtaining precise measurements from photographic or other records is not as easy as it seems; second, in such complex situations there are a great many uncontrolled variables that may influence results (e.g. the presence of other people in the vicinity); and finally, many psychologists have ethical objections to the observation of individuals who have not had the opportunity to give informed consent to their participation, considering it to be an invasion of privacy.

Characteristics of personal space

Although originally described as bubble-like, it is now thought that personal space is shaped more like an irregular cylinder (Hayduk, 1981). It appears to vary in size according to which part of the body is being focused on and whether measurements are taken from in front, to the side or behind. It has been divided by Hall (1966) into 4 different zones, based on his observations of personal space use in different cultures. Interactions between people take place at one of these 4 distances, which are shown in Box A.

Box 4.1   Hall's zones of interpersonal space

Intimate (0–18") is reserved for full-contact relationships (such as those involving comforting or lovemaking) or occasionally for relationships governed by rules (e.g. wrestling) or for heated arguments.

Personal (18"–4') is for friends involved in conversation, where touching may occur.

Social (4'–12') is for business interactions, formal and informal and more formal social interactions, where people are not acquainted and not especially friendly.

Public (12'–25'+) would be used for very formal interaction, e.g. between speakers and audiences, or defensively where interaction is not desired.

The distances quoted in Box 4.1 are based on observation of white middle-class Americans and a visual depiction is given in Figure 4.3. Hall observed that they may vary in different individuals as a result of experience and also show cultural differences. This leads us into a consideration of the factors affecting personal space preferences.

FIGURE 4.3 *Views of a person using intimate distance (a), personal distance (b), social distance (c) and public distance (d)*

Variables influencing personal space

Personal space can vary in both size and shape as a result of the influence of a wide range of factors. These can be divided into situational, personal and cultural.

Situational factors are of two types: social factors, which are to do with the nature of the relationship between individuals; and physical factors, which are to do with the physical environment in which the interaction takes place. The first *social* factor is the degree of attraction or liking between the individuals concerned. Little (1965) found that outline figures of people described as good friends were placed closer together. People are generally more comfortable when a friend or someone similar to them (e.g. in age or race) stands close to them. Women in particular reduce interpersonal distance to indicate attraction (Edwards, 1972). Insults and criticism lead to dislike and increased interpersonal distance (Guardo and Meisels, 1971). Interactions with stigmatised persons, e.g. obese, facially disfigured or amputees, also involve increased distance (Wolfgang and Wolfgang, 1971). Status is also important; for example, in the military, the greater the difference in rank, the greater the interpersonal distance (Dean et al., 1975). It is up to the higher status member of the pair to move closer.

Where the *physical* environment is concerned, the over-riding principle appears to be that if space is limited or escape difficult, more space is required. For example, more space is required indoors than outdoors, in the corner than in the centre of a room and in small, low-ceilinged rooms (Cochran et al., 1984).

Personal factors are evident in the range of different responses to the same situation. Gender, age and personality are the best researched of these. *Gender* differences are complex. Females seem to prefer closer distances in same-sex interactions, whilst males in pairs tend to prefer a greater distance (Aiello, 1987). This may reflect differences in the amount of socialisation to be affiliative received by each sex or male concern with avoiding allegations of homosexuality. Where there is threat or discord, females prefer greater distance than males. Mixed-sex pairs tend to be closer, if the relationship is intimate, than same-sex pairs but if they are just friends they tend to be in between the female and male same-sex pairs. In the middle of menstrual flow, females keep a greater distance from males than they do at other times during the cycle. Since their behaviour with females does not change in this way, this may be a way of indicating that they are not sexually receptive (Gallant et al., 1991).

Age affects personal space preferences more predictably. By 18 months, infants are showing changes according to the person and the situation (Castell, 1970); by the time they are about 12 years old, they have fully developed the adult norms (Aiello, 1987). In general, personal space increases as the child gets older, although it can be inconsistent in younger children (Figure 4.4).

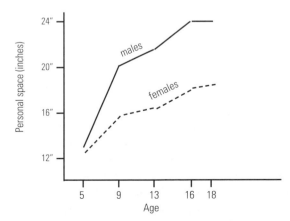

FIGURE 4.4 *Personal space increases with grade in school, with males showing larger increases than females (based on Tennis and Dabbs, 1975)*

Personality affects personal space in predictable ways. Extraverts or people high in need for affiliation with others have smaller personal space zones (Cook, 1970); anxious people tend to require more (Patterson, 1973), as shown by studies of psychiatric and criminal populations. Schizophrenics, for example, have larger and more variable personal space requirements (Horowitz et al., 1964) and violent prisoners also require more personal space, especially behind them (Hildreth et al., 1971).

Culture, as previously mentioned, was studied by Hall (1966), who divided cultures into 'contact' (e.g. Mediterranean, Arabic, Hispanic) and 'non-contact' (e.g. North European, white American) and suggested that the latter group preferred greater interpersonal distance. There are also subcultural differences; for example, members of the same ethnic group interact more closely than those from different ethnic groups (Willis, 1966). However, there have been many conflicting research findings in this area and results can be affected by socioeconomic status (Scherer, 1974) and the choice of language to use in the interaction (Sussman and Rosenfeld, 1982).

Effects of personal space on behaviour

If personal space is important to us, interfering with it should have noticeable effects on behaviour. Inappropriate distance can be created by either standing too close to someone (invasion of personal space) or by keeping too distant from them. Effects of these changes on attribution and impression formation, attraction, helping behaviour, working in groups, arousal, emotion and flight have been considered.

Attribution about psychological characteristics has been investigated by asking for judgements about the status of people seen in films. When personal space is manipulated in the films, people are judged as being more equal in status if they interact at closer quarters (Burns, 1964). *Impressions* of others can be related to their choice of distance; people who choose to sit at greater distances are viewed more negatively (Patterson and Sechrest, 1970). Choice of appropriate distance facilitates *attraction*. Fisher and Byrne (1975) found that students of both sexes liked a female who sat closer better than they did a male, which fits in with the gender differences mentioned earlier.

Helping behaviour has been investigated by invading personal space. In this situation, people are less likely to help, for example by picking up an object that is dropped (Konecni et al., 1975). However, if the 'invader' requests help and appears to be in great need, then more help is likely in this situation (Baron, 1978). Co-operation and productivity in *group work* have been investigated and related to how closely group members sit and whether they sit facing one another or side by side. Effects are complex but the overall conclusion is that there is more co-operation when people are close or face one another. Competition is more likely when they are more distant or less face to face and can in this situation lead to greater productivity (Gifford, 1987).

Arousal levels change when personal space is invaded and can be used as an indicator of the level of discomfort experienced. A controversial study demonstrating this was carried out by Middlemist et al. (1976), who invaded personal space by standing next to a male using a urinal. This led to urination taking longer to begin and occurring more quickly, usually regarded as an indicator of tension. People have also been found to cross the street more quickly if their personal space is invaded while waiting for lights to change (Konecni et al., 1975). Invasion of personal space by a friendly person has positive effects, however, indicating that cognitive interpretation of the arousal produced is a key factor (Storms and Thomas, 1977). If the arousal can be attributed to a source other than the space invasion (as it might be at a football match, for example) then there are no negative effects (Worchel and Yohai, 1979).

Box 4.2   The effects of personal space invasion

Emotion and flight were studied by Sommer (1969) in a classic study in which men sitting alone had their space invaded by a researcher who sat 6–20 cm away; 30% moved within one minute and 55% within ten minutes, compared with 0% and 25% of control subjects who had not been invaded. This was originally carried out with mental patients, but later confirmed in a college library with a student population.

Theoretical explanations have also been offered to explain the origins and functions of personal space and why disruption has so many negative effects. There are two theories about the *origins* of personal space. *Ethological models* (e.g. Evans and Howard, 1973) suggest that, because all humans seem to have a need for personal space, it may be genetic in origin. *Social learning models* (e.g. Duke and Nowicki, 1972) focus on the differences between individuals and argue that personal space is learned as a result of the processes of observation, imitation and reinforcement. This accounts for its gradual acquisition in children and for cultural differences, but not for where it came from in the first place!

Most theories focus on the *functions* of personal space and have suggested four possibilities. *Comfort* was suggested to be the main purpose by Sommer (1959), who argued that being either too close or too far away from others is uncomfortable. The problem with this idea is that 'comfort' is a difficult concept to define and measure. *Protection* was suggested by Dosey and Meisels (1969), who considered that personal space protects the individual against aggression and helps to maintain self-esteem and behavioural freedom. This fits in with the work of Hildreth et al. (1971) on violent prisoners, who were found to have 'body buffer zones' up to four times those of non-violent prisoners.

Communication and the regulation of intimacy have also been proposed as functions. Not only is it easier to pick up sensory information when at the appropriate distance, but personal space itself is a form of non-verbal communication, providing information about the relationship between individuals (e.g. attraction, relative status) and the nature of their interaction (whether it is informal or formal and business-like). Smaller distance generally indicates more interest in communicating with the other person.

Another possible function is to provide *optimal stimulation/arousal level*. This is generally achieved by the regulation of sensory input, including that from other people. Thus in an amusement park, where there is already a high level of stimulation, Nesbitt and Steven (1974) found that a brightly dressed and heavily perfumed confederate was given more space (i.e. avoided!) than a more modest confederate. This could explain the variation in personal space requirements quite well, since there will be considerable variation in cognitive interpretations of a situation and whether or not it is regarded as stressful as a result.

The last theory is *intimacy equilibrium theory* (Argyle and Dean, 1965), which suggests that we have conflicting inclinations when in the presence of others; we want to approach them and be friendly but we also want to avoid them in case they are dangerous. This creates an approach–avoidance conflict, leading to a point of equilibrium which represents the level of intimacy in the relationship. If this is interfered with, for instance if someone moves too close, you will try to re-establish equilibrium by compensatory behaviours such as moving away or avoiding eye contact. This can be seen readily in lifts or on crowded underground trains. Generally, this theory is considered sound, but there have been several revisions proposed.

First, there is the concept of *social penetration*. This refers to the idea that we may not necessarily use compensatory behaviours when we want relationships to change. If someone moves closer, for example, we may reciprocate if we like them and desire greater intimacy (Altman and Taylor, 1973). There are also compensation limits (Aiello, 1977), which mean that if changes are too great it is impossible to restore equilibrium. Whether we reciprocate or compensate is determined by the way that we cognitively label the increase in arousal that occurs if our space is invaded (Patterson, 1976). If it is labelled positively, we reciprocate; if it is labelled negatively, we compensate. This is known as *arousal cognition* theory and is illustrated in Figure 4.5. Finally, Knowles (1980) suggests that our response to change depends on the relative strength of our approach–avoidance tendencies in that situation; do we want to get closer more than we want to get away? When the two are not in balance, we will feel uncomfortable.

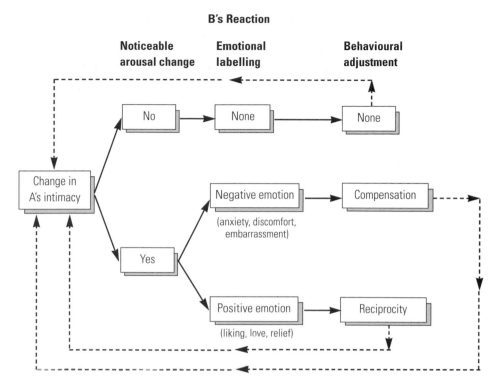

B's Reaction

FIGURE 4.5 *Patterson's arousal model of interpersonal intimacy (from Patterson, 1976)*

Overall, then, it can be concluded that personal space functions to aid communication and maintain optimum levels of intimacy, stimulation and arousal and to reduce threats from stress and danger. As such, it has major implications for behaviour and is an important consideration when designing the environment, as we shall see in Chapter 5.

TERRITORY

This term was first applied by Howard (1948) and popularised by Ardrey (1966). It refers to an area that is visibly bounded, in the sense of being obviously 'staked out', habitually used and defended and relatively stationary; it tends to be home-centred. Unlike personal space, it is often visible, does not move with us and is generally much larger. Territoriality, then, can be defined as behaviour by which an organism characteristically lays claim to an area and defends it against intrusion by members of its own species (Veitch and Arkkelin, 1995).

Measurement of territory

Measurement of territorial behaviour is difficult since by definition, it cannot be done in the laboratory. Most of the research has been carried out on animals; what research there is on humans has employed field studies and experiments, surveys and interviews and naturalistic observation.

Field studies look at naturally occurring associations between variables, whilst field experiments attempt to manipulate variables in the real world and observe the consequences. For example, a field study by Smith (1981) found that on beaches females tended to claim (by using towels, radios, etc.) smaller territories than males. In a field experiment, Taylor and Lanni (1981) found that students who took part in discussions in their own rooms had more influence on the decisions made than did those who were visitors. Surveys and interviews are useful for exploring people's thoughts, but rely heavily on responses being accurate. For example, Brower et al. (1983) showed people different drawings of properties with changes in such aspects as fences and plants, to see how they felt these affected the likelihood of theft from the property, and found that the presence of such features was felt to be a deterrent. Naturalistic observation can cover a range of different environments, such as refectories and playgrounds. Measures can be taken of marking (use of personal property such as a coat or beach towel to indicate territory) and personalisation (altering or decorating territory to demonstrate ownership, e.g. by erecting fences, naming houses, putting up posters in bedrooms).

Territoriality in animals is considered by many to be a basic drive, important in mating and the raising of young. It serves the purpose of spreading individuals out so that food resources are not overloaded, reduces the spread of disease and minimises fights. If boundaries are clearly marked, for example by urinating (in dogs) or vocalisation (in birds), then other individuals are being warned off. Even if there is an encounter, the *prior residence effect* keeps fighting to a minimum; the animal which is on home territory is generally at an advantage and will chase off the intruder. (This may also be seen in competitive sports in humans – the home team or even individuals on home territory seem to do better (McAndrew, 1992).

In animals which have a *lek* system (Gould, 1982), territorial behaviour does lead to aggression. A lek is an area where males gather to compete for territories and fight to lay claim to a patch of ground. The more central areas are more coveted and the males that claim them obtain more access to females.

Territoriality in humans is different in that it uses symbolic markers such as possessions and signs to indicate boundaries, rather than physical markers such as scent. Humans also invite others into their territory.

Types of territory

Altman (1975) distinguished primary, secondary and public territory in humans. The differences are explained in Box 4.3.

Box 4.3   Different types of territory

Primary territories e.g. homes, generally have clear boundary markers and personalisation. They are owned and/or used by the individual for an extended period of time and are considered to be under the control of the owner, so that others are only allowed there by invitation. As such, they form an important part of the individual's self-identity and self-esteem.

Secondary territories, such as a seat in class, are used regularly but shared with others. They are occupied on a temporary basis and the occupants do not have complete control over them. Sometimes they are referred to as semipublic areas. Use is governed by norms and informal rules and is generally not defended.

Public territories are accessible to everyone and used only on a temporary basis, so if the individual is not present his rights lapse. Examples are parks, beaches and libraries. Markers may be used to try and reserve locations, such as coats on chairs in a library and these arc usually respected by others.

Factors affecting territorial behaviour

Factors affecting territorial behaviour can be divided into personal, situational and cultural. *Personal* factors include gender; research shows that males tend to have larger territories than females. For example, Mercer and Benjamin (1980) asked students to draw on a plan of a shared room which space was theirs and which their roommate's and found that when males were sharing they tended to regard a larger portion of the room as their own territory. In the home, the wife typically has the kitchen as her own territory (Sebba and Churchman, 1983). Another personal factor is intelligence and it appears from the Mercer and Benjamin study mentioned above that more intelligent individuals tend to mark off larger territories for themselves. *Situational* factors include both physical and social aspects of the situation. The best known physical factor is the concept of defensible space, proposed by Newman (1972). This proposes that if there are barriers, either real or symbolic, people feel more secure, e.g. from crime. Clear views, providing opportunities for surveillance, also increase feelings of security. This was confirmed in the study by Brower et al. (1983) mentioned as an illustration of the use of an interview technique. The most important social influence is legal ownership, which appears to increase territorial behaviour, as shown by the level of personalisation (Greenbaum and Greenbaum, 1981).

Culture appears to be a significant influence as well. Smith's (1981) beach study showed that, compared to the French, the Germans were more territorial, using more marking (towels to reserve places, building sandcastles as barriers) and laying claim to larger territories. Another study by Worchel and Lollis (1982) found that Americans were more likely than Greeks to remove litter from the sidewalk outside their houses, as they regarded it as a semi-public rather than a public space. American street gangs are also more territorial than their British equivalents (Campbell et al., 1982).

Effects of territory on behaviour

Territorial behaviour can be seen in the form of personalisation and marking, aggression and defense and dominance and control. All of these have important applications, as the following section shows.

FOCUS ON APPLICATION ...

institutions and crime

Personalisation and marking, when applied to primary territories, represent the individual nature of the owner of the territory (Brown, 1987). Secondary and public territories are marked in more straightforward ways with anything that is available, but even then personal possessions seem to be more effective than objects like newspapers that might be mistaken for rubbish. Markers are nearly always respected by others, although when space is invaded people rarely defend it, as shown in Becker and Mayo's (1971) study of invasion of seats in a refectory. More personal markers are more effective when there is more demand for space (Sommer and Becker, 1969) and male possessions are more effective than female ones (Shaffer and Sadowski, 1975). The positive effects of personalisation are shown by improvements found in the social atmosphere of a psychiatric ward when residents were encouraged to personalise their territories (Holahan 1972); the same thinking lies behind the trend in residential homes for the elderly to allow residents to

keep their own furniture as far as possible. Similarly, more harmonious families have been found to have clearer territorial agreements (Sebba and Churchman, 1983). Another positive effect is to reduce the fear of crime (Normoyle and Lavrakas, 1984).

Aggression and defence are uncommon in human territorial behaviour, unlike the position in animals. Group territories such as countries are defended more, but disputes tend to be settled through negotiation and legal proceedings instead of overt aggression. People who have defensive displays outside their houses (such as signs saying 'Private Property' have been shown to respond more quickly to a knock on the door (Edney, 1972), suggesting that they are more vigilant. There is some legal acknowledgement of the right to defend territory, insofar as shooting a burglar is dealt with more leniently by the courts than shooting anyone else. Burgled houses have been shown to differ from non-burgled houses (Brown and

Altman, 1983) in that they have fewer territorial markers such as fences, walls, house names, parked cars and less visibility. However, research by McDonald and Gifford (1989), which asked the opinions of convicted burglars about different properties, found agreement that they were less likely to burgle the highly visible properties, but the territorial markers simply served to indicate that there was probably property worth stealing!

Dominance and control are related issues: dominance implies rank or standing within a group and is important in animal territorial behaviour; control refers to the level of influence over resources within the territory and is more important when considering the behaviour of humans. This control may be active (e.g. in the form of aggression) or a passive resistance to influence by others (e.g. taking a boundary dispute to court).

Dominance has been demonstrated by Esser (1968) in psychiatric patients, whose dominance ratings corresponded to the size of their territories. The upper third in the hierarchy used all the space on the ward, the middle third had large central territories and the lower third had small territories on the periphery of the ward. Similarly, Paslawskyj and Ivinskis (1980) found that the more dominant members of a group of retarded women had larger territories and those who were adjacent in the dominance hierarchy had territories that were further apart, which would possibly serve to minimise aggression. Box 4.4 contains further illustrations of this relationship.

When control is considered, Taylor and Stough (1978) have reported that people feel more in control in primary territory such as a bedroom than in secondary or public territory. They are also less likely to move furniture in public territory than in primary or secondary territories. One reason why burglary is often so traumatic, apart from the feelings of shock and defilement, is the associated feelings of loss of control, especially when personal objects have been taken (Brown and Harris, 1989).

Box 4.4   The link between territory and dominance

Another illustration of dominance can be seen in the 'home court advantage' (Schwartz and Barsky, 1977) whereby a variety of sports teams have been shown to do better when playing at home (Figure 4.6). This has been attributed to fan support and the fact that the effect is stronger for indoor than for outdoor sports has been attributed to the magnification of sound made by fans. It has further been suggested that in court the prosecutor may be at an advantage because he is typically placed nearer the jury, giving the impression that they share the 'same side' (Austin, 1982).

Theories about territory

The origins of territorial behaviour may be instinctual (Ardrey, 1966) or it may be learnt. The former proposal is supported by its universality and its occurrence in all animals. Even herd animals have a group territory and commune dwellers have their own space (although the great apes pose a problem, as they do not appear to be territorial). The latter proposal is supported by the extent to which it varies between cultures. Most researchers consider it to be a combination of the two, basic behaviours being instinctually determined and

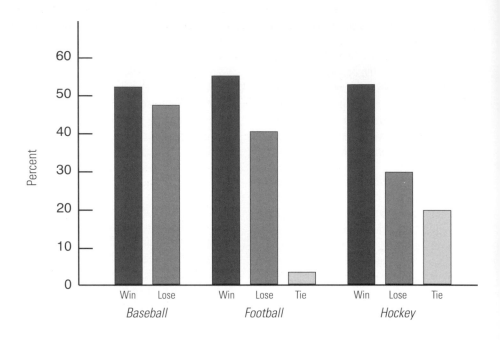

FIGURE 4.6 *Outcomes of home games in three professional sports. Differences in winning percentages are not large but with ties as possible outcomes to their games, hockey teams lose much less often at home than do baseball teams (from Gifford, R., Environmental Psychology, 2/E. Copyright © 1987 by Allyn & Bacon. Adapted by permission.)*

more complex ones learnt (Esser, 1976), as with many other behaviours. Esser argues that territoriality is governed primarily by the brainstem, with more complex aspects such as cognitive mapping being organised by the right cerebral hemisphere, which is generally responsible for spatial behaviour.

As regards functions, territorial behaviour is thought to operate primarily as an organiser in humans (Edney, 1975). Having control over our environment means that life is more predictable and we therefore know how to behave in different environments because we know the rules that are laid down by those who have control over that territory. We also know where to find other people and how to obtain privacy when we want to get away from them (Gold 1982). We are enabled to develop a sense of self-identity and self-esteem, particularly as our control enables us to operate in effective ways, at least in our own territory. Thus people who work for others would generally rather work for themselves and there is also pressure to achieve home ownership. As they get older, children soon want to have their own room, if at all possible.

Another view, proposed by Schrodt (1981), is that territory is a byproduct of conflict. Conflict originates between individuals who are dissimilar (e.g. in religion, ethnicity or politics) and this can lead to conflict between nations.

The winner will be the individual or group who has the most supporters (gang members). The territory on which the fight took place then becomes the property of the winner and so territory develops even though it was not the prime aim of the conflict (Figure 4.7).

In (a), the original units (e.g. individuals, families, ethnic groups, nations) are randomly distributed. Conflict is assumed to be possible when any individual gets upset for any reason. When this unit is adjacent to a different kind of unit, conflict will occur (although conflict is not necessarily violent; it might merely be the pressure of a majority ethnic group on a minority ethnic group to change their language). The conflict results in victory for the unit with the most units of the same type in the immediate vicinity. The losing unit surrenders its territory. In a computer simulation of this process, stage (b) was reached after 351 such conflicts and stage (c) was reached after 403 conflicts. By stage (d) (524 conflicts), most potential conflicts do not lead to actual conflict because most units are now adjacent to units of their own kind. Only sporadic border conflicts occur and the territories remain more stable (Gifford, 1987).

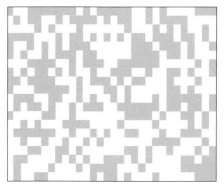

a) Initial distribution

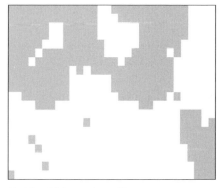

b) After 351 actual conflicts

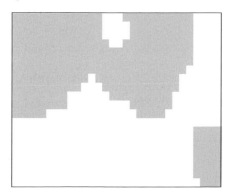

c) After 403 actual conflicts

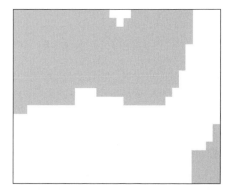

d) After 524 actual conflicts

FIGURE 4.7 Schrodt's street-gang theory of territory development (from Gifford, R., Environmental Psychology, 2/E. Copyright © 1987 by Allyn & Bacon. Reprinted by permission.)

PRIVACY

This can be *defined* as having control over the amount of interaction we choose to have with others (Derlega and Chaiken 1977). Eight features of privacy have been identified by Altman (1975), the most important of which are outlined in Box 4.5.

Box 4.5   Altman's features of privacy include the following:

- *Optimal level of interaction* being sought, so too much privacy is as bad as too little. In this respect, it can be regarded as a form of homoeostatic behaviour, related to attempts to maintain an optimal arousal level by controlling the amount of stimulation received from other people.

- *Selective control* being exercised, so there is a balance between seeking (approach) and restricting (avoidance) interaction according to our present needs.

- *Interpersonal boundary control* is also exercised, so that both the amount and the type of input received from others and our own output to them can be determined at will. For example, we will not discuss personal matters (self-disclosure) with just anyone.

Types of privacy

Westin (1970) argues that there are four *types* of privacy. The first of these, *solitude*, refers to being alone and unobserved; *intimacy* involves being in a small group or pair, separated and away from others; *anonymity* is the process of being detached from others, for example being unrecognised in a public place; finally, *reserve* is evident when we keep a psychological distance between ourselves and others, being with them but selectively tuning them out of awareness.

These types can be seen as forming two major *orientations* (Marshall, 1972):

1 *general withdrawal* covers solitude and intimacy, both situations involving being away from others, e.g. hiking alone or in a couple.

2 *control of information* covers anonymity and reserve, where what is avoided is self-disclosure, e.g. a stripper could maintain this aspect of privacy despite revealing all in public.

Measurement of privacy

Measurement of privacy is difficult, primarily because it is a complex concept involving both social and informational aspects. Behaviour can be observed (e.g. Weinstein observed use of privacy booths erected in a school classroom), but most investigations have used surveys and questionnaires. For example, a factor analytic study of questionnaire data by Marshall (1972) found support for Westin's typology of privacy and also added *seclusion* (living out of sight and sound of others) and *not-neighbouring* (not wanting to have contact with neighbours and actively disliking having them drop in).

Mechanisms used to maintain optimum levels of privacy have been described by Altman (1975). The most obvious of these are the *verbal* mechanisms, e.g. 'Go away!' or 'Would you like to go to the pictures?'. *Non-verbal* mechanisms include facial expressions (e.g. a welcoming smile), gestures (handshakes and hugs of greeting), fidgeting (usually considered a sign of boredom), posture (leaning towards people to show interest or away to show reserve) and eye contact (again, a sign of interest). Clothing can be considered as part of this group as well, e.g. wearing veils in Muslim countries, use of sunglasses and possibly even personal stereos, can all be seen as ways of cutting down inter-action. *Environmental* mechanisms include physical features such as territorial markers which serve to indicate that entry is by invitation only, closed doors and the use of locks on rooms.

Factors influencing privacy

Factors influencing the need for privacy can be divided into personal, situational and cultural. *Personal* factors such as experience lead to individual differences being apparent, as shown by Marshall (1972). People who grew up in crowded homes were found to prefer anonymity and reserve as adults; city dwellers preferred anonymity and intimacy. (Of course, there may well be exceptions to this, as with other generalisations in both psychology and common sense theorising – so some city dwellers may not prefer anonymity, for example.) There are also gender differences. Females generally disclose more to others and prefer environments that permit this to take place (Firestone et al.,1980). Dormitory studies have shown that men show less interest in solitude when in high-density dorms and stay away more from shared rooms (Walden et al., 1981). Another influential factor is personality; people who are more anxious and have less sense of well-being have greater privacy needs (McKechnie, 1974), as do those who have lower self-esteem (Pedersen 1982).

Situational influences can be divided into physical and social aspects. One of the major aspects of the physical situation that has been investigated is the use of open-plan interiors. Sundstrom et al. (1982a) found that there was less satisfaction with privacy in open-plan offices, whereas Marshall (1972) found that residents in open-plan houses preferred less privacy. These conflicting results may reflect a difference in the measurement taken (satisfaction versus preference) or may be the result of genuine differences resulting from the nature of the other occupants – workmates may be less desirable contacts than other family members. Another study by Firestone et al. (1980), set in a nursing home, found that residents who were in private rooms preferred more privacy than those in open wards, which could reflect a process of adaptation to the two situations.

Research on the social setting has investigated people's ideas about informational privacy, particularly in respect to who should have access to personal information. Stone et al. (1983) found, for example, that credit companies were considered to have more rights than employers and employers more rights than law enforcement agencies. Most people feel that there has been an invasion of privacy if information is obtained for negative purposes, without permission and subsequently disclosed to outsiders (Tolchinsky et al., 1981). The key issue here would appear to be that of control.

Cultural variation appears to be large, but this may only be the case when considered on a superficial level. Patterson and Chiswick (1981), for example, studied the Iban of Borneo, who live in long houses where there appears to be little privacy. Their conclusion was that the Iban in fact have the same privacy needs as most Westerners, but they achieve it in different ways, e.g. through the use of special techniques for changing clothes in public. A study of gypsies by Yoors (1967) revealed that in the morning, they only wash their faces when they are ready to interact; until this happens, others will not approach them, demonstrating that privacy is a two-way process.

Theories of privacy

Theories of privacy relate mainly to its functions. Westin (1967) has proposed four basic functions outlined in Box 4.6.

Other theories of privacy behaviour have proposed different explanations. Altman (1975) has suggested that it operates to provide *selective control over access to the self*. As previously described, this involves boundary controls and seeking of optimal interaction levels. Laufer and Wolfe (1977) have related privacy

---

Box 4.6 The functions of privacy

- *Protection of communication*; interaction can be managed by finding private places for sharing confidences.

- *Control and autonomy*; providing a choice about when to see others, which can be an important determinant of health and well-being. A wilderness solitude study by Hammitt (1982) found that this type of setting is preferred by some people because it gives them freedom to decide for themselves what they are going to do.

- *Personal identity* can also be re-established when alone; we can assimilate information received from others and develop our sense of self.

- *Emotional release* is possible in a way that it is not in public; we can drop our social roles and masks and have a good cry if we want to.

needs to stage in the life cycle. Children have little sense of privacy but as the sense of self develops, so do privacy needs; by adolescence, there will be strong needs. A theory proposed by Archea (1977) looks to the environment as an important determinant of privacy needs, seeing it primarily as an *information distribution process*. The physical layout of the environment governs the way that information can be distributed, for example, whether or not it provides visual or acoustic screens. Finally, it can be seen as involving a *hierarchy of needs*, according to Sundstrom et al. (1982b), who perceive different aspects of privacy as having different degrees of importance for different people. For example, at the lowest level of an organisation employees are highly visible and work in close proximity to one another, so their needs are to keep other people out – social control. In the middle ranks, there may be visual screening (e.g. in an office) so their needs will be to eliminate noise from others so that they can concentrate. The higher ranks' needs are mainly for autonomy and freedom from control by others. Thus, in this analysis, status is an important determinant of privacy needs.

CROWDING AND DENSITY

Density is an objective measure, referring to the number of people in a given space, e.g. England has 325 people per square kilometre. It can therefore be altered (Stokols, 1972) by changing the number of people (social density) or the size of the space (non-social or spatial density). According to Zlutnik and Altman (1972), it is also possible to differentiate inside density (the number of people in a residential space) from outside density (the number in a larger area).

Crowding refers to the psychological experience of density, hence it is a subjective measure which will vary according to individual and social factors (Stokols 1972). For example, being in an enclosed space with one person may in certain circumstances feel more crowded than being with thousands of people at a football match.

Effects on behaviour

Effects on behaviour can be explored by looking at animal and human studies. *Animal studies* have either looked at naturally occurring population cycles or at the results of experimental manipulations of population density. In the first group, the best known example is the research on lemmings (e.g. Dubos 1965). These are Scandinavian rodents which appear to migrate to the sea and drown themselves in large numbers every 3–4 years; this behaviour has been explained as a *population limitation mechanism*. However, it is now known that they breed prolifically and as population density increases so a malfunction of the adrenal gland develops, which leads to hyperactivity and accidental drowning. Another naturalistic study by Christian et al. (1960) followed the progress of Sitka deer released onto a small island. An initial dramatic increase in the population was followed by a dramatic decrease and then the level stabilised. The deer which died were found to have adrenal glands that were up to ten times the size of those in control deer and this was suggested to be the result of stress caused by overcrowding. Another study is outlined in Box 4.7

Box 4.7 The behavioural sink

The most famous experimental study is that of Calhoun (1962), who studied rats kept in a restricted space and allowed to breed. The dominant rats took up most of the space, others being restricted to what became known as the 'behavioural sink'. The latter group showed increased aggression, poorer nest building and infant care (leading to 96% mortality before weaning), greater physiological change and incidence of tumours. These findings have since been confirmed in a range of other animals.

When it comes to research on *human participants*, correlational and survey methods have been the most popular, but there have been some experimental studies of laboratory performance. The effects of crowding on physiological responses and health, task performance and social interaction have been the main areas of focus.

Regarding *physiological responses and health*, both short-term laboratory and long-term field studies have shown that increasing density leads to stress and arousal (Epstein, 1982). Health is affected by high inside density but not high outside density (Freedman, 1975), as shown in studies of prisons and student dormitories (McCain et al., 1976).

Task performance effects depend on the type of task; high density appears to affect performance of complex but not simple tasks (Evans, 1979). The effects are particularly noticeable if social interaction is required during the task or if the high density level is unexpected. For example, Saegert et al. (1975) found that subjects were less able to give directions (i.e. to use their cognitive maps) in high density situations such as crowded department stores or railway stations. Karlin et al. (1979) discovered that high density in university accommodation was related to lower grades being achieved; grades improved when less crowded accommodation was provided. It was suggested that high densities may affect performance of higher level cognitive tasks by impairing information-processing ability. There may also be an effect on decision-making, as shown by Rodin (1976), who found that children raised in high density conditions were less likely to make their own choices about the type of sweet they wanted.

Social interaction is affected in different ways, depending on the circumstances; a crowded party is perceived very differently from a crowded lift, for example. Freedman (1975) proposed the density–intensity model, which suggests that increases in density intensify the affective state produced by the social and situational factors. This can be illustrated with reference to the effects of density on attraction, altruism and aggression.

Interpersonal attraction is reduced in high density conditions, especially in male participants (Griffit and Veitch, 1971). People also show more social withdrawal, less eye contact and are generally less talkative, as shown by Baum and Valins (1977) in their dormitory studies. *Altruistic behaviour* is also decreased; for example, it has been found that stamped addressed envelopes dropped in crowded dormitories were less likely to be posted. Holahan (1977) argues that this is due to fears for personal safety, which could perhaps account for the reduced levels of helping in urban compared to rural areas. Other explanations that have been proposed relate to attentional differences and differences in lifestyle that could lead to, for example, different amounts of time being available for helping.

Aggression may be increased by high density conditions, provided that the tendency is there anyway. Thus, Rohe and Patterson (1974) found that high density led to increased aggression in children in a situation where there weren't enough toys to go round. Prison research also shows a high correlation between density and violence (Cox et al., 1984); a 30% reduction in the prison population led to a 60% reduction in assaults on other inmates, especially in male prisoners.

Factors influencing response

Factors influencing response to crowding can be divided, as elsewhere in this chapter, into personal, situational and cultural variables. Looking firstly at *personal* factors, it has been found, perhaps predictably, that sociable people (those who like to be with others) suffer less from crowding (Miller and Nardini, 1977). Research into locus of control has yielded contradictory results, however. McCallum et al. (1979) found that people with an internal locus of control, who believe that they are in control of their lives rather than being at the mercy of external forces, were affected less by crowding. It has also been shown by Baum and Valins (1977) that persons given control (in this case by being near the control panel in a lift) feel less crowded. Other research, however, indicates that people with an external locus of control may be less affected because they give up easily and therefore suffer less stress. Gender studies show that men are more affected than women in terms of negative changes in mood, attitudes and behaviour. Dormitory studies show that they cope by leaving their rooms more than women in crowded situations (Aiello et al., 1981). Previous experience of crowding may help people to cope physiologically (Booth (1976) found reduced stress responses) but not behaviourally (Rohe (1982) found that it led to increased arguments with others). Finally, expectations are also important; Womble and Studebaker (1981) showed that campers in an Alaskan park who expected high densities reported that the area was less crowded than those who did not.

When it comes to *situational* factors, we can focus on social and physical elements separately. Socially, there are well-known effects of the presence of others and their behaviour on performance, whether they are watching the individual or not or interfering with activities or not. The *social facilitation effect* shows that performance of simple, well-learnt tasks is improved, while performance of complex, incompletely learnt tasks is hindered (Zajonc, 1965). When individuals interact, the opportunity for social support to be created through the formation of coalitions arises. The other side of this coin is that some individuals may then become isolated, which is in itself stressful (Aiello et al., 1981). Thus four-person rooms may be psychologically healthier than five-person rooms because there are less likely to be isolates (Reddy et al., 1981). Where others are thought to share the same views, less crowding will be experienced (Schaeffer and Patterson 1980).

The physical arrangement of the environment and its use of space can also affect perceptions of crowding. Long corridors lead to greater perception of crowding and more stress in dormitories (Baum et al., 1978). High-rise buildings also increase perceived crowding, leading to negative attitudes and poorer relationships with others (McCarthy and Saegert, 1979). This is especially the case for those on the lower floors, who have less opportunity for visual escape as there is little by way of a view from the windows. Rooms that receive more sunlight are perceived as less crowded by females (Schiffenbauer et al., 1977). Rectangular rooms with more doors and partitions (Desor, 1972) and higher ceilinged rooms (Savinar, 1975) are perceived as less crowded.

Finally, there appear to be *cultural* differences in response to density increases. When placed in dormitories, Mediterraneans seem to experience more crowding than Asians; both are higher than Americans (Nasar and Min, 1984). Gove and Hughes (1983) found that blacks were more sensitive to crowding than whites, while Hispanics were least sensitive, seeming to have a cultural preference for closeness. Some cultures do, however, seem to adapt to a situation. For example, despite the greater density in China, there is less crime, mental illness and disease (Schmitt, 1966). Mitchell (1971) argues that this is because they have developed tighter family controls on behaviour and tend to show less emotion.

Theories

An overall model that summarises the research on crowding is presented in Fig 4.8. Theories have been proposed that deal with the antecedents, psychological processes and outcomes of crowding. *Antecedent* theories take three forms.

1 The *ecological approach* (Barker, 1968) argues that each behavioural setting has an optimum number of people it requires to function well; too few and it is understaffed, too many and it is overstaffed. Both of these can cause problems, e.g. overstaffing can lead to a shortage of resources such as desks in a classroom. Here the behaviour setting is the most important factor.

2 The *social physics approach* (Knowles, 1983) looks at how people are distributed in space, whether there are partitions in the room, whether there is an audience watching the person, etc. Here the people are important as well as the behaviour setting.

3 *Density–intensity theory* (Freedman, 1975) proposes that the effects of crowding are to magnify existing responses to that situation, so again the situation is crucial.

Theories about *psychological processes* take two approaches. Control models (e.g. Schmidt and Keating, 1979) suggest that high density affects people because it decreases their feelings of control. This control may be behavioural (the ability to act as we want and work towards our own goals, e.g. choosing whether to leave or remain at a football match), cognitive (the ability to process information and think clearly) or decisional (the amount of choice we have, e.g. about where to sit in a cinema). Overload models (Cohen, 1978) suggest that when density is high, as in cities, people may be less able to process information. This, in turn, would lead to a reduced feeling of control and also to feelings of stress and arousal because the preferred level of stimulation has been exceeded. Milgram (1970) suggested that this overload leads to the tendency to withdraw from others.

Consequence models focus on the concept of arousal and are therefore related to the overload models. High density has its effects by increasing arousal, which affects task performance and social behaviour in turn. Worchel and Teddlie (1976) introduced a 2-factor theory of crowding based on this idea, whereby invasion of personal space initially increases arousal levels. If this increase in arousal is then attributed to the other people present, we will feel crowded, if we can blame something else, such as an exciting film, we will not feel crowded.

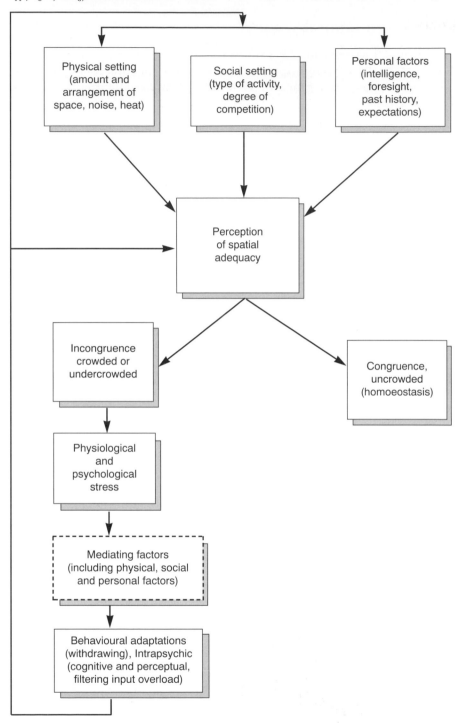

FIGURE 4.8 *An integrative model of crowding (from Moos, R.H. The Human Context: Environmental Determinants of Behaviour. Copyright © John Wiley & Sons, Inc. Reprinted by permission.)*

CHAPTER SUMMARY

To conclude this chapter, it is clear that the social element of our environment is an important determinant of four inter-related aspects of our use of space – personal space, territory, privacy and crowding. In each case it is important to consider how to define and measure the concept, how it originates, influences behaviour, is influenced in turn by other variables and how it can be theoretically explained. All these issues affect our relationships with others, both strangers and friends, and have important implications for the design of the environment, which is what we will be considering in the next chapter. As an overview, it is useful to conclude with Altman's diagrammatic outline of the relationship between these concepts, shown in Fig 4.9.

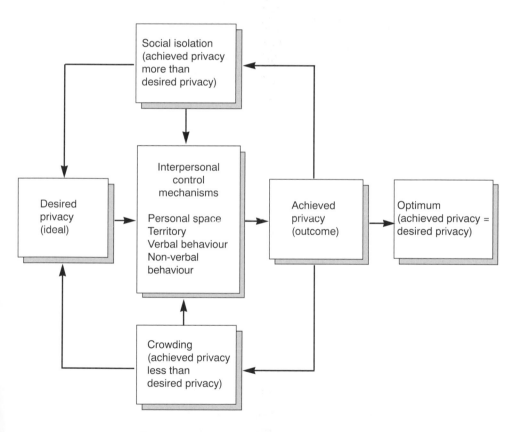

FIGURE 4.9 *Overview of relationships among privacy, personal space, territory and crowding as postulated by Altman (1975)*

chapter five

THE BUILT ENVIRONMENT

CHAPTER OVERVIEW

In the previous chapters, we have been considering the ways that people perceive and think about their environment and the effects that the physical and social aspects of that environment can have on their behaviour. Continuing with this line of thought brings us to focus next on the way that the environment can be manipulated or designed to meet particular needs and the consequences that this can have for the people who use it. More than any other animal, human beings have developed the ability to adapt the environment to their needs, building homes and workplaces, schools, prisons and hospitals; when enough of these buildings are clustered together, they will form a city. In this chapter we will be looking at the importance of designing buildings that meet the needs of those who will be using them, whether they are houses, workplaces, institutions or cities.

IMPLICATIONS FOR DESIGNERS

The fact that many buildings may change their purpose from that originally intended and that cities evolve gradually as well means that in many cases the design is not always appropriate. The complexity of our needs means that it may not have been successful in the first place in meeting its aims. Buildings are constructed to fulfil certain functions and although many functions are common to all (e.g. provision of security and shelter from the weather), their primary purpose will generally result in quite different design needs. A house, for example, will be designed, at least in part, to keep out people other than the residents; a prison focuses more on keeping people in. This will lead to quite different physical and spatial characteristics (for example, in terms of how much they are separated from other buildings) and these in turn give the building a meaning and result in it providing cues about the particular social activities that will take place there. For example, it is obvious, from its appearance, that a particular building is a church and what sort of activities will take place there. There will also be an aesthetic response – is it attractive? – and an affective or emotional response – do you like it?

A designer will need to take all of these aspects into consideration. Coventry Cathedral, for example, has upset many traditionalists who do not feel that it looks sufficiently like a cathedral – unlike, for example, Canterbury. You can compare the two in Figure 5.1. The architect Le Corbusier (1963), the designer of the high-rise flat, overlooked such factors when he argued that buildings were merely machines to live in. The fact that such buildings ultimately proved unacceptable to their occupants is an indication of the importance of the psychological aspects of design. Buildings are more than just practical items and they are even more than simply aesthetic. They have social and cultural significance to their users and designers who ignore this cannot expect their buildings to be successful, even though they will inevitably be used because they have been invested in. For example, Patri (1971) found that when natives living in one-room houses in Guam were provided with new houses, they still only made use of one room in them; the houses had to be redesigned after building to meet the cultural needs of the occupants. The fact that these needs are constantly subject to ever-accelerating changes means that the environment in which we live, which changes more slowly, may in fact be one that was designed for the needs of previous generations (Studer, 1970). For example, schools traditionally provided with individual desks find it difficult to organise students to carry out group activities.

FIGURE 5.1 *Cathedral designs may be traditional or more radical*

All this implies that designers have a great responsibility to think very carefully about what they are creating, because of the impact their designs will have on the users. Another reason for caution here is the possibility of *architectural determinism* — the idea that design can be manipulated to shape behaviour directly. For example, painting walls soothing colours to reduce anxiety; or utilising spatial characteristics to create feelings of solemnity in a church or courtroom. This extreme viewpoint has been rejected because it ignores factors such as individual differences, the ability people have to alter the environment to suit their needs (e.g. by moving furniture) and the generally active nature of our response to the environment.

At the other extreme is *environmental possibilism* (Porteus, 1977), which sees the environment as giving us possibilities and setting limits on behaviour; the individual thus has a greater role to play and prediction regarding environmental influence is difficult. The most acceptable position, *environmental probabilism* (Porteus, 1977) is a compromise between these, arguing that prediction is possible on the basis of our research-based knowledge of how design and psychological factors interact in determining behaviour. Thus it is quite likely that many people would reject the idea of living in a high-rise block of flats but if they wanted to be in a particular area, if the flats were especially well decorated or if they were penthouses in London's Docklands development, then the response would be different.

Before we move on to consider some examples of design issues, it is important to mention individual differences. Design tends to work in a normative manner, being based on the average person rather than on individual needs. Like off-the-peg clothes, it may not exactly fit the individual who eventually becomes the wearer. The standards on which it is based are both physical and sociocultural. Thus equipment and spaces are designed to fit the average human body using *anthropometric standards* so that, for example, doorways are always the same height and width and lighting in many buildings reaches the regulation levels. This may vary according to the situation; for example, the amount of leg room between seats in the cinema would be considered unacceptable at work. There may also be cultural differences — minimum temperature requirements for many workplaces are 70°F in the USA and 63°F in England. In Japan, flats are typically very small and any attempt to build larger ones merely results in subletting!

What this means is that there are inevitably compromises. For example, the standard bathroom toilet represents a compromise between the anatomical needs of males (standing/squatting) and females (squatting) and does not suit either sex perfectly (Kira, 1976). In some instances, the fit between person and environment will be poor, requiring adaptation; this in turn requires energy and can therefore prove stressful (Wheeler, 1967), as we shall see in Chapter 7. Such people have been referred to as the *environmentally disenfranchised* — children, the elderly and the handicapped are all limited by size, mobility, strength, perceptual power, or speed of movement. For example, they may be unable to reach items on high shelves, read notices in small print, turn handles easily or get through doorways while using a Zimmer frame.

Now we can consider the way that designers attempt to take account of all these issues. The applications we will look at are design of rooms, residences, workplaces, institutions, neighbourhoods and cities. In all these cases, Lang (1987) has pointed out that architects are trying to make their designs fulfil three purposes: commodity (What function will the building be serving?); firmness (Is it structurally sound? Will it last?); and delight (Is it aesthetically pleasing?). From the psychological viewpoint, designs can be assessed in terms of their habitability or congruence, which refers to how well they fit the needs of their users (Nelson, 1976). Clearly, there are two sides to this and many architects have come to realise that consultation with users is an important part of the design process (Kaplan and Kaplan, 1982). Feedback is also important and this is obtained through postoccupancy evaluation.

DESIGN OF ROOMS

Room design can be considered in terms of space, colour and materials, lighting and windows, furnishings and aesthetics.

Space requirement will depend on the nature of the activities to be carried out in the room; a ballroom and a bathroom will have different demands, for example. Perceived size is affected by shape (a rectangular room seems larger than a square room of the same area, as shown by Sadalla and Oxley (1984)), colour (Baum and Davis (1976) found that light-coloured rooms appear to be larger) and contents (Imamoglu (1973) showed that rooms containing more furniture appeared to be smaller). Space also relates to privacy needs and the opportunity to establish territory by personalisation. Features that encourage personalisation, such as noticeboards, will be favoured, as will those that enable space to be partitioned, such as plants, room dividers and furniture such as bookcases. Another important consideration is freedom from intrusions, both visual (being overlooked) and auditory (being overheard). Sundstrom et al. (1994) have reported that freedom from auditory intrusion may well be more important to people than freedom from visual intrusion. The overall importance of privacy is demonstrated by the study of Vinsel et al. (1980), showing that college students who dropped out were more likely to complain about lack of privacy (e.g. shared rooms) than those who remained at college.

Colour has had surprisingly little research devoted to it. Apart from its effect on space perception, described above, the only notable research is that on perception of temperature. People have learnt to associate red and orange with warmth and blue and green with coolness (Ross, 1938), but when they are asked indirectly to rate their perception of the room temperature in different coloured lights, they do not show any differences (Berry, 1961). Materials used for building and decorating may also have particular associations, for example Sadalla and Sheets (1993) found that wood on the outside of houses was linked with feminine and emotional owners. Inside, soft surfaces have been found to increase social interaction in autistic children.

Light levels appear to affect conversation; for example, Gergen et al. (1973) found that interacting in darkness led to less conversation and reduction of volume, generally increasing intimacy in people who were not previously acquainted. However, there is some conflict in research findings here, indicating that this aspect of behaviour may be learnt. Lighting preferences depend in general on the context, as well. Low levels will not be preferred if walking through an inner-city area at night, for example. An important consideration, as we have seen in Chapter 3, is the amount of control provided over the level of lighting, a greater degree of control being preferable. *Windows* are essential; other than bathrooms, where privacy is desired, rooms without windows are greatly disliked (Collins, 1975) and have a negative effect on mood (Karmel, 1965). Hospital patients have been shown to do better when they are in rooms with pleasant views (Ulrich, 1984). Windows seem to be particularly important in smaller rooms (Butler and Steuerwald 1991).

Furnishings and their arrangement can also affect social interaction as described in Box 5.1.

Box 5.1 Sociopetal and sociofugal environments

Osmond (1959) described environments as sociopetal or sociofugal, according to whether they encouraged or discouraged interaction. Sociopetal environments encourage interaction by having movable furniture and face-to-face seating, e.g. chairs arranged in a horseshoe rather than in rows in a classroom (Sommer, 1969). Sociofugal environments have fixed furniture that makes communication difficult, e.g. church pews, benches in shopping centres (Figure 5.2). Sommer and Ross (1958) found that the level of interaction could be manipulated in a geriatric hospital; placing chairs around the walls reduced interaction, whilst arranging them in small groups increased it.

Aesthetics also affect social behaviour. If people find the room that they are in attractive, they will interact more with others (Russell and Mehrabian, 1978), find others more attractive (Maslow and Mintz, 1956) and be more altruistic (Sherrod et al., 1977). If they are uncomfortable in a room, on the other hand, they are more likely to blame this on the people they are with (Aiello and Thompson, 1980).

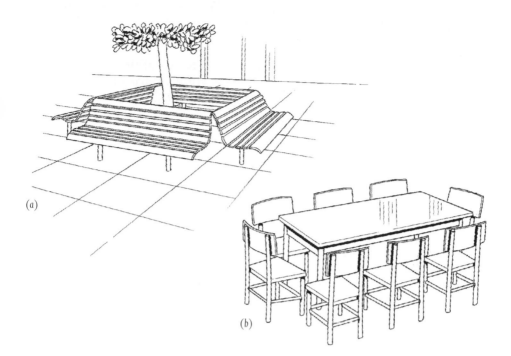

FIGURE 5.2 (a) *Sociofugal environments are designed to keep people apart* (b) *Sociopetal environments are designed to bring people together*

RESIDENTIAL ENVIRONMENTS

As well as providing shelter, the place that we live in is a centre for many of our daily activities (such as socialising, eating and washing), an important part of our identity (signalling status, for example) and often has significant memories associated with it. Therefore we often feel a certain bond with it, referred to as a *place attachment* (Altman and Low, 1992). As with attachment to people, we may feel anxious when away from it (homesickness) or if we have lost it as a result of natural disasters or accidents, as shown by Holman and Silver's (1994) study of earthquake victims in Los Angeles. This attachment may extend to furnishings, possessions and cars as well as the home itself (Belk, 1992). Social networks also form part of this place attachment (Fried, 1982), which appears to be one reason why people from lower socio-economic groups often have strong place attachments. Interestingly, even the homeless can have a strong attachment to the place where they live (Bunston and Breton 1992). Moving is well known to be a highly stressful experience

(Holmes and Rahe, 1967), often evoking feelings akin to grief. Thus we speak of moving to a new 'house'; it is not until we have settled in and formed a place attachment that we will refer to it as 'home'.

Housing comes in a variety of different forms and five different dimensions along which it differs, both within and across cultures, have been identified (Altman and Chemers, 1980; Altman and Gauvain, 1981):

1 whether it is *permanent* (most common in our society) or *temporary* (e.g. caravans and mobile homes);

2 whether it is *differentiated*, so that different rooms have different functions (e.g. bathroom, bedroom), or *homogeneous* (e.g. bedsit);

3 whether it is *communal*, with several generations or families living in one house, or *non-communal* (more common in our society);

4 whether it has *identity*, reflecting the personal characteristics of the owner, or *communality*, reflecting the cultural stereotype. Most houses, even if mass-built, will have some element of personalisation (Figure 5.3);

5 whether it displays *openness* or *closedness* to outsiders. In the latter case it will be walled or hedged.

FIGURE 5.3 *In this street, personalisation has given originally identical houses a lot more individual identity*

Satisfaction and preferences

Given the wide range of options available – houses, bungalows, terraces, semidetached, detached, flats, bedsits, caravans, etc. – there has been a lot of research into people's preferences. In the USA and Britain, it has generally been found that most people prefer a detached, single-family home in the suburbs (Cooper, 1972). The main reason given is that this prevents unwanted interaction with neighbours (Michelson, 1977); the physical separation is felt to give greater interpersonal boundary control (Altman, 1975). Housing choices in practice may, however, be determined by a range of other factors such as economics, availability of transport, schools and other facilities, proximity to work and shops, status, crime rates, etc.

Given these constraints, satisfaction must be assessed in terms of whether the chosen housing meets needs adequately, not in terms of whether it is ideal. Gifford (1987) presents a model of influences on and outcomes of residential satisfaction (Figure 5.4), which gives a good idea of the range of personal (observer) and environmental characteristics (both objective and as perceived by the observer) which can influence such feelings.

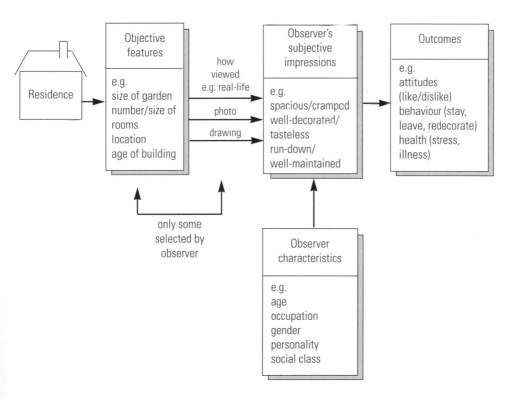

FIGURE 5.4 *A research model of residential satisfaction, behaviour and well-being (based on Gifford, 1997)*

Personal influences can be seen in terms of age and stage in the life cycle. Younger and older people are more likely to be satisfied with a flat in the town centre (Michelson, 1977). An individual's role is also influential; for example, husbands and wives often disagree (Michelson found that 40% of wives but only 5% of husbands were satisfied after a move to a town centre flat). Personality may also have some bearing; Wiggins (1975) found that more sociable people prefer design features that facilitate this behaviour.

Environmental influences have been found to be important determinants of dissatisfaction. Thus it has been found to be associated with small house size, small living and dining areas and badly designed bathrooms (Kaitilla, 1993), as well as poor plumbing, heating, kitchen design and lack of storage space (Galster and Hesser, 1981). Strong social ties (often found in cul-de-sacs) are associated with satisfaction and are reflected in an increase in the amount of exterior decoration, e.g. at Christmas (Oxley et al., 1986). Dissatisfaction is associated with stress, which has consequences for behaviour and health and may lead to a decision to move. In a five-year period, approximately 36% of Britons will move house. Not all of these move because of dissatisfaction, but they will all experience stress as a result (Stokols et al., 1983). However, those who are unhappy but choose not to move may experience even more stress.

Interior design and use of space

In differentiated homes, different rooms serve different purposes. There are some consistencies in the way that this is organised; for example, Black (1968) has reported that leisure reading is usually done in a living room and is least likely in a kitchen or dining room. Bedrooms are the most frequently occupied rooms (Parsons, 1972) and as they are intended to be quiet, private space, they are often physically separated from the rest of the house, e.g. by being upstairs. The average size of bedrooms has increased in recent years, which has been attributed by Hasell and Peatross (1990) to the increasing tendency for women to go out to work, which means that they have to dress at the same time as their husbands. Women are also more likely than previously to have their own private study.

Privacy needs are an important determinant of the use of space. Altman et al. (1972) have divided families into open and closed according to how they achieve this; closed families rely more on locked doors. Thus the two types of family would require different designs, but as a general principle private and group spaces are located in different parts of the house. The bathroom has over 30 different functions (Kira, 1976) and may serve in addition as an important source of privacy.

Each particular type of area within the house needs to be designed to optimise use of space, according to its function. Here, we are going to look at group and private space, support space and support systems. Considering *group and private spaces* first, the areas used for leisure and socialising require comfortable chairs arranged in a circular pattern, neither too close together (under 3 feet) nor too far apart (over 10 feet). Tables and shelves close by for objects such as cups to be deposited on will be useful and the light level needs to be adjustable but generally at a moderate level. Particular furniture arrangements may be needed to facilitate TV viewing, listening to music and reading. Children's play areas will have different requirements, needing to be of adequate size to permit play, easily supervised and with strong surface materials to prevent damage (Faulkner and Faulkner, 1975). The dining area needs to be close to the kitchen and should open into at least one other area of the house as well as the kitchen; it needs a table 30 inches high. The bedroom is used primarily for sleeping and dressing, but also for reading and relaxing. The bathroom needs to be arranged so that the door does not hit any of the fitments when opened, the toilet itself will be screened when the door is opened, there is adequate storage and ventilation and the window is conveniently placed.

Support spaces are areas that deal with maintenance, e.g. the kitchen, utility and storage spaces. The kitchen can be divided into a refrigerator centre, mixing centre, sink centre, cooking centre and serving centre, all of which need to be arranged in a logical sequence. Standard sizes exist, e.g. the mixing centre should be at least 3 feet wide, but these need to be adapted to the requirements of the chief user. Utility rooms, such as the laundry, sewing room and workshop, all need tool storage, sinks and electrical outlets. The laundry needs airing space, the sewing room primarily light and the workshop should additionally be isolated from the rest of the house.

Support systems include lighting, heating and wall and floor coverings. Lighting needs to provide adequate direct sunlight – too little will be gloomy, while too much will produce glare, excessive amounts of heat (as in a greenhouse) and insufficient privacy. It can be controlled by thinking carefully at the design stage about the orientation of the house on its site and making use of trees, skylights and window coverings as appropriate. Artificial illumination must be adjusted to suit the activities taking place. Switches need to be placed near doors and a mixture of general illumination from ceiling fixtures and local illumination from spotlights and table lamps is best. General illumination ensures that there are no harsh contrasts, but may be too diffuse for some activities; local illumination can be used to create atmosphere and emphasise objects as well as providing extra light for reading, for example.

Heating again can be partly controlled by considering the orientation of the house in terms of the prevailing sun and wind. Large glass areas should face south or south east and the opposite side should be well insulated; the north west needs particular protection from excessive wind and sun. Wall and floor coverings are an important determinant of privacy, as they can provide a good deal of sound insulation. Wallpaper is generally considered more interesting than painted walls, as well as being a better insulator, along with cork and fabric.

Other design considerations revolve around the organisation of space. Firstly, there is a choice between a one- and a two-storey building. One-storey buildings avoid the problem of stairs and give easy access to outside space; two-storey buildings are cheaper to build and to heat and give more privacy. Then there is a choice between open- and closed-plan interiors. Closed plans give greater privacy and provide separate spaces for different activities to take place without interfering with one another; open plans create more noise transfer and reduce privacy, but give a feeling of spaciousness. Examples of good and poor designs can be seen in Figure 5.5.

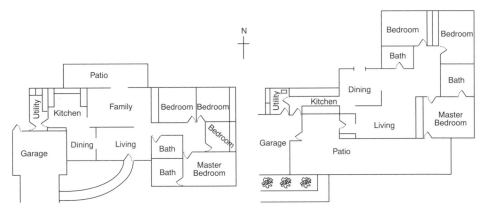

Plan A

Some major rooms and patio face north; others face the street
Bedrooms are adjacent (loss of acoustic privacy)
Front door opens into the living room
No inside access from garage to house

Plan B

Major rooms and patio face south; none face the street
Bedrooms are not adjacent
Front door doesn't open directly into the main living room
Inside access from garage to utility and kitchen

FIGURE 5.5 *Plan A contains some serious problems. Plan B is relatively problem free*

Different types of residence

Single-family houses are typical of Western industrialised societies. At least in the middle and upper socioeconomic groups, houses are an important part of the owner's self-image and in general, they demonstrate the personality and economic status of the owners. This is particularly true of the living room, as shown by Sadalla et al. (1987), who found that homeowners' evaluation of the image projected by their homes was independently verified by students who were just shown slides of the interior and exterior of the house. Goffman (1959) argued that the front regions of the house, especially the front garden, are more important in this respect than the back regions that are not so obviously on display to others. This is reflected in the use of the back door by family and friends and the front door by everyone else. Inside, there are also front regions that are on display (especially the living room) and back regions that are not, such as the kitchen (Altman and Gauvain, 1981). Formal rooms are often reserved for entertaining and real living goes on in the kitchen. Gender roles differ so that males are traditionally considered responsible for the condition of the exterior of the house and females the interior.

Flats generally offer less space per family and have less auditory privacy due to their thinner walls, so people feel more crowded (Aiello and Thompson, 1980). Their layout dictates friendship choices; Festinger et al. (1950) found that friendships were most likely with the family next door and friendships with those further away became progressively less likely unless their entrance was passed on the way into or out of the building (e.g. if they lived near the staircase).

FOCUS ON APPLICATION ...
high-rise flats

High-rise flats have been the subject of a great deal of investigation; generally they are associated with less social interaction (Yancey, 1971) and a greater likelihood of and fear of crime. Newman (1972) attributed this latter to the lack of *defensible space* (shared or semipublic space) and others have pointed to lifts and stairs which cannot be kept under surveillance and provide escape routes and hiding places. A good example of this is the Pruitt-Igoe project in St Louis (Yancey, 1971),

illustrated in Figure 5.6. This consisted of 43 11-storey blocks that were built in 1954 and demolished 18 years later because the levels of crime, vandalism, rape and drug abuse had resulted in many of the apartments becoming unoccupied. Other research, summarised by Halpern (1995) has concluded that flat dwelling, especially in high-rise blocks, is associated with higher levels of mental illness, especially in females, who may feel more vulnerable.

FIGURE 5.6 *The Pruitt-Igoe public housing project*

As a result of these findings, high-rise designs are now avoided. Current design focuses on positioning windows to improve surveillance and subdividing open spaces in ways that encourage territorial marking and defence.

Dormitories occupied by students, where room sharing is the norm, have also been studied. The main use of rooms is for studying and socialising, which are generally conflicting activities, privacy being a high priority for studying. It has been found that smaller halls of residence are preferred to high-rise blocks and that rooms where furniture can be moved around and personalisation is possible are preferred (Schiffenbauer et al., 1977). Suite designs, where several rooms open into a shared lounge and bathroom, are preferred to corridor designs, where each room opens into a corridor leading to the bathroom; they also lead to greater sociability (Valins and Baum, 1973).

Homes for the elderly are becoming more important as the numbers of elderly people increase. Retirement housing complexes which are low-rise and age segregated are preferred (Devlin, 1980) and associated with greater sociability, self-esteem, activity and satisfaction. There are no significant effects on health; the drawback is that the users may become site oriented, increasingly reluctant to leave their base. Easy access to outdoor space and shopping facilities is essential, as many users will have limited mobility. For the same reason, there also needs to be a great deal of emphasis on safety, with handrails, easy access to cupboards and shelves, shallow steps, knobs that are easy to turn, non-slip flooring and security from fire and intruders (Bell et al., 1990). Space that encourages social interaction, both inside and outside, is essential, since many elderly people live alone (Lawton 1987). Paths need to be wide and well maintained and all obstacles (such as overhanging foliage) cleared. Elderly people are generally more sensitive to physical aspects of the environment discussed in Chapter 3, such as pollution, temperature variation and noise, so these need to be controlled as far as possible.

WORK ENVIRONMENTS

Work environments have been researched in some detail with regard to the physical aspects of the environment discussed in Chapter 3. This research goes back to the Hawthorne studies (Roethlisberger and Dickson, 1939), where physical changes such as illumination were investigated to determine their effects on performance. The major finding was termed the Hawthorne effect, whereby virtually any change was found to improve performance for a short time, until the novelty of it was lost. Box 5.2 gives a critique of these studies.

Box 5.2 Have the Hawthorne studies been reported accurately?

An article by Rice (1982) has cast serious doubts on the existence of the Hawthorne effect. Several objections have been raised to the original report as a result of further examination of the data and interviews with ex-workers from the plant. Firstly, the Hawthorne plant was the subject of several studies between 1924 and 1932, some of which do not support the existence of the Hawthorne effect. Studies in the mica-splitting department showed that the introduction of rest periods improved output; studies in the bank-wiring department showed no increase in output as a result of the changes that were introduced. The effect was only found in a study of five telephone relay assemblers and two of these were replaced by others in the middle of the study because they were too slow. This, and the fact that there were greater financial incentives and more feedback about performance in that department, could have resulted in improved performance over time. Since the research took place over a five-year period, it is of course quite likely that as time went on the women would get better at the job!

Another general principle that has emerged is the *Yerkes-Dodson Law*, which refers to the inverted-U relationship between arousal and performance (shown in Figure 5.7), such that performance is best at moderate levels of arousal and decreases when arousal is either too low (tired or drowsy) or too high (anxious or agitated). Many physical changes in the environment affect performance at work via this change in arousal, which they induce. Changes in arousal also affect the ability to pay attention to input (Kahneman, 1973) and the motivation to seek stimulation is reduced (Berlyne, 1960). Herzberg (1966) has referred to the physical environment as a hygiene factor, which relates to job satisfaction in such a way that when the physical environment is one in which they are not comfortable (e.g. it is too hot or too noisy), people feel dissatisfied at work (Sundstrom et al., 1994). Music is generally liked because it creates a pleasant atmosphere but it can also be distracting and so it may not necessarily improve performance (Sundstrom, 1986).

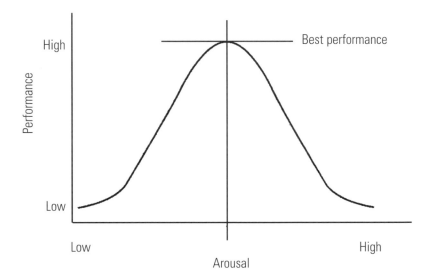

FIGURE 5.7 *The Yerkes-Dodson Law*

Lighting is a complex aspect to deal with, as it is necessary to take into account the amount, colour, type and location of the light source, the amount of reflectance provided by the walls and ceilings and the contrast with surrounding areas. Standards exist that give recommended levels of illumination for different tasks and environments, avoiding both glare as a result of too much light and lack of clarity of vision as a result of too little (Kaufman and Christensen, 1984). Use of video display units (VDUs) with computers has emphasised the importance of adequate lighting. Their use is associated with complaints about eyestrain, headaches and back pain (Turnage 1990); some of these complaints may be the result of factors such as fewer breaks and the poor ergonomic design of many seats, however, rather than the VDUs themselves. Windowless settings are not only disliked (Collins, 1975) but have been found in underground factories in Sweden to lead to complaints of headaches (Hollister, 1968).

Use of space in the workplace has also been investigated. For example, desks can not only give status but can be used to make a barrier between the occupant and any visitor (Joiner, 1971). Decorated spaces are generally found to be more comfortable and environments that are rated as pleasant are associated with increased helpfulness (Sherrod et al., 1977). Too much socialising, of course, may not be desirable at work! Having an *assigned workspace*, e.g. being responsible for a particular machine, encourages personalisation and territorial behaviour and also improves responsibility (Sundstrom, 1986). Arrangement of space also determines *workflow*, which refers to the way that work is moved around. An assembly line is a good example of an arrangement that facilitates this (Hicks, 1977). Related office departments also need to be adjacent to one another, for the same reason.

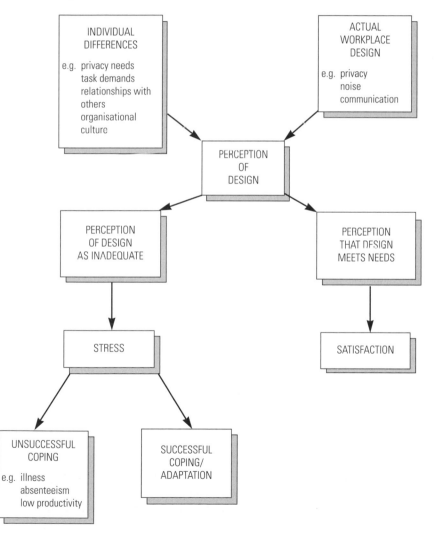

FIGURE 5.8 *Environmental issues in workplace design: a model (based on Bell et al., 1996)*

Open-plan offices have become more popular since the 1960s, but can also cause problems in terms of privacy, which is another important component of satisfaction at work (Sundstrom, 1986). Such offices have no internal partitions from floor to ceiling, which makes communication easier and improves performance on simple tasks (Block and Stokes, 1989). However, there is a lack of visual and auditory privacy and noise can actually interfere with communication, so they have generally been found to reduce job satisfaction and motivation (Oldham and Brass, 1979). Figure 5.8 gives a summary of environmental considerations in workplace design.

Institutions

Institutions are the last type of building that we will consider here. These can take a wide variety of forms, such as schools and nurseries, hospitals, residential homes, prisons, museums and zoos.

Investigations of *schools and nurseries* have shown that simple physical changes, such as using soft carpeting and illuminations, cushions and comfortable chairs, increase class participation (Sommer and Olsen, 1980). Windowless classrooms have interesting effects, in that students dislike them, teachers like them because there are fewer distractions, but performance appears to be unaffected (Larson, 1965). Size of class is a determinant of density and how much competition there is for resources. Glass et al. (1982) found that small classes were better in terms of attitudes, interaction and achievement; increase in size above about 20–25 made little difference, however. When school size is considered, it is clear that smaller schools are better in several respects: there is less anonymity, so deviance is reduced, there is better partic-ipation and more social interaction (Gump, 1987). Increases above 500–600 pupils make very little difference (Garabino, 1980).

Use of space can also be considered here. Pupils who are put at the front participate more and are more attentive (Montello, 1988), although their achievement is not necessarily better. As in offices, open-plan classrooms have been introduced in many schools since the 1960s, the idea being that different activities could take place in different areas of the room. They have generally been found to increase interaction, but can lead to more distrac-tion, more time spent moving around and less time focused on the task (Gump, 1987). Lack of privacy is again a common complaint.

Playground design is an important determinant of the style of play adopted by the children. Where there is little equipment, play revolves around unstructured activities and ball games. When equipment is provided, there is more activity, sometimes at the expense of social interaction, but also more territorial conflict over equipment use (Weinstein and Pinciotti, 1988). The variety and complexity of equipment is also important and Hayward et al. (1974) have identified three types of playground:

1 traditional playgrounds have swings, slides and seesaws;

2 modern playgrounds have novel equipment, sand pits and water fountains, often designed to be aesthetically pleasing;

3 adventure playgrounds have unconventional equipment, such as tyres, paints and digging equipment and are often landscaped. These can have different effects on children's behaviour, as Box 5.3 shows.

Box 5.3 The effects of playground type on play

A study by Hayward et al. (1974) observed children of different ages in the different types of playground. Preschoolers made most use of traditional and modern playgrounds and 6–13-year-olds made more use of adventure playgrounds, building things and playing imaginary games. Adults did not like the adventure playgrounds because they felt they were unattractive to look at. Overall, there was less physical activity in the modern playground (Hart and Sheehan, 1986). This indicates that the age and other requirements of the child need to be matched with the correct type of playground; variety is therefore essential.

Hospitals are often designed for staff ease of use rather than for patient comfort (Ronco, 1972) and aim to give patients minimal control over their space. This can lead to dependency, which does not promote rapid recovery from illness. More recent designs have attempted to overcome such negative effects. Ward designs, shown in Figure 5.9, have been researched by Trites et al. (1970). Radial designs were found to be better in terms of staff satisfaction and time spent with patients than single and double corridor designs, perhaps because less time was spent walking to and fro. This finding has not always been confirmed, however. Design will also influence patient movement and interaction, which is generally to be encouraged unless they are in intensive care. Reducing the number of beds on a ward and using sociopetal furniture arrangements (see Box 5.1) has been shown to increase social interaction (Ittelson et al., 1970). As in dormitory studies, research carried out in a mental hospital by Cherulnik (1993) found that suite designs (2–3 people to a room with internal partitions) were preferred to a corridor design with 1–2 to a room; they also increased alertness and interaction. Windowless rooms are associated with more postoperative problems (Wilson, 1972) and noisy rooms with greater use of painkillers and complaints about pain (Minckley, 1968). A room with a pleasant outlook onto a natural setting, on the other hand, can lead to a shorter postoperative stay and reduced use of painkillers (Ulrich 1984). Apart from staff and patients, design needs to take visitors into account. Studies have shown, for example, that many hospitals are difficult for visitors to find their way around (Carpman et al., 1984).

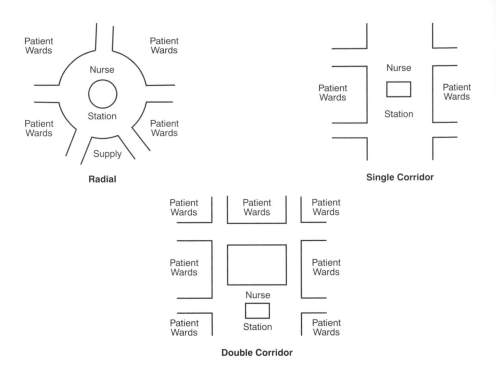

FIGURE 5.9 *These designs represent three types of hospital ward. The radial unit appeared to be the most desirable in terms of staff satisfaction and amount of time spent with patients (adapted from Trites et al., 1970)*

Residential homes for the elderly share the difficulties faced by designers of retirement housing for the elderly. They may take the form of community housing with services such as medical care, meals and activities being provided or nursing homes. In most of these, there are the additional problems that the occupants may be deprived of privacy and their freedom of choice may be restricted. Deprivation of privacy is particularly likely where the person must be kept under surveillance (e.g. for health reasons or because they are suffering from dementia) and can lead to social withdrawal in an attempt to restore the balance. Privacy can be increased by carefully regulating the number of beds per room and by providing opportunities for the marking of territory and retention of personal possessions as far as possible. Freedom of choice can be essential to maintaining self-esteem and satisfaction with life, which in turn relate strongly to activity levels and socialisation, as well as longevity. Allowing people to determine their own activities and routines and giving them responsibilities will help to reduce feelings of helplessness. Removing barriers to participation, such as long corridors which discourage mobility and ensuring that they can easily find their way around by, for example, colour coding doors and floors will all increase their feelings of being in control.

Communal kitchens are another good way of encouraging independence and communal space for socialising. Careful design of such communal spaces is essential, as shown in a study by Howell (1980), details of which are given in Box 5.4.

Box 5.4   Use of communal space in residential homes

Use of communal space was investigated at three sites, where the design differed significantly, as shown in Figure 5.10. Site A had communal space which was just beside the main pathway to rooms; site B had communal space that had to be walked through to get to other rooms; site C had communal space that was set well away from other rooms. Contradictory to expectations, the most popular space was that in site A, whilst site B was felt to be too public.

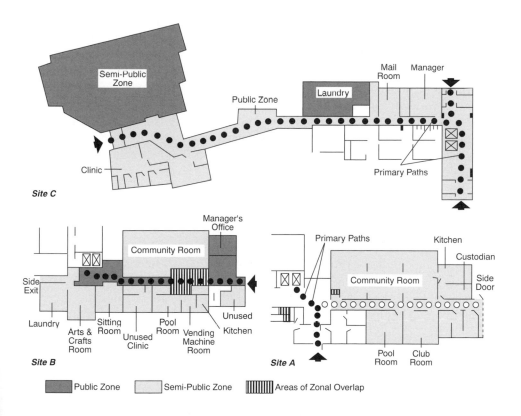

FIGURE 5.10   *The sites investigated in Howell's study of residential homes for the elderly*

Outside areas also need careful design to provide protection from the weather — shade from the sun, screens from the wind — and landscaping to encourage people to go outside. Wheelchair ramps must be provided, as well as garden furniture, to provide further opportunities for socialisation.

Prisons are designed to keep people in, on the other hand, but the type of design traditionally used to accomplish this can have repercussions for behaviour and health. Smaller numbers sharing cells and use of partitions to provide privacy have been found to improve health (Cox et al., 1982). Newer designs try to achieve separation from society at large in more subtle ways than prisons like Alcatraz. Instead of bars, rooms may be provided with several narrow windows. Colour and light have been improved, with individual control of lighting being provided instead of staff turning it all out at a certain time each night. This has been estimated to reduce violence by 30–90% (Wener et al., 1987), as well as vandalism and graffiti.

Museums and zoos share the need to display exhibits carefully and guide visitors around them. Museum buildings are often large, formal rooms, which reduce activity and feelings of pleasure (Mehrabian, 1976a), so the rooms often benefit from being partitioned in some way. Improving legibility by providing maps and routes to follow, possibly colour coded, helps to increase participation and enjoyment. These work best if they take advantage of the natural tendency people have to move to the right when exploring rooms. The problem of 'museum fatigue' (Robinson, 1928) is a reduction in enjoyment that results when attention is concentrated on the exhibits for long periods. This can be alleviated by introducing a 'cognitive breather', e.g. by changing the nature of the exhibits occasionally (Thomson, 1986) or offering an interactive display. Although modern museums have made great efforts to do this, it is still up to the visitor to take advantage of the opportunities provided for such breaks.

Zoos have similar problems, but because their exhibits are alive they have to consider the comfort of the animals as well as that of the visitors (Martin and O'Reilly, 1988). Since the motivation of visitors is not primarily to learn, but to relax and socialise, the zoo environment must not be too demanding. This suggests that signs and information need to be eye-catching and brief. Interactive exhibits are useful and popular (Derwin and Piper, 1988), as in museums. Campbell (1984) refers to three generations of zoo exhibits: first-generation exhibits were those kept behind bars; second-generation exhibits employed barless enclosures, where the animals were contained by a moat (these are still the most common); third-generation exhibits display animals in their natural habitat, kept in groups of compatible species (Figure 5.11). Thus there has been a gradual improvement in the extent to which the needs of the animals are being met, although no difference has been detected in visitor enjoyment between the second- and third-generation exhibits (Shettel-Neuber, 1988). The most attractive exhibits tend to be those where

FIGURE 5.11 *A first-generation zoo exhibit*

there are infant animals, water, where the animals are clearly visible, large, active and close to the visitor (Bitgood et al., 1988). Knowing this, strategies can be introduced such as bringing smaller animals closer to visitors and spreading out the attractive ones to reduce the crowds.

NEIGHBOURHOODS AND COMMUNITIES

A neighbourhood is an area which is defined by its residents as existing, with some agreement on its name, boundaries and characteristics. Thus it is larger than the home but smaller than the city and has a sense of community associated with it. Chavis et al., (1986) define a sense of community as being 'a feeling that members have of belonging and being important to one another and a shared faith that members' needs will be met by their commitment to be together'.

Warren (1978) identified six *types of neighbourhood*: integral, parochial, diffuse, stepping stone, transitory and anomic, depending on how much interaction there is between residents, how much they interact with outsiders and how much of a sense of identity they have. Integral neighbourhoods are most interactive in general and most cohesive, whilst anomic are completely disorganised. Thus the different types give a different sense of community to those who live there. In general, there will also be less sense of community in areas with multistorey flats than in those with single-family dwellings (Weenig et al., 1990). Satisfaction is related to density, social compatibility of neighbours and availability of facilities (Zehner, 1972). Safety from traffic and crime are also important. Ebbesen et al. (1976) refer to some people as having an 'environmental spoiling effect', in that they can create a negative feel throughout an entire area. Community organisations can increase satisfaction by improving communications and interaction and giving inhabitants a joint purpose (Wandersman, 1981).

CITIES

Cities are currently home to more and more people, although Sears et al. (1991) have reported that only about 21% actually choose to live there. Other research by Bell et al. (1990) puts the figure as low as 9%. Milgram (1970) points out that there is a very large amount of stimulation in cities, which can lead to stimulus overload. Some of this is positive, as in the cultural and other facilities, but other aspects, such as the large numbers of vehicles and pedestrians, can operate in negative ways to reduce social interaction and involvement; for example, it has been found that helping behaviour is reduced. City dwellers are therefore less satisfied with their neighbourhoods than those who live in the suburbs or in small towns (Cook, 1988).

The implications are that reducing traffic flow by, for example, using traffic-calming measures or rerouting strategies, will improve satisfaction. Access to open space, particularly if it is semipublic, is also helpful to restore a sense of control and responsibility (Brower, 1977). Parks themselves are often disliked and underused because they are vandalised and perceived as unsafe.

CHAPTER SUMMARY

To summarise this chapter, we have considered how research on the physical and social aspects of the environment can be used to promote positive behaviours through appropriate design of residences, institutions and workplaces. We have also mentioned the importance of a sense of community and how people respond to the conditions associated with city life. In Chapter 7 we will return to these issues when we consider the negative effects that the environment can have. In Chapter 6, by way of a complete contrast, we will be taking a look at responses to the natural environment rather than the built environment.

chapter six

THE NATURAL ENVIRONMENT

CHAPTER OVERVIEW

R esponse to the environment depends to a large extent on how natural it is perceived to be. A natural environment is difficult to define, since man-made parks and landscapes can confuse the issue. Sebba (1991) has pointed out three important differences between natural and manmade environments, which may be helpful here. First, natural environments have a greater *variety of shapes*, which are also softer and rounder than those in man-made environments. Second, *stimulus intensity* (e.g. temperature) shows more variation in natural environments and is less controllable. Third, natural environments show more *change* and contain more *moving inanimate objects*, such as clouds and the sun. In this chapter, we will be looking at attitudes to and preferences for different types of environment and at the applications of this type of research to the use of the environment for recreation and travel.

ATTITUDES TO NATURE
AND THEIR DETERMINANTS

Research has been carried out into the link between our attitudes and preferences and use of the environment in terms of recreation, conservation, etc. Attitudes have been defined and their nature and origins described in Chapter 2. Although primarily learnt, there may be genetic factors, such as influences on personality, which make some attitudes more likely than others (Keller et al., 1992). In general, observation and imitation of others (social learning), rewards and punishments (operant conditioning) and the formation of associations (classical conditioning) will all be major influences on our attitudes. Direct personal experience is more potent than the relayed experience of others (Fazio et al., 1982), which has important implications for changing attitudes.

According to consistency theories, we like to be consistent and feel uncomfortable when we are not. This implies that our attitudes should be related to our behaviour. Unfortunately, there is a great deal of research that indicates that this is not always the case; for example, La Pière (1934) found that hotels in America allowed a Chinese couple to stay, even though their expressed policy at the time was that such persons would not be admitted. Looking at environmental issues, it is clear that at present many people have positive attitudes towards the environment; despite this, few are actively involved in recycling or energy conservation and few would intervene if they observed someone littering. One reason for this is that attitudes need to be measured quite specifically if they are to be linked successfully with behaviour. Not all environmentalists are convinced that water use needs to be restricted or that use of garden chemicals can be avoided, for instance. Exploring a range of behaviours may also show more consistency, allowing for the fact that environmentalists may choose to make their contributions in different ways.

Another important factor (Fishbein and Ajzen, 1975) is that social norms affect attitudes and behavioural intentions. Even where there are social norms that favour conservation of the environment, people may voice these without really agreeing or intending to take action; alternatively, they may wish to take action but find themselves restricted by social norms, e.g. about taking regular baths. Fishbein and Ajzen's (1975) *theory of reasoned action* suggests that attitudes and social norms combined produce behavioural intentions, which will lead to behaviour only if that behaviour is easy to carry out, as shown in Figure 6.1. This has been confirmed in studies of attitudes towards the use of nuclear energy versus coal in the production of electricity. Measuring perceptions about control over the situation can be a way of discovering the extent to which the individual feels that there are obstacles in the way of carrying out intended behaviours. So if there are conflicting social norms, pressure from significant others and behaviour is difficult to carry out for any reason, it will be less likely to occur. Attitudes also need to be activated in order to influence behaviour in particular situations (Fazio, 1990). If they do not seem to be relevant, they will have little effect on behaviour – hence 'conservationists' have been observed cutting down trees to get wood for campfires!

Another line of thought (Festinger, 1957; Bem, 1971) is that attitudes follow behaviour, so if we can be made to change our behaviour, a change in attitudes should follow. Thus if friends can persuade us to join in a demonstration, we are more likely to adopt the appropriate attitude as a result. A practical example of this is the introduction of fines for littering. The problem with this is that the behaviour change needs to be voluntary for this to work; O'Riordan (1976) has found that legislation requiring cars to be fitted with emission control devices does not affect attitudes to air pollution.

The preceding discussion relates primarily to the attitudes of individuals and makes the important point that social norms are a major influence on both attitudes and their links with behaviour. This in turn raises a question about the origins of the social norms themselves.

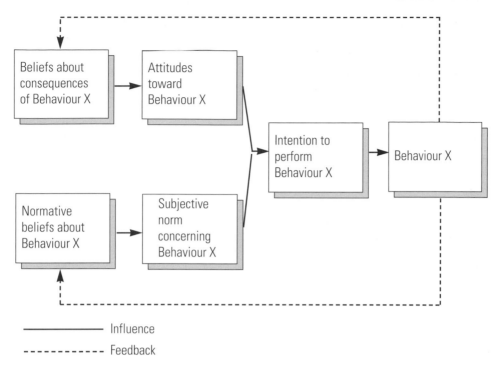

FIGURE 6.1 *Fishbein and Ajzen's Reasoned Action Model shows the influence of social norms and attitudes on behaviour* (from Understanding Attitudes and Predicting Social Behavior *by Ajzen/Fishbein,* © 1980. *Adapted by permission of Prentice-Hall, Inc. Upper Saddle River, NJ.*)

It has been suggested by White (1967) that religion has been an important determinant of the way that we relate to the environment; it dictates how we think about ourselves in relation to the physical world and thence indicates to us how important the physical world is. Western industrialised societies are at present predominantly Christian and the Christian tradition is that humans, being made in God's image, are set apart from the rest of nature. Humans have a non-physical spirit, which means that eventually the physical aspects of life will be unimportant. The Bible explicitly states that humans were instructed by God to 'fill the Earth and subdue it; and have dominion over the fish of the sea and the birds of the air and over every living thing that moves upon the Earth' (*Genesis* 1:28). In addition to this, the Hebrews were predominantly nomadic, a lifestyle that relies on utilising resources and then moving on.

In the Middle Ages the natural world was viewed with fear (Burke, 1985), as can be seen in numerous fairy tales about dark, impenetrable woods where none dared venture. The early American settlers also viewed the wilderness as something to be conquered (Nash, 1982), which has been described as a *homocentric* view. It was not until the advent of romanticism, in 18th-century and early 19th-century Europe, that attitudes changed. Other cultures have been less homocentric, as can be seen in their art; wilderness landscape paintings, unpopular in the West until relatively recently, have been created by Chinese and Japanese artists for thousands of years. North American Indians have also perceived themselves as part of the natural world to a greater extent, with a duty to live in harmony with it and watch over it.

More recently, the realisation that resources are limited and that irrevocable damage is being done to the environment, has led to the ethical reconsideration of what the relationship between people and the natural environment ought to be. One approach is *resourcism*, which aims to conserve and manage natural resources for future use. Another is *preservationism*, which aims to preserve as intact wholes particular ecosystems such as wilderness areas. Unlike resourcism, this is not an economically based approach, but it is still based on the argument that this may benefit humans in some way, e.g. by maintaining a diversity of species, some of which may prove to be useful to us (medically, for example) in the future. The most radical approach, *ecocentrism*, argues that all life and ecosystems have equal merit and therefore deserve protection.

Two important considerations in this debate are the issues of biophilia (Wilson, 1984) and biophobia (Ulrich, 1993). These are considered to be genetically determined influences which have evolved because of their survival value. *Biophobia* refers to a predisposition to dislike environments in which we cannot function well. It is like Seligman's (1970) concept of preparedness to learn, which argues that some associations are easier to form because they have survival value and have therefore become part of our genetic make-up. For example, snake phobias are quite common, despite the fact that many people rarely encounter, let alone have unpleasant experiences with, snakes; in the past, however, it may have been valuable to fear and avoid snakes as a matter of course. Individuals who learnt this readily for genetic reasons would have been more likely to survive and pass on their genes to their offspring. Similarly, a dislike for certain types of environment could have become genetically programmed because it aided survival at some time during evolution.

Biophilia refers to the human need to have close contact with nature. Ulrich (1993) suggests that this shows itself in a liking for the natural environment and in improved physical and psychological performance and well-being as a result of being in it. For example, Kaplan (1977b) describes factory workers who drive some distance at lunch-time to find some trees and grass where they can eat lunch. Support for this idea comes from research into the restorative effects of environments, which shows that peaceful scenes (of lakes, for example) can reduce stress levels (e.g. examination stress; Ulrich, 1979) and aggression and improve health (e.g. postoperative recovery was found to be faster in a study by Ulrich, 1984).

ENVIRONMENTAL PREFERENCES AND THEIR ORIGINS

Are some natural environments more attractive than others? Are there individual differences in preference? Before we can explore this, we need first of all to mention how the environment can be assessed.

As mentioned in Chapter 1, some physical aspects of the environment (e.g. pollution, noise) can be measured objectively using the Environmental Quality Index (EQI). A Perceived Environmental Quality Index (PEQI) gives a subjective measure of how the individual concerned perceives that aspect of the environment (Craik and Zube, 1976). The Environmental Emotional Reaction Index (EERI) can be used to show emotional responses to the environment such as pleasure (Russell and Lanius, 1984). This is the instrument most commonly used in the research that we will discuss next. Another technique used in preference studies is to show people slides and ask them to choose their favourite scene or rate how much they like each one.

Some general principles have emerged in preference studies. Firstly, considering the physical features of the environment, outdoor settings are clearly very important to many people. For example, Sebba (1991) found that when asked to identify the place that was most important to them in their childhood, 97% of a sample of students and teachers identified an outdoor setting such as a seaside or a park. Scenes with high levels of contrast are preferred, e.g. snow-capped mountains and green valleys, blue sea and golden sands, blue skies and white icebergs (Kaplan and Kaplan, 1989). Scenes showing human influence were lowest in preference, although small structures in a natural setting (such as a log cabin) were quite popular (Miller, 1984). Similarly, natural elements, such as trees, in urban scenes also improve ratings (Sheets and Manzer, 1991). Neither extreme openness nor dense, blocked views (e.g. by tall grass) are popular. Open forest and parkland scenes score highly (Kaplan, 1984). Kaplan and Kaplan (1989) argue that the preferred scenes are 'those where it is easiest to extract the information needed to function'. Very dense scenery is potentially obscuring a lot of information and very open areas make it difficult to pick individual things out, so in these cases it will be difficult to work out what to expect and how safe it will be to explore.

Content is also important. Waterscapes are often highly preferred, as is 'ruggedness' (Palmer and Zube, 1976). Water must, however, be associated with freshness and clearness, so that mountain lakes and streams will be popular but swampy stagnant water will not (Kaplan, 1984). Sounds appropriate to the scene, such as those made by birds and animals, enhance liking.

Research into psychological factors determining preferences has focused on concepts such as complexity and ambiguity, which are rated by judges as they view slides and can then be independently related to preferences and liking. As mentioned in Chapter 2, the general organisation of a scene is referred to as its *collative properties* (Berlyne, 1974); these include complexity, novelty, incongruity and surprisingness. Berlyne relates these to the extent to which the scene promotes exploration, either specific exploration (aimed at satisfying curiosity) or diversive exploration (aimed at alleviating boredom). On the basis of the Yerkes–Dodson law mentioned earlier in the book, it might be expected that we would prefer intermediate levels of complexity, novelty, surprisingness and incongruity, but this does not appear to be the case. Wohlwill (1976) found that we prefer:

- intermediate complexity in the built environment (but overall we prefer the less complex natural environment);

- greater novelty;

- greater surprisingness;

- less incongruity.

Whether this would apply to real-life situations as well as to photographs is a matter for debate.

Litton (1972) has looked at other collative properties – enframement, convergence and contrast – and argues that we like scenes that direct our attention to important areas. *Enframement* is found where there are natural borders to the scene, such as vegetation (Figure 6.2). *Convergence* is where lines draw together and focus attention on a particular point, e.g. rivers running into a lake. *Contrast* refers to differences in colour, texture, etc., between different

FIGURE 6.2 *Enframement enhances the attractiveness of a landscape by helping the observer organise their perceptions of the scene*

parts of a scene, which allow the background and foreground to be easily distinguished. Rolling, featureless landscapes like prairies or fens will not be popular because they lack all of these things.

As mentioned in Chapter 2, Kaplan and Kaplan (1989) have produced a *preference model* that is an extension of the above ideas. This relies on the principle that in order to survive, we have to process information successfully and that stimulation in the form of information to process has therefore become important to us. The information contained in a scene has been examined in terms of four factors, as outlined in Box 6.1.

Box 6.1   Preference for scenery

- *Coherence.* To what extent is the scene organised into a coherent whole?

- *Complexity.* How many different elements are there in a scene? The above features both refer to immediately visible features of the scene and are similar to Berlyne's collative properties. The next two factors refer to its potential if explored.

- *Legibility.* How easy is it to understand, or explore without getting lost?

- *Mystery.* How likely is it that there is hidden information that would be revealed on exploration. Complexity and mystery are illustrated in Figure 6.3.

These factors may not be equally important, but all appear to contribute to our preferences; the more coherent, complex (up to a point), legible and mysterious (unless it implies danger) the scene is, the more it will be preferred.

Origins of environmental preferences

These have been attributed to learning, based on experience and cultural values (Knopf, 1987). Few cross-cultural studies have been carried out, but Hull and Revell (1989) found that Balinese natives and Western tourists evaluated Balinese landscapes in similar ways, indicating that the strongest predictor of preference is not culture. The evolutionary view, on the other hand, sees preferences as being dependent on survival value – to be able to recognise and seek out appropriate environments for survival (Charlesworth, 1976). Thus, water, light and vegetation are all important qualities. Appleton (1984) talks in terms of environments offering *prospect* (unrestricted views) and *refuge* (safe hiding places). This can be seen in children's preferences for playing in enclosed spaces (Boschetti, 1987) and in the preference shown by diners in restaurants for the tables alongside walls or windows (Eibl-Eiblesfeldt, 1988). Support is also provided by research showing that animals have genetic preferences for specific habitats, e.g. Wecker (1964) found that mice born in captivity to parents captured in woods or fields showed a preference for the environment the parent was taken from.

FIGURE 6.3 *Complexity (left) and mystery (right)*

Individual differences can also be seen and emphasise the fact that in humans at least, experience may be an important factor. Research has been carried out into *environmental personality* – differences in typical ways of behaving that have implications for the way we interact with the environment. Thus, for instance, sociability and activity levels will lead to different preferences and different personalities will feel more or less secure in different environments. One early writer on this topic was Angyal (1941), who refers to autonomy and homonomy. *Autonomy* is the tendency to strive to manipulate and master the environment, e.g. by creating and maintaining a very neat garden; *homonomy* is the tendency to use the environment very much as it is, e.g. collecting wild mushrooms.

Before we can look at individual differences, we need to look at how they have been measured. Eight different approaches can be identified here.

1 *Person–thing orientation scales* (Little, 1976) measure the extent to which people are attuned to people (person specialists) or to objects (thing specialists). There are also people who are interested in both (generalists), interested in neither (non-specialists) and interested mainly in themselves (self-specialists).

2 The *Environmental Personality Inventory* (EPI) (Sonnenfeld, 1969), measures four factors:

■ environmental sensitivity, i.e. how much impact the environment has on the individual;

■ environmental mobility, i.e. how much people want to travel and how risky they think places are;

■ environmental control, i.e. how much people think they control the environment or vice versa;

■ environmental risk taking, i.e. how much people want to take risks and whether they think different activities are risky or not.

3 The *Environmental Response Inventory* (ERI) (McKechnie, 1974), which consists of eight scales, each containing about 20 questions, as shown in Box 6.2. A children's version, the CERI, has been produced by Bunting and Cousins (1983).

4 The *Environmental Preference Questionnaire* (EPQ), produced by Kaplan (1977a), assesses preferences in seven areas:

■ nature (enjoyment of outdoor activities such as camping);

■ romantic escape (getting away from urban living);

■ modern development (such as modern housing);

■ suburbs (preference for suburban activities such as mowing the lawn and watching sport);

■ social (preference for being with people);

■ passive reaction to stress (going to sleep or eating as responses);

■ city scale (preference for the stimulation of city life).

5 *Stimulus screening* (Mehrabian, 1976a) and *noise sensitivity* (Weinstein, 1978) scales deal with how the individual processes incoming information. The stimulus screening scale identifies screeners, people who can filter out irrelevant stimuli and are therefore less prone to being overaroused by them; the noise sensitivity scale looks at emotional responses to noise.

6 *Sensation seeking* (Zuckerman, 1980) has four scales which look at interest in physical activities and risk taking, pursuit of new sensory and mental experiences, pursuit of pleasure and susceptibility to boredom. This appears to be genetically based and a moderate amount may be adaptive. It influences social behaviour, travel, participation in outdoor activities, consumer behaviour and occupational choice. An example is given in Box 6.3.

Box 6.2 The Environmental Response Inventory

Pastoralism. The tendency to oppose land development, preserve open space, accept natural forces as influences and prefer self-sufficiency.

Urbanism. The tendency to enjoy high density living and appreciate the varied interpersonal and cultural stimulation found in city life.

Environmental adaptation. The tendency to favour the alteration of the environment to suit human needs and desires, oppose development controls and prefer highly refined settings and objects.

Stimulus seeking. The tendency to be interested in travel and exploration, enjoy complex or intense physical sensations and have very broad interests.

Environmental trust. The tendency to be secure in the environment, be competent in finding your way around and be unafraid of new places or of being alone.

Antiquarianism. The tendency to enjoy historical places and things, prefer traditional designs, collect more treasured possessions than most other individuals and appreciate the products of earlier eras.

Need for privacy. The tendency to need isolation, not appreciate neighbours, avoid distraction and seek solitude.

Mechanical orientation. The tendency to enjoy technological and mechanical processes, enjoy working with your hands and care about how things work.

Source: from Gifford, R. *Environmental Psychology, 2/E.* Copyright © 1987 by Allyn & Bacon. Reprinted by permission.

7 *Personal projects analysis* (Little, 1983) asks people to list and give details, including locations, of personal projects they are undertaking, both short- and long-term – learning to swim, for example. This gives some idea of personality (e.g. active/passive) and relationship with the environment.

8 *Place identity* (Proshansky, 1978) looks at the way certain places, such as the home, can become important parts of the self-concept.

The research into individual differences can be grouped according to whether it focuses on dispositions (characteristic ways of behaving), personal constructs (characteristic ways of thinking), information-processing (characteristic differences in the amount and kind of stimulation preferred) or demographic variables such as age and sex.

Research on *dispositions* has focused on traditional personality dimensions, such as introversion/extraversion. For example, outgoing individuals are generally found to prefer closer interpersonal distances than reserved individuals (Altman, 1975) and they also use open furniture arrangements which are sociopetal (McElroy et al., 1983). They perceive environments as more active (Feimer, 1981) and are better able to give directions (Bryant, 1982).

Box 6.3 *Sensation Seeking Scale* A sample of items from the SSS and a scoring procedure

Each item contains two choices. Choose the one that best describes your likes or feelings. If you do not like either choice, mark the choice you dislike the least. Do not leave any items blank.

1 A I have no patience with dull or boring persons.
  B I find something interesting in almost every person I talk to.

2 A A good painting should shock or jolt the senses.
  B A good painting should provide a feeling of peace and security.

3 A People who ride motocycles must have some kind of unconscious need to hurt themselves.
  B I would like to drive or ride a motorcycle.

4 A I would prefer living in an ideal society in which everyone is safe, secure and happy.
  B I would have preferred living in the unsettled days of history.

5 A I sometimes like to do things that are a little frightening.
  B A sensible person avoids dangerous activities.

6 A I would not like to be hypnotised.
  B I would like to be hypnotised.

7 A The most important goal of life is to live to the fullest and experience as much as possible.
  B The most important goal in life is to find peace and happiness.

8 A I would like to try parachute jumping.
  B I would never want to try jumping from a plane, with or without a parachute.

9 A I enter cold water gradually, giving myself time to get used to it.
  B I like to dive or jump right into the ocean or a cold pool.

10 A When I go on a vacation, I prefer the comfort of a good room and bed.
   B When I go on a vacation, I prefer the change of camping out.

11 A I prefer people who are emotionally expressive even if they are bit unstable.
   B I prefer people who are calm and even-tempered.

12 A I would prefer a job in one location.
   B I would like a job that requires travelling.

13 A I can't wait to get indoors on a cold day.
   B I am invigorated by a brisk, cold day.

14 A I get bored seeing the same faces.
   B I like the comfortable familiarity of everyday friends.

Scoring: Count one point for each of the following items that you have circled: 1A, 2A, 3B, 4B, 5A, 6B, 7A, 8A, 9B, 10B, 11A, 12B, 13B, 14A. Add your total for sensation seeking and compare it with the norms below:

0–3 Very low	6–9 Average	12–14 Very high
4–5 Low	10–11 High	

Source: Atkinson et al. (1993)

Research on *personal constructs* has looked mainly at locus of control, which is the extent to which people feel that they determine what happens to them (internal locus of control) or that they are controlled by outside influences (external locus of control). Those who have an external locus of control prefer a larger interpersonal distance from strangers (Duke and Nowicki, 1972) and have less tolerance of high densities (Sundstrom, 1978). They also take fewer precautions in the face of a tornado than do internals. Recyclers (Arbuthnot, 1977) and antipollution activists (Trigg et al., 1976) tend to be internals; internals generally believe that environmental problems are their responsibility, though they are less likely to feel that they can have any impact on the situation. Externals prefer romantic architecture (e.g. baroque) and internals classical architecture, perhaps because this latter is more subdued and controlled.

Some research has also been done using the specialist environmental personality scales. Using person–thing orientation scales, it has been found that thing specialists use more physical constructs to assess places than do any of the other types (Little, 1976). Using the ERI, Gifford (1980) has found that pastoralists, antiquarians and mechanically-oriented people prefer pictures of buildings without people. Pastoralists and antiquarians also dislike modern architecture. The EPQ has been used by Kaplan (1977a) to show that scores on different scales relate to differences in choice of activities and to the reasons given for choices. For example, people high on the nature scales like to be outdoors and prefer peace and quiet.

Information-processing differences have also been revealing. Thus stimulus screeners are less affected by a disliked setting than are non-screeners (Mehrabian, 1978); screeners also adapt better to crowding (Baum et al., 1982). Sensation seekers are more strongly attracted to pleasant settings than those who do not seek sensation (Mehrabian, 1978) and are more likely to engage in dangerous activities such as sky-diving and motorcycling (Brown et al., 1974). They are also more likely to be interested in travel to risky and exotic places (Zuckerman, 1979).

Research into *demographic variables* has concentrated largely on age. Zube et al. (1983) have shown that young children are least affected by the presence of human influences in a landscape and middle-aged people are most affected, with the elderly in the middle. Children are especially attracted to water, whilst young adults and middle-aged people are most attracted to complexity. Children prefer less complex landscapes (Bernaldez et al., 1987) and like savannah (open grassland) with occasional trees (Balling and Falk, 1982); 11-year-olds show less liking for darkness and roughness as features than 16-year-olds, which could be because they are associated with fear.

APPLICATIONS TO
OUTDOOR RECREATION

It almost seems paradoxical that, having improved the standard of our housing and developed new technologies to the extent that we can completely shut ourselves off from the environment, we are turning more and more to outdoor leisure activities such as camping and caravanning, watersports, walking, rock climbing, off-road driving, golfing, fishing, parachuting and so on, and to holidays that take us away from the environment we have chosen to live in and invested in so heavily.

The use of the environment for recreation implies that on a temporary basis, we are carrying out activities that we have chosen to do for their own sake, i.e. they are intrinsically motivated. People who carry out such activities seem to have identifiable characteristics and needs and it is these that we will consider next.

Characteristics of users

In the USA, national and state park users have been found to have higher incomes than average, be in professional and technical occupations, have higher levels of education and come from urban areas (Lime, 1986). Stankey (1972) classified users as 'purists' or 'non-purists', according to the extent to which they preferred the natural environment to be free from human influences. Purists also have stronger needs for solitude and tend to be male, highly educated and raised in an urban environment (Cicchetti, 1972). Rural residents are more likely to see the environment as a resource to be utilised and are more used to seeing evidence of industry in the form of agriculture, mining and forestry (Buttel et al., 1987). There is some evidence that wilderness users are lower in need for affiliation with other people (Rossman and Ulehla, 1977) and possibly higher on autonomy and awareness of sensations and feelings (Driver and Knopf, 1977). Despite this, it is apparent that the main determinant of use is not personal characteristics but other factors such as availability of facilities (Marans, 1972).

Motivations of users

The motivations of wilderness users have also been explored. In general, visiting natural areas allows us to indulge in behaviours that we cannot carry out in everyday life. Knopf (1987) has suggested that these motivations can be grouped into four categories. First, we may be seeking *peace* and *restoration* through escaping from the complexity and sheer quantity of stimulation we are confronted with in everyday urban life. Kaplan (1977b) suggests that this positive response to nature has been programmed into us during the evolutionary process. Support for this as a major motivation comes from Mandell and Marans (1972), who found that tension relief was the most important reason given for participation in outdoor activities. Rossman and Ulehla (1977) found the need for solitude to be so important that satisfaction is greatly reduced if other people are encountered in wilderness areas.

The second possibility is that this type of activity can be used for *building confidence*. It provides an opportunity to assess personal strengths and weaknesses and master new skills, for example, survival skills such as trapping animals for food and cooking on campfires. This mastery could in turn enhance self-esteem.

A third possibility is that it is a method of *seeking stimulation*. Even people who like urban life find a 'change of scene' stimulating and the natural environment provides a different kind of stimulation to that available in cities. High-risk outdoor activities take this increase in arousal still further by giving what is now known as an 'adrenaline rush' – consider the effects, for example, of bungee jumping, white-water rafting and parachuting.

Lastly, the natural environment can be used to *confirm our basic values*. Nature has a symbolic value for most people, being regarded as mysterious, fundamental and the giver of life. To 'keep in touch with nature' is regarded by many people as spiritually important and a way of making a statement about the self. Nature's aesthetic qualities often lead to emotional experiences, as is evident in the phrase 'a breathtaking view'.

Despite the above analysis, it is clear that motivations vary, even amongst people engaged in the same activities; Brown et al. (1977) demonstrated this in a study of deerhunters, some of whom wanted stimulation whilst others primarily sought solitude. Some differences are, however, evident between those who participate in different activities: crosscountry skiers want solitude and snowmobile users adventure (Knopf et al., 1973); anglers want relaxation and hunters exercise (More, 1973).

In 1987 the President's Commission on Americans Outdoors studied 2000 individuals and distinguished five groups in terms of their motivations. Their results are detailed in Box 6.4

A final motivation for outdoor activity is *social pressure*. According to Cheek and Burch (1976), 96% of people who visit wilderness areas are in groups and over half of them are there because someone else wanted to go! Thus affiliation with others is an important factor.

Box 6.4   Motivation for outdoor activities

The first group identified by the Commission were the *health-conscious sociables* and these made up one-third of the sample. The median age was 49 and they enjoyed picnics, barbeques, sightseeing and light exercise. The second group, the *get-away actives*, made up another one-third of the sample and had a median age of 35. Their preference was for quietness and solitude and they liked activities such as hiking and canoeing. The third group was the *excitement-driven competitives*, who made up 16% of the sample and had a median age of 32. These people enjoyed risky activities such as mountain climbing. The next group, the *fitness driven*, comprised 8% of the sample and preferred strenuous activities such as sport – marathon runners are a good example. The final group, referred to as the *unstressed and unmotivated*, constituted 8% of the sample and they were not interested in outdoor activity at all.

Benefits

The benefits of outdoor recreation, not surprisingly, relate to these motivations. Again, researchers have tried to categorise the benefits and Tinsley and Johnson (1984) have identified nine categories:

1   intellectual stimulation (for example, new knowledge about how to do things);

2   catharsis (release of energy, through sport for example);

3   expressive compensation (self-expression in different ways such as camping and hiking);

4   hedonistic companionship (socialising for pleasure);

5   supportive companionship (friendship maintenance, e.g. barbecues with friends);

6   secure solitude (e.g. hiking alone);

7   routine temporary indulgence (e.g. a round of golf);

8   moderate security (e.g. bowling);

9   expressive aestheticism (artistic and creative self-expression, as in painting and photography).

A large number of studies also confirm that wilderness experiences have therapeutic benefits. For example, Slotsky (1973) found improvements (such as less dependency and fewer reports of feeling helpless) in psychiatric patients taken hiking in the mountains for five days. Hartig et al. (1991) randomly exposed participants to either a wilderness trip, a non-wilderness holiday or no holiday at all. The wilderness group reported greater feelings of happiness and well-being and showed improved performance on a proofreading task. Cardiovascular benefits have also been reported (Froelicher and Froelicher, 1991) and some people report a mystical or 'peak' experience, which is considered by writers such as Maslow (1954) to be important for personal growth (Csikszentmihalyi and Kleiber, 1991).

Management of outdoor recreational areas

Given that different people have different needs, depending on age, sex, personality and socioeconomic status amongst other things, it is obvious that a wide range of facilities need to be made available. Some leisure activities can only take place in particular areas (e.g. skiing and white-water rafting) and therefore these need to be carefully provided for. Since solitude (or at least, given that most wilderness users are not alone as such, lack of contact with strangers) is important to most people, the number and size of recreational areas is obviously a prime consideration. Where meeting others is part of the motivation, the area can be more confined, e.g. a campsite.

The quality of the area provided is important to most users. They will be less satisfied with it if there is evidence of littering, pollution or other signs of use; this is especially true of users from more educated groups (Cicchetti, 1972). For many groups of users, technology (such as the presence of motor vehicles)is associated with reduced satisfaction; for example, Lucas (1964) has shown that canoeists dislike motorboats and skiers dislike snowmobiles. Expectations are another important determinant of satisfaction so, for example, if users meet other people when they are not expecting to, or if anglers do not catch any fish, they will be less satisfied (Driver and Knopf, 1976). The facilities provided also determine satisfaction, as is clear if a campsite is considered.

FOCUS ON APPLICATION ...
greenlock

Looking at recreation from the viewpoint of the environment, it is obvious that overuse could destroy the natural resource concerned. For example, the Grand Canyon has an aircraft pass over every four minutes in peak periods (Bell et al., 1996). Pitt and Zube (1987) have argued that each natural environment has a recreational carrying capacity, defined as the number of people who can be served before the environment becomes adversely affected. To estimate this, it is necessary to take into account the amount of ecological damage (e.g. walkers wearing fresh footpaths), the availability of facilities (e.g. at campsites and visitor centres) and the amount of social interaction resulting from the number of people in the area. The extent of the problem can be seen by examining statistics. In 1990, 60 million people visited American national parks (Coates, 1991); 90% of this visitor use was concentrated in just 10% of the available area (Hendee et al., 1978). Thus overcrowding or *greenlock* can be a severe problem. Accessibility is another: traffic increases pollution and traffic jams decrease satisfaction. Yosemite national park has a 21-cell jail to cool off people who have lost their tempers waiting in traffic jams! Restricting access to prevent overload is one solution to crowding, but that may not be economically feasible.

Another management issue is how much to interfere with the natural environment. Some users prefer it to be totally natural ('unspoilt') while others, such as campers, require it to be developed to provide washrooms and restaurants. The needs of different groups may therefore clash and choices will have to be made, possibly between the wishes of the majority and the desires of a minority. Another perspective on this is that the land and its inhabitants are not just commodities to be exploited by humans, but have their own needs and rights which may require human usage and interference to be restricted.

APPLICATIONS TO TRAVEL

Spending extended periods away from home, whether for business or leisure, constitutes travel. Fridgen (1984) has pointed out that there are five stages involved in this:

1 anticipation and planning (often done far in advance and in itself a source of satisfaction);

2 travel to the destination;

3 on-site behaviour;

4 return travel;

5 recollection.

Motivation to travel is an interesting and little-researched topic and one reason for this is that motivation is likely to be different at different stages of the process outlined by Fridgen. Another is that it cannot be studied in isolation from the rest of the person's life, as the same general influences are likely to be predominant. Thus it is also likely that different types of traveller will have different motivations; compare, for example, tourists, businessmen and volunteer workers. The discussion that follows deals mainly with tourists, whose motives may be more related to the environment and less to financial or ideological aims.

Types of traveller

Research by Dann (1977) made a distinction between anomie and ego enhancement tourists. *Anomie* tourists are mainly married middle-class people, who need to feel that they are part of a caring community and travel because they do not feel this way when at home. *Ego enhancement* tourists are mainly older females from the lower socioeconomic groups, who want to feel greater power and social status than they do when at home. Another analysis is presented in Box 6.5.

Box 6.5 Types of traveller

Work by Crompton (1979) identified nine motives, based on both research and a literature review, which could be divided into a social psychological and a cultural group. The social psychological group consisted of seven motives: escaping from a mundane environment; self-evaluation; relaxation; status; regression; improving family relationships; facilitating social interaction. The cultural group consisted of two motives: novelty and education. This latter group were, partly at least, related to choice of destination, while the former group were not related to this at all.

Motivation

Pearce (1982) has related the motivation to travel to Maslow's (1954) hierarchy of needs, which proposes that we have to satisfy a range of needs, from basic biological ones such as food and sleep to the complex need for self-actualisation, which is the realisation of our full potential. In between these are safety needs (the need to feel physically secure), love and esteem needs (wanting to be liked and respected by others), and cognitive needs (needs for stimulation and beauty). According to Maslow, we must satisfy the basic needs first but once this is done we will move up to the next level in the hierarchy. Reasons for travel, then, will relate to our position in the hierarchy – some people will travel to satisfy their belongingness needs, others to increase their self-esteem, others to satisfy aesthetic needs and so on (Table 6.1). Pearce goes on to categorise tourist travellers into five types: exploitative (e.g. business persons); pleasure first (e.g. holidaymakers); high contact (e.g. journalists and students); environmental (e.g. explorers and conservationists); and spiritual (e.g. pilgrims and missionaries).

Such analyses suggest that what matters to people is not so much the range of facilities at the destination, the climate or the culture but the extent to which it meets their psychological needs at the time. Destinations may be more appropriately grouped in brochures according to whether they promote social interaction or culture, for example, which may lead to better choices and greater satisfaction provided that people are clear about what they want.

Research on destinations has found that they fit into six categories: homes of family and friends; resorts (often in sunny climates); rural locations; cities; planned leisure developments (e.g. Disneyland); religious shrines. What people do when they get there depends on their traveller type (Pearce, 1982) (Table 6.2).

Table 6.1   Reasons for travel destinations of 5000 Canadians

Reasons for destination choice	Respondents giving each reason (%)
To visit friends or relatives	50
Relaxing atmosphere	33
Scenery	41
For oceans and beaches	19
Sports facilities	10
Good campsites	11
Good weather	24
Not too many tourists	10
To get better buys	4
Low cost of vacations	11
Warm, friendly people	22
Good roads	13
Outstanding food	7
Attractive customs, life	7
Foreignness	7
Nightlife	6
Easier to have fun there	13
Cultural activities	5
Attractive advertising	5
Don't know much about own province's attractions	2
Don't make fun of English	3
Kicks of getting something back through customs	1
None of above	9

Source: Pearce (1982)

Impact of tourism

This can be considered in terms of the traveller, the hosts and the environment. From the perspective of the traveller, people generally report that they have gained enriched knowledge and new experiences, made new friends and feel refreshed and ready to return to a more routine existence. A study by Morris (1982) found that depression and anxiety declined after a pilgrimage to Lourdes and remained significantly low for ten months afterwards, so in this type of traveller at least there appears to be a positive emotional outcome. Satisfaction is generally related to expectations and preferences, characteristics of the area visited, social relationships, relaxation and the absence of negative conditions like pollution, crowding and noisy fellow travellers (conclusions reached by Dorfman (1979) in a study of campers).

Although travel should be enjoyable and Furnham (1985) has shown that it is one of the main reasons why people save money, negative experiences are not uncommon. The journey itself may involve discomfort (consider a 12-hour plane trip, for example) and illness or theft is not always avoidable. Furnham (1984) reports bewilderment, boredom, disgust, rage, anxiety and stress as negative responses. Iso-Ahola (1986) points out that travel is often a compromise between the needs we have for novelty and for familiarity; too much novelty can lead to what Furnham and Bochner (1986) have described as *culture shock*, a term first introduced by Oberg (1960). The effects are described in Box 6.6.

Box 6.6 The effects of culture shock

This involves strain caused by the need to adapt, feelings of being rejected by the new culture, confusion about how to behave, about personal identity and roles, anxiety and even disgust about differences in food and cleanliness, feelings of loss and despair ('homesickness'), deprivation of status, social support from friends and material possessions such as cars and feelings of loss of control, impotence and inability to cope. Such responses can lead to negative moods at the start of the holiday, withdrawal and possibly minor health problems while away (Pearce, 1981). Hence many resorts try to reduce this by providing a familiar diet and surroundings. An example of this is a Turkish resort which has a bar called the 'Rovers Return'; similarly, Tangiers offers fish and chips direct from Yorkshire.

Although these effects can be considerable, they are less extensive than those on the people of the host country. Tourists are only away for a short time on the whole, they group together for support, use guides and travel company representatives as intermediaries and have less need to participate in normal everyday life. Where host communities are small, isolated and unsophisticated, e.g. Bali, Iceland and rural areas in Europe, tourists are often disliked (Pearce, 1982). There may be interpersonal friction and stress as a result of the increased noise, pollution and environmental degradation. The effects are reduced when the host culture is similar to that of the visitors in terms of technological and economic status but even then it has been noted that, for example, city dwellers become more aggressive during the tourist season.

Finally, the host environment itself may suffer in similar ways to recreational areas in the travellers' country of origin. The availability of tourists will lead to building activity to provide accommodation and food outlets. Crime typically increases compared with that in similar areas with fewer tourists (Walmsley et al., 1983). There may also be damage to cultural attractions, such as that experienced by the cave paintings at Lascaux in France as a result of so many tourists breathing on them.

Table 6.2 The five major role-related behaviours for 15 traveller categories

Traveller category	The five clearest role-related behaviours (in order of relative importance)
Tourist	Takes photos, buys souvenirs, goes to famous places, stays briefly in one place, does not understand the local people
Traveller	Stays briefly in one place, experiments with local food, goes to famous places, takes photos, explores places privately
Holidaymaker	Takes photos, goes to famous places, is alienated from the local society, buys souvenirs, contributes to the visited economy
Jetsetter	Lives a life of luxury, concerned with social status, seeks sensual pleasures, prefers interacting with people of his/her own kind, goes to famous places
Business person	Concerned with social status, contributes to the economy, does not take photos, prefers interacting with people of his/her own kind, lives a life of luxury
Migrant	Has language problems, prefers interacting with people of his/her own kind, does not understand the local people, does not live a life of luxury, does not exploit the local people
Conservationist	Interested in the environment, does not buy souvenirs, does not exploit the local people, explores places private, takes photos
Explorer	Explores places privately, interested in the environment, takes physical risks, does not buy souvenirs, keenly observes the visited society
Missionary	Does not buy souvenirs, searches for the meaning of life, does not live in luxury, does not seek sensual pleasures, keenly observes the visited society
Overseas student	Experiments with local food, does not exploit the people, takes photos, keenly observes the visited society, takes physical risks
Anthropologist	Keenly observes the visited society, explores places privately, interested in the environment, does not buy souvenirs, takes photos
Hippie	Does not buy souvenirs, does not live a life of luxury, is not concerned with social status, does not take photos, does not contribute to the economy
International athlete	Is not alienated from own society, does not exploit the local people, does not understand the local people, explores places privately, searches for the meaning of life
Overseas journalist	Takes photos, keenly observes the visited society, goes to famous places, takes physical risks, explores places privately
Religious pilgrim	Searches for the meaning of life, does not live a life of luxury, is not concerned with social status, does not exploit the local people, does not buy souvenirs

Source: Pearce (1982)

CHAPTER SUMMARY

In conclusion, we have explored our relationship with the natural environment from many angles. We have looked first at attitudes and how they relate to behaviour, at their origins and at the need for ethical decisions about the correct way to regard the environment. Then environmental preferences, their origins and the range of individual differences that affect them were touched on. The need for outdoor recreation, its benefits and management issues have been considered, followed by a section on the motivation for and consequences of travel. This last section has raised the issue of negative responses to the environment in the form of stress and it is to this that we will devote the next chapter.

chapter seven

THE ENVIRONMENT AND STRESS

CHAPTER OVERVIEW

In this chapter we will be looking at some of the ways in which the environment can be damaging to our mental and physical health by contributing to stress. We will start by examining the nature of stress and its effects and move on to look at the aspects of the environment that are generally associated with stress and at the factors that influence these effects. The applications of this research to city life, work, natural and technological disasters and extreme environments will be considered and finally we shall look at theories and models of stress.

THE NATURE OF STRESS

We have acquired, through the course of evolution, a response to dangerous situations, known as the 'fight or flight response' (Cannon, 1929), which generally operates to assist our survival. However, when this response operates inappropriately – for too long or in response to the wrong things, for example – it can be harmful. This is basically what happens in stressful situations, whether they are natural disasters, accidents, long-term problems like noise or pollution, travel, living in crowded urban areas or in extreme environments like outer space, the fundamental nature of the response is the same.

So how can we define stress? Broadly speaking, stress implies that the environment is felt to be making demands on people that exceed their ability to cope. A possible *definition*, then is that stress is a situation or condition which places the individual under some pressure, involves adjustment in behaviour and can cause changes which are unpleasant, sometimes maladaptive and even associated with physical damage. The situation itself is referred to as the *stressor* and the resulting behaviour as the *stress response*. One important point about this view of stress is that it must be regarded as a process involving environmental stressors and the individual's psychological and physical responses to them. Between the two, and a very important part of the process, is the individual's cognitive evaluation of the situation or environment, known as an *appraisal*. This includes an assessment of the threat posed (e.g. by an impending storm or a dangerous job), of the extent of loss or harm suffered (e.g. of damage to crops after a frost) and of the possibility of coping with the stressor (e.g. how best to respond after an earthquake warning). This appraisal process is a very important part of stress and represents a fundamental part of the *transactional model* of stress (Cox, 1975), which sees stress as resulting from the interaction between the individual and the environment (Figure 7.1).

FIGURE 7.1 *The three aspects of the stress process* (from McAndrew, 1993)

Although this approach emphasises the individual nature of stress, it is possible to generalise about the nature of stressors to some extent. There are four general points that we can make. First, stress can result not only from *unpleasant* and *threatening* situations but also from *intense, pleasurable* experiences. Taking the family on holiday, for example, is well known to be stressful! Second, stress is often linked with *lack of control* over the stressor, as in the example of noise given in Chapter 3 where it was noted that our own noise is not nearly as disturbing as that created by our neighbours. We need not exercise this control, it is enough that we think that we have it. The most famous example here is the work by Seligman (1975) on learned helplessness, which showed that animals subjected to electric shocks from which they could not escape appeared to give up trying and became helpless. Another example can be found in a study which compared 22 old people put into a residential home by their families with 18 who applied themselves. Despite being equivalent in terms of health initially, 19 of the first group had died after one month, compared with only four of the second. Thus being forced to move had increased stress and mortality rates.

The third important determinant of stress is the *predictability* of the event. Generally, unpredictable events such as noise are found to be more stressful (Glass and Singer, 1972), but in some instances very predictable events can be stressful – just think about the effects of a dripping tap! The final component, which is common to many stressful situations is *threat and loss*, as is evident in natural disasters which threaten home and family.

To summarise, then, stress results from stimuli that are highly pleasant or unpleasant, uncontrollable and unpredictable (or highly predictable) and pose a threat in some way. We will return later to examine the nature of environmental stressors in more detail, but first it would be useful to consider the ways in which we are affected by stress, both physiologically and psychologically.

Physiological responses to stress

Regardless of the nature of the stressor, the response is generally the same. Selye (1956) described it as occurring in 3 stages, which he called the General Adaptation Syndrome (GAS), illustrated in Figure 7.2 and described in Box 7.1.

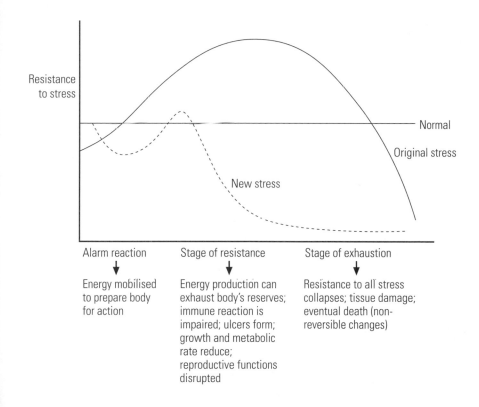

FIGURE 7.2 *The General Adaptation Syndrome*

Box 7.1   The General Adaptation Syndrome

The first stage is the alarm reaction, in which the body is stimulated to mobilise its resources and prepare for fight or flight by the sympathetic branch of the autonomic nervous system. This leads to an increase in heart rate and blood pressure, respiration rate, muscle tension, pupil dilation and increased blood flow to the brain and muscles, blood being diverted away from the digestive organs in order to achieve this (leading to a 'sinking feeling' in the stomach or even feeling sick). This process is brought about by adrenaline and noradrenaline, substances released by the adrenal glands near the kidneys.

If the stress continues, the body enters the stage of resistance, where the pituitary gland, under the control of the hypothalamus, produces hormones which in turn stimulate the adrenal cortex to produce glucocorticoids. These act to maintain a higher metabolic rate and blood glucose level and lead to an increased production of red blood corpuscles. The body starts to consume its energy stores, which can lead to hypoglycaemia if they become exhausted. Other effects are less useful. The activity of the immune system is reduced and bodily repairs are decreased, so infection and damage become more difficult to deal with. The production of some hormones is reduced: for example, somatic (growth) hormone and hormones associated with reproduction, such as testosterone. This may lead to loss of sex drive and, in females, disruption of the menstrual cycle and an increase in miscarriages (Kennedy et al., 1990).

Overall, then, there is a considerable reduction in bodily activities involved in growth, reproduction and resistance to infection and an overwhelming increase in those which prepare the person for energetic action. There will be feelings of weariness and possibly illness at this stage, but if the stressor is removed the individual will return to the original prestress state. Note that if an extra stressor is added at this point, resistance to that will be very much reduced, as shown in Figure 7.2. If stress continues, the individual enters the third stage, that of exhaustion, where resistance to all forms of stress collapses, there is widespread damage to tissues (e.g. in the adrenal glands), illness such as high blood pressure, strokes and possibly death (Welch, 1979). For example, people are twice as likely to catch a cold after a prolonged period of stress. The physiological basis of these processes is shown in Figure 7.3.

Psychological changes

These will vary in nature and extent according to the nature and intensity of the stressor, the predisposition and previous experience of the individual and the degree of social support the individual receives from friends and family. Some of the possible responses follow.

Changes in general levels of arousal may be shown in behaviour as increased tension, anxiety and depression (Byrne, 1979). Fidgeting and overly emotional reactions may be seen, possibly leading to increased aggression and hostility. Behaviour may become disorganised, so reasoning powers may be reduced as well as the ability to carry out skilled tasks. Increased rigidity may lead to excessive dependence on routine, to rituals and stereotyped behaviours; this

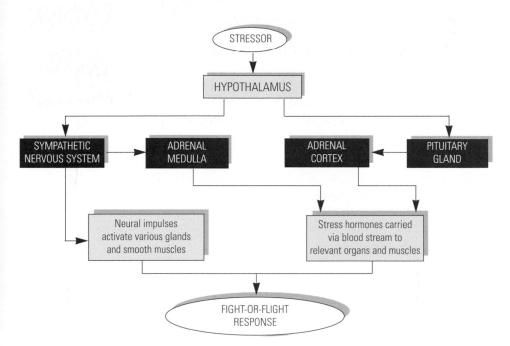

FIGURE 7.3 *Pathways of stress*

can be seen in confined zoo animals which pace along the same path repetitively. Coping responses may be shown in an attempt to reduce discomfort (e.g. the stressful situation may be avoided), although these could themselves be dysfunctional in the longer term, for example by leading to the development of phobias (Eysenck and Rachman, 1965). Other ways of coping are more clearly maladaptive, e.g. substance abuse (Keane and Wolfe, 1990). In the longer term, mental illness is a distinct possibility (Halpern, 1995).

Given, then, that we have established in general terms what stress is, what kinds of events and stimulation can act as stressors and what is involved in the stress response, we can now go on to establish specific links between stress and some aspects of the environment that we have explored in previous chapters.

TYPES OF ENVIRONMENTAL STRESSOR

Stressors can be categorised in various ways and it is important to remember that what is stressful to one person may not be to another, depending on their cognitive appraisal of the situation. Evans and Cohen (1987) have identified the following four types of stressor, which can be distinguished according to how long they persist, how severe they are and how many people they affect.

1 *Daily hassles* (or microstressors) are minor everyday events which, cumulatively, can have a big impact on the individual (Lazarus, 1966). They are mostly of short duration and focused on the individual. Included in this category would be dripping taps, overcrowded buses, traffic jams, losing keys, annoying neighbours, etc. A group of middle-aged adults studied by Kanner et al. (1981) reported their most frequent hassles to be concerns about weight, the health of family members, rising prices, home maintenance, having too many things to do and losing things.

2 *Life events* (or life stressors), researched by Holmes and Rahe (1967), are events that many people experience at one time or another. If too many occur over a short period, they can lead to stress and illness. They are focused largely on the individual and may be of short or long duration. Examples are divorce, moving house, going into hospital or on holiday and starting a new job.

3 *Ambient stressors* are relatively minor, generally long-term and affect everyone in the vicinity. They include all the physical and social conditions in the environment that can cause discomfort, such as wind, pollution, noise and overcrowding.

4 *Cataclysmic stressors* are major upheavals that are generally acute in duration (although the aftereffects may not be) and affect large segments of the population. They include natural disasters such as tornadoes and floods and technological catastrophes such as Chernobyl and the Gulf War.

Based on the above, a useful categorisation of stressors has been produced by Halpern (1995), an adaptation of which is shown in Table 7.1.

Table 7.1 A categorisation of stressors

	Minor	**Major**
Acute	Hassles, e.g. crowding, noise	Cataclysmic stressors, e.g. earthquakes
Chronic	Ambient stressors, e.g. pollution, ongoing noise, heat	Long-term difficulties, e.g. produced by life events or disasters, such as poverty or homelessness

MEASUREMENT OF STRESSOR AND STRESS RESPONSE

The first step in carrying out research in this area has been to devise ways of measuring both the stressors and the stress responses and it is to these that we turn next.

Stressor measurement

Measurement needs to cover intensity, duration, rate of occurrence and controllability of the stressor. *Intensity* of some stimuli, such as the ambient stressors (wind speed, noise, temperature) can be measured easily using existing scales. Disasters and catastrophes can be measured using statistical data such as the number of people killed or homes destroyed; earthquakes can be measured by the Richter scale. Such objective measures can be compared if required with subjective reports, e.g. of experienced air quality. Life events and hassles can be measured using scales devised by Holmes and Rahe and Lazarus respectively; the former, the Social Readjustment Rating Scale, gives a weighting to each life event as an indicator of its severity, based on ratings by independent judges (Table 7.2). How recently the event occurred can also be noted, to indicate its likely current impact on the individual – a bereavement a week ago is likely to have more impact than if it happened a year ago, for example.

Duration needs to be measured for all stressors; some may be weak in intensity, but have major effects on the individual because they are longlasting, e.g. air pollution. The *rate* and *regularity* of occurrence of the stressor also determines its impact. Does it occur once and then become unlikely to recur (e.g. a nuclear accident) or is it something that is repeated at regular intervals (like floods in certain areas, or tornados in 'tornado alley' in the USA)? Is it predictable, like a passing train, or comparatively random, like a tornado? Finally, it is important to measure the event's *controllability* or, at any rate, how controllable it is perceived to be. Natural disasters and life events are largely beyond our control, whereas ambient stressors such as temperature can be controlled to some extent and their effects reduced (e.g. use of air-conditioning to control temperature).

Stress response measurement

This needs to take into account both the physiological and psychological aspects of the response. *Physiological* measures can be taken of many of the components of the GAS, such as levels of adrenaline and noradrenaline (jointly referred to as catecholamines), corticosteroids in blood and urine, heart rate and blood pressure and changes in arousal shown by skin conductance (galvanic skin response or GSR) and muscle tension (electromyograph or EMG). Longer term effects can be demonstrated by looking for signs of illness such as heart disease and hypertension. For example, Eliot and Buell (1979) found that young employees on the space program at Cape Kennedy showed a 50% increase in sudden death (attributed to heart failure) compared to the norm for their age group. Another indicator is illness that is associated with impaired immune system functioning, such as cancer (Morris et al., 1981) and respiratory infections (Jemmott et al., 1983). The functioning of the immune system itself can be tested by looking for the presence of lymphocytes and antigens in the body.

Table 7.2 Social Readjustment Rating Scale

Rank	Life event	Mean value
1	Death of spouse	100
2	Divorce	73
3	Marital separation	65
4	Jail term	63
5	Death of close family member	63
6	Personal injury or illness	53
7	Marriage	50
8	Fired at work	47
9	Marital reconciliation	45
10	Retirement	45
11	Change in health of family member	44
12	Pregnancy	40
13	Sex difficulties	39
14	Gain of new family member	39
15	Business readjustment	39
16	Change in financial state	38
17	Death of close friend	37
18	Change to different line of work	36
19	Change in number of arguments with spouse	35
20	Mortgage over $10,000	31
21	Foreclosure of mortgage or loan	30
22	Change in responsibilities at work	29
23	Son or daughter leaving home	29
24	Trouble with in-laws	29
25	Outstanding personal achievement	28
26	Wife begins or stops work	26
27	Begin or end school	26
28	Change in living conditions	25
29	Revision of personal habits	24
30	Trouble with boss	23
31	Change in work hours or conditions	20
32	Change in residence	20
33	Change in schools	20
34	Change in recreation	19
35	Change in church activities	19
36	Change in social activities	18
37	Mortgage or loan less than $10,000	17
38	Change in sleeping habits	16
39	Change in number of family get-togethers	15
40	Change in eating habits	15
41	Vacation	13
42	Christmas	12
43	Minor violations of the law	11

Source: Holmes and Rahe (1967)

Psychological responses that can be measured include psychiatric symptoms, coping responses and task performance. Psychiatric symptoms can be measured using instruments such as the State–Trait Anxiety Inventory (Spielberger, 1972) to give an indication of emotional responses such as depression and panic, thought disorders such as intrusions and repetitive worries and associated behaviours such as loss of appetite and insomnia. Coping responses can be measured using inventories which give an indication of whether individuals focus on managing the problem (e.g. by trying to change the situation) or on dealing with their own feelings (e.g. by talking to others). One such inventory produced by the Center for the Study of Neuroses at the University of California, San Francisco, asks people to what extent statements such as the following apply to them:

- I tried to find new interests;
- I sought increased emotional support from others;
- I welcomed some time alone to think about what had happened.

Performance on cognitive tasks can also be assessed to see if stress has caused any deterioration in cognitive ability, or in the way that people respond to others. For example, Glass and Singer (1972) demonstrated that noise could affect task performance and Cohen (1980) found an increase in tendencies to withdraw and be aggressive and a decrease in sensitivity to others.

Clearly, then, the assessment of stress is a complex affair. Nevertheless, there is now a considerable body of research that links stress with different aspects of the environment and it is to this that we turn next. We will look at the effects of each of the major groups of stressors in turn, divided into ambient stressors (physical and social) and their practical application to housing and hazards at work and then go on to study the cataclysmic stressors (natural disasters and technological catastrophes). A detailed consideration of life events and hassles is beyond the scope of this book, although in practice many of these will be associated with ambient and cataclysmic stressors.

AMBIENT STRESSORS
AND THEIR EFFECTS

In Chapter 3 we considered the general effects of the physical aspects of the environment on behaviour and in Chapter 4 the effects of social factors. Here we are focusing on what happens when this stimulation reaches levels that prove stressful. We will be considering physical stressors such as seasonal changes in light, temperature, barometric pressure, wind, weather in general, air quality and noise and social stressors, such as crowding, crime and lack of social support.

Seasonal changes in light lead some individuals to experience severe depression in the autumn and winter. This syndrome, known as *seasonal affective disorder* (SAD), is associated with overeating and oversleeping. It appears to disappear spontaneously in the spring and has been thought to be caused by the lack of light during the winter months when days are shorter. The main effect may be on the production of melatonin by the pineal gland, a substance which is known to affect mood and energy levels. Another general effect of seasonal change is on the rate of physical illness; in Britain there are 40,000 more deaths in the winter than in the summer (Lowry, 1991). Although this could result from several different factors, it has implications in turn for psychological well-being.

Temperature has been linked in several studies (e.g. Rotton and Frey, 1984) with the rate of psychiatric emergencies, warm days leading to an increase. Aggression and even riots are more likely when the temperatures are moderate to high (Bell and Greene, 1982), falling again when the temperatures reach higher levels.

Barometric pressure is difficult to assess in isolation, since changes are typically associated with changes in other aspects of the weather, but it has been shown that low pressure has been associated with an increase in reported levels of depression and medical complaints (Briere et al., 1983) and an increase in suicide rates and complaints to the police (Fisher et al., 1984). Wind that is warm and dry is associated with high levels of positive ions and also with an increase in depression, nervousness and irritability (Sommer and Moos, 1976). These findings can be put together to suggest that a stressful weather pattern is one that is associated with warm, low pressure days; Briere et al. (1983) found that this was linked with emergency admissions for depression, particularly when there was also cloud cover.

Air pollution has been linked with mental health; Klitzman and Stellman (1989) found that perceived air quality was strongly associated with mental health in a study of 2000 office workers. Bullinger (1989) showed that individuals living in more polluted areas experienced more negative moods and they also showed more adverse reactions to negative life events (Evans et al., 1987). Rotton and Frey (1984) found an increase in psychiatric emergencies on days when pollution was higher; this was especially true for carbon monoxide, ozone and nitrogen dioxide levels. Most of these studies have controlled for the effects of other variables and show strong effects of relatively small fluctuation in pollution levels.

Noise effects appear to be complex and have been studied in relation to workplace and aircraft noise primarily. In the workplace, it is clear that those exposed to higher levels of noise show an increase in nervous and psychosomatic illness and anxiety and higher levels of social conflicts (e.g. Cohen, 1969). Welch (1979) found that employees exposed to unpredictable noise for three years or more and whose work requires mental concentration, have a 60% increase in their chances of suffering from cardiovascular disease. The problem with all of these studies is that the effect of noise is confounded with that of other factors in the workplace – where there is noise, there are usually other stressors too.

Aircraft noise has also been investigated by looking at its effects on people who live in the vicinity of airports. This research is outlined in Box 7.2.

Box 7.2 The effects of aircraft noise

Early work showed links with drug-taking, cardio-vascular problems, hypertension and psychiatric hospital admissions, e.g. Abey-Wickrama et al. (1969). More recent research has tried to ensure that other differences between people who live in quieter and noisier areas have been controlled for, and this has produced a rather more complex picture. Tarnopolsky et al., (1980) argue that it is only those people who describe themselves as annoyed by aircraft noise who seem to show these effects and have therefore suggested that some people may be noise sensitive. This in turn may be related to neuroticism (Broadbent, 1972).

A similar result has been obtained by looking at the effects of road traffic noise (Halpern, 1995). Overall, it is concluded that noise, although annoying, does not relate very strongly to mental ill health. Halpern (1995) attributes this to the fact that it is easy to track down the source of the noise and therefore to cope with it in appropriate ways; compared with some of the other variables we are considering, it is easier to control.

The first of the social ambient stressors that we shall consider is crowding. This research was stimulated by the 'behavioural sink' studies of Calhoun (1962), which showed that high density living in rats led to behaviour disturbances, disease and a decrease in successful reproduction and rearing of offspring. Studies of humans have shown varying effects, but Levy and Herzog (1974) in the Netherlands found population density to be strongly correlated with aggressive offences and other crimes, death, psychiatric and hospital admission rates and fatal coronaries in males. Other research in Chicago and Hong Kong, however, has found no adverse effects (Galle et al., 1972; Mitchell, 1971). In Britain, Halpern (1995) reported data on 7500 people and found that high density dwellers were more likely to report sleeplessness, depression, irritability and nervousness. It seems likely from this that there may be sizeable cultural differences leading to these conflicting findings.

Household density effects are variable according to the level of density being examined. Both very low density (people living alone) and very high density are associated with poorer mental health, as shown in Figure 7.4. Halpern (1995) has proposed that those who live alone may be at risk because they lack social support, possibly due to recent bereavement. Mitchell's (1971) Hong Kong study found adverse effects of high density only when dwellings were shared by non-kin (unrelated people); this led to poorer emotional health and increased levels of hostility. When people can escape from the house, the effects are reduced. For example, Ruback and Pandey (1991) found in India that females suffer from the effects of density more than men and suggested that this was because they spend more time in the house.

To summarise, population and household density are associated with mental ill health, but this is variable across cultures. They are also associated with crime (not necessarily causally), but the effects can be reduced if escape is possible. Living alone may have even worse effects. The effects of density have also been explored in dormitories and prisons, where people are forced to share with strangers. One of the best studies of shared student accommodation is that of Lepore et al. (1991), who looked at 175 students over an eight-month period. At the end of the study, those in more crowded rooms reported more psychological distress, disagreements and hassles and reduced perceptions of control. Baum and Paulus (1987) found that common areas and sociopetal designs led to an increase in negative effects because interaction is unavoidable. In prisons, Cox et al. (1984) have shown that larger institutions have increased suicide, death and psychiatric admission rates. Double occupancy is associated with worse effects than living in a single cell. Although many of these studies have been criticised, a well-controlled study by Wener and Keys (1988) found an increase in sickness rates when a prison unit was increased in density.

Crime can be both a result of stress and a cause of it; here, the emphasis is on its contribution to social factors causing stress. Fear of crime is stressful, leading to a chronic anxiety state which includes a sense of helplessness. White et al. (1987) found a negative association between perceived crime levels and mental

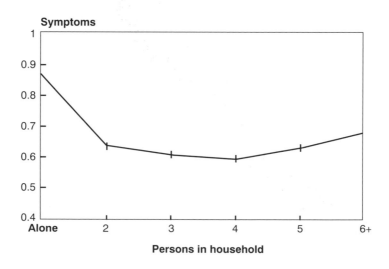

FIGURE 7.4 *Average symptom levels by household size*

health, so that mental health was lower where there was perceived to be a high crime rate. Crime can also lead to social withdrawal and the undermining of social support networks. Hearing about crime from others (such as neighbours and friends) increases fear (Tyler, 1980), especially if the reported crime is in the locality (Box et al., 1988). Thus a socially cohesive community will spread more fear (Bastlin et al., 1988). Direct experience of crime as a victim leads to serious long-term effects for 35% of victims and moderate effects for 31% (Maguire, 1982). Victim support groups have confirmed these findings and have shown that the effects are worst for females who live alone.

Fear of crime is also linked to the number of strangers (often referred to as pedestrian traffic) passing through the area (Hunter and Baumer, 1982) and with building size. Larger buildings are associated with more fear (Newman and Franck, 1982) even though the actual crime rate is not higher.

Social support is an important factor in mental health, better support being available to those with better mental health. The direction of causation in this relationship (whether social support leads to improved mental health or good mental health leads to a bigger network of friends) is still uncertain (Cohen and Wills, 1985). Individual differences in social support have been researched and some findings are presented in Box 7.3.

Box 7.3   Individual differences in social support

Most people have a social network of 25–30 people, of whom they may know 6–10 well and these people also tend to know each other (20% of possible links between different individuals in the network usually exist in practice). Neurotic individuals, however, have networks of between 10–15 people and they tend not to be interconnected. Psychotics have very small, dense (i.e. interconnected) networks of 4–5 people, most of whom are relatives (Mueller, 1980). Network size will of course vary considerably in different individuals (some are simply more sociable than others, for example, and will have larger networks) and may also vary from time to time in any given individual according to factors such as age, nature of employment, geographic location, interests, etc. It is suggested that these networks are protective and mental illness is therefore more likely in those who lack them, although mentally ill people may also undermine the networks they do have (Levy, 1983). To the extent that the characteristics of the environment influence social contact and hence the formation of social networks, it can be seen to have an indirect influence on the development of mental illness.

Social support may be instrumental, involving practical help and advice, or emotional, providing support, encouragement and the opportunity to express feelings. These different types of social support may come from different sources: for example, family members may give financial help, friends emotional help and neighbours immediate practical help. Neighbouring can be encouraged by social homogeneity (encouraging interaction by ensuring that neighbours are similar in terms of race, economic status, etc.), proximity (Festinger et al., 1950) and by designing new developments so that houses are arranged in cul-de-sacs or in short, narrow roads with little traffic (Halpern, 1995). Neighbourliness is reduced by high density living, lack of public space in which to socialise (as shown by Yancey's (1971) study of the Pruitt-Igoe development) and take charge of as defensible space (Newman, 1972) and the presence of mixed land use (such as commercial and industrial buildings) in the area (Halpern, 1995), this last being thought to lead to increased traffic flow. Neighbours must also feel that they can decide for themselves whether they want to interact (i.e. they must be able to regulate the interaction) or there will be hostility instead of good will, leading to feelings of both lack of privacy and loneliness and ultimately to increased stress. Figure 7.5 provides a summary.

INFLUENCE OF PHYSICAL
ENVIRONMENT ON CONTACT

	Prevents privacy	**Allows privacy**
Heterogeneous	Conflict or withdrawal	Little contact
Homogeneous	Conflict or withdrawal	Good relationships

(Row axis label: TYPE OF SOCIAL ENVIRONMENT)

FIGURE 7.5 *The influence of physical and social environments on neighbours' relationships*

Factors affecting stress

Our discussion so far has suggested that there are several determinants of whether or not stress is experienced in a situation. We will now look briefly at some of these: appraisal of the stressor, perceptions of control, personality, social support and coping responses.

Appraisal has been mentioned briefly elsewhere in this chapter. Objective measurement, e.g. of noise levels, has been found to relate very poorly to subjective ratings of annoyance; approximately 30% of the variability in response can be accounted for by different attitudes to noise (Tracor, 1971). This may relate to the perception of risk as well. Fear of plane crashes is associated with greater feelings of annoyance about airport noise, for example. Similarly with nuclear power, where studies of people living near Three Mile Island nuclear power plant in America have shown that those who feel that it is of economic benefit are less likely to be negative in attitude and they also suffer less stress.

Perceived control over the stressor has been related to a reduction in its effect for example in Glass and Singer's (1972) study of the effects of noise. Phifer (1990) showed that having control over environmental stressors reduced susceptibility to infection, headaches and gastro-intestinal disorders. Having accurate expectations (e.g. about crowding) has been shown to be associated with less stress (Baum et al., 1981). In medical settings, being given a choice of treatments has a similar effect (Miller and Mangan, 1983). Halpern (1995) has suggested that feelings of having a choice about where to work and live may be an important contributor to whether or not environmental stress is experienced.

Personality has been linked with the above research by exploring differences in locus of control. Individuals with an internal locus of control, who perceive that they have more control over their lives, are more likely to perceive difficulties as challenges. They are often physically fitter and better equipped physiologically to withstand stress (McGilley and Holmes, 1988). Kobasa (1979) described them as being higher in hardiness. They seem to be more constructive in the face of difficulties, have lower blood pressure and suffer from less illness (Contrada, 1989).

Social support networks, as discussed earlier, can be helpful in various ways: they can help solve practical problems and can encourage self-disclosure and emotional expression (Cohen and Wills, 1985). *Coping responses* can range from withdrawal and denial to anger and aggressive problem solving. A useful form of coping is relaxation, which acts to counteract the physiological effects of the stress response (Benson, 1975). Adopting a comfortable position in a quiet environment and employing a repetitive mental device such as the chants used in some forms of meditation, or imagining peaceful scenes, leads to decreased cortical activation, muscle tension, heart rate, blood pressure and respiration rate.

PRACTICAL APPLICATIONS

So far in this chapter we have dealt with the groundwork in terms of physical and social conditions that contribute to stress; in the previous chapter we have mentioned that changing environments, as experienced when travelling for example, can also be stressful. Before we go on to look at the effects of drastic change, as seen in natural disasters and technological catastrophes, we need to examine briefly the way in which combinations of stressors can lead to stress being experienced in everyday situations – housing developments and work environments.

Housing developments

It has already been noted that high-rise flats are associated with feelings of both loneliness and lack of privacy and that people who live in them have more psychological problems than average. Certain council housing estates, even though not high rise, are also associated with psychiatric distress and high levels of crime and vandalism, some of which can be attributed to their design characteristics. The solution to such problems is not always straightforward, however, as research detailed in Box 7.4 demonstrates.

Box 7.4   The effects of intervention in housing estates

Halpern (1995) gives the example of the Southgate estate in Cheshire (Figure 7.6), which was scheduled for demolition in 1989, planners having assumed that the physical character of the estate was responsible for its poor reputation. This announcement resulted in an increase in reported levels of physical illness and psychiatric problems and a campaign by residents to save the estate, demonstrating that the community spirit was intact despite the poor physical environment. Another example is the Eastlake estate, in one of the new towns, which suffered from problems such as vandalism, crime, violence, withdrawal, distrust and general unpopularity, which appeared to be design related. Over a three-year period, refurbishment was carried out, including road narrowing and building speed ramps, providing double-glazing, better security, improved street lighting, rebuilding garages, resiting parking areas and provision of play facilities. Interviews with residents showed that their perception of the estate improved (although they still felt that outsiders viewed it as terrible). Social relationships also improved, as shown by more evidence of social support and neighbouring and so did mental health, as indicated by a fall in the rate of probable depression cases from 25% to 4% (Figure 7.7).

Some of these responses are clearly design-related and the significance of design in determining social support levels and crime rates is well established. However, two other important points arise from this. Firstly, the environment has a *symbolic* aspect, which means that it, like the people who inhabit it, can be labelled and that label can become self-fulfilling. If an estate gets a reputation as a problem area or a dumping ground for undesirables, it will have an adverse effect. The other important point is that well-being is affected by the size of the *discrepancy* between what people have and what they want, and it is well documented that private ownership of a detached house is what most

FIGURE 7.6 *The Southgate estate*

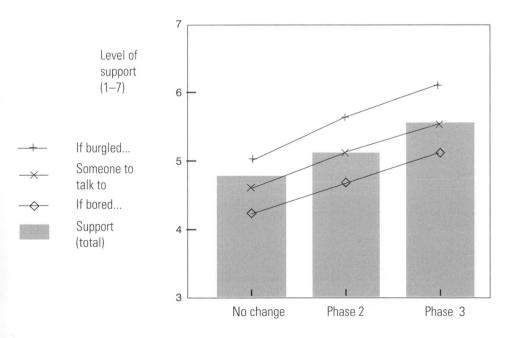

FIGURE 7.7 *Eastlake: social support from neighbours by phase of redevelopment*

153

people aspire to. Therefore the objective nature of the environment is only part of the picture.

Hazards at work

As mentioned in Chapter 3, research has identified a cluster of problems known as *sick building syndrome* (Woods, 1988), where there are symptoms of illness and other psychological problems but no underlying disease, which differentiates it from building-related illness (physical illness produced by exposure to a toxic environment). Typical symptoms include eye, nose and throat problems, skin irritation, headaches, nausea, etc. They seem to relate to a range of work and environmental variables such as stress, VDU use, job satisfaction, pollutants and satisfaction with the physical environment. This is shown clearly in the model produced by Hedge et al. (1989).

On a more specific level, it is clear that some occupations are associated with significantly more stress than others. The highest injury and fatality rates occur in the construction, agriculture, forestry, fishing and manufacturing industries, suggesting that manual work, especially if undertaken outdoors, is one problem area. Another is nursing and police work, which carry the risks of contracting illness or being the victim of a physical attack respectively. Psychological research has given some insights into other reasons why some jobs may be more stressful than others, as follows. Research by Zimolong (1985) found that construction workers tended to underestimate risks associated with familiar work situations. Jermier et al. (1989) showed that physically dangerous police work was perceived to be risky and was also associated with fear and anxiety. Mearns and Flin (1996) found that those people who perceive themselves as being in control tend to underestimate risks. All this research suggests that the nature and familiarity of the work environment and the amount of control we feel we have over it, contribute to our assessment of the risks involved and hence to stress levels. A similar situation applies when considering fear of crime.

Another aspect of work-related stress that is relevant to environmental issues is commuting. Driving is the most popular way to get to work, being the preferred option of 85% of workers in North American cities (Stokols and Novaco, 1981). Most commuters travel alone, which could be regarded as an example of territorial behaviour, in which case it may be difficult to change. Driving is known to create physiological reactions characteristic of stress, such as chest pains (Aronow et al., 1972). Commuters who drive longer distances have more negative feelings, reduced tolerance for frustration, reduced satisfaction with life and higher blood pressure. Those who have to cross more interchanges on the way to work have more frequent illness, especially colds and 'flu, more illness-related absence from work and more days when they are ill enough to be hospitalised. The phenomenon of *road rage*, reported by Turner et al., as long ago as 1975 as being experienced by 12% of male drivers and 18% of females, is another illustration of the stress associated with driving.

CATACLYSMIC STRESSORS

According to Cvetkovich and Earle (1995):

'Hazards are a special kind of environmental event that pose threats to humans and the things that humans value. They represent the potential occurrence of extreme conditions of the natural environment or the misfunctioning of the human-built technological environment.'

This definition emphasises the classic distinction made in the study of hazards between natural hazards (often referred to as disasters) and technological hazards (often referred to as catastrophes). Although Cvetkovich and Earle criticise this distinction for being simplistic and consider a classification based on causes, characteristics and responses to be more useful for the purposes of hazard management, it is the simplified twofold system that we will use here.

Natural hazards

Natural disasters include volcanic eruptions, earthquakes, floods and hurricanes; worldwide, these claim around 250,000 lives every year (Burton et al., 1978), as well as causing considerable damage to property and personal disruption for many more people. They are not evenly distributed geographically; for example, in the USA, earthquakes are more common in California, hurricanes in Florida and tornadoes in the South-East and Mid-West ('tornado alley'). Britain, by comparison, is relatively trouble-free, although the gales which swept the south of England in 1987 are a memorable exception.

When is an event classified as a disaster? One key criterion is *destruction*; disasters tend to be associated with damage and death to a sufficient extent to warrant government intervention. This means that they can be related to population density, in the sense that if few people are affected the event will not be perceived as a disaster. Another criterion is the degree of *disruption* to functioning, which also tends to rule out damage that occurs in isolated areas. Finally, disasters are generally regarded as *uncontrollable*. Disasters vary in many ways; perhaps the most important (Kates, 1976) is the degree to which they are *intensive* (sudden, brief, powerful and unpredictable, e.g. earthquakes) or *pervasive* (widespread and longer lasting, e.g. drought).

Which characteristics of disasters are important in determining how people will react? Four major factors have been identified and are outlined in Box 7.5.

Box 7.5   Determinants of response to disaster

First, *event duration* is important, longer lasting events generally having greater effects. This is obviously partly dependent on *intensity*, however; a tornado, for example, is very brief but powerful. The third factor is whether or not there is a *low point* after which things improve and clearing up can begin (Baum et al., 1983). It is clear, for example, when a tornado has passed, whereas earthquakes often have aftershocks. The low points of pervasive disasters such as floods and drought are more difficult to ascertain. Finally, the amount of *warning* is important (Fritz and Marks, 1954). Lack of warning tends to make the consequences worse, although the usefulness of the warning is itself dependent on how effective the communication is and how well the event has been prepared for, e.g. in terms of evacuation procedures. Other contributory factors include the degree of social cohesiveness of the community, the effects of the event on family and friends, the extent of financial and property loss and damage, whether separation from family occurs and whether the distress of others is witnessed.

Perception of natural hazards

The issue that is being raised here is the extent to which people are aware of the risks they are facing. In general, the magnitude of the threat is underestimated; even those who are aware are unlikely to have taken any precautions (Sims and Baumann, 1983) unless they have previous first-hand experience of similar situations (Kates, 1962). After the Second World War, for example, rationing led to the stockpiling of food by the older generation for many years subsequently. After a disaster, many people move back into the disaster area, for social and economic reasons (Burton et al., 1978).

Perception of natural hazards can be measured using the Environmental Appraisal Inventory (EAI), developed by Schmidt and Gifford (1989) to measure the extent of perceived threat to the self and environment and the level of perceived control. Four factors appear to be mainly responsible for hazard perception. First, there is the *crisis effect*, whereby awareness is greatest immediately after the disaster and subsequently reduces. Second, the *levee effect*, so-called because the erection of a levee (barrier) to keep out flood waters typically induces people to resettle areas previously considered to be dangerous; in general, protective measures reduce perception of risk. A parallel can be seen in the increased risks taken by motor-cyclists after they purchase protective clothing (known as risk homeostasis theory)! *Adaptation* is also important; in earthquake-prone areas people appear to be less concerned (Kates, 1976), although there is less adaptation when the hazard threatens income or health. Finally, *personality*, particularly locus of control (Rotter, 1966), determines perception of risk. People who have an external locus of control and trust to luck, fate or help from external agencies such as the government, are less likely to take precautions. So, for example, there are more tornado-related deaths in the deeply religious areas of the southern USA than in the Mid-West, despite the fact that the Mid-West has more tornadoes (Sims and Baumann, 1972).

Psychological effects

The psychological effects of disasters are difficult to ascertain, as it is often difficult to determine the predisaster level of functioning for comparison. There is a lot of individual variability as well, but some general conclusions can be reached despite these problems.

During the event there are negative effects such as fear, but few people panic (Quarantelli and Dynes, 1972). Some may withdraw or appear stunned but in general a range of responses from constructive helping to random activity can be seen. Antisocial behaviour such as looting may occur, but at the other extreme there may be an increase in social cohesiveness (Bowman, 1964). Immediately after the event there is considerable distress, anxiety, depression, nightmares, mental health problems and other signs of emotional trauma, the extent of which is related to the extent of the disaster. Rubonis and Bickman (1991) concluded that in general, a 17% increase in psychopathology could be observed. Perceived levels of social support decrease, partly due to families and communities being disrupted and partly because there has been an increase in need in a large number of individuals (Kaniasty and Norris, 1993).

Most of the stress-related problems are short term, lasting up to a year, although they may remain evident 16 months after the event (Steinglass and Gerrity, 1990). There are individual differences, but effects are generally stronger in those directly affected by the disaster; 25–30% seem to suffer for some months. Chronic stress, often called *post-traumatic stress disorder* (PTSD), is unusual and involves intrusive thoughts, avoidance of thinking about the event, sleep disturbances, social withdrawal and increased levels of arousal (Solomon and Canino, 1990). It may be more likely in those with previous psychiatric problems. Difficulties may be particularly evident in those who have recently retired. For example, Hunt (1997) reported that 19% of a sample of World War II veterans still showed war-related health problems, dreams and traumatic recollections. Joseph et al. (1993) found that survivors of the Herald of Free Enterprise disaster, in which 193 people died showed increased consumption of alcohol, cigarettes, sleeping tablets, antidepressants and tranquillisers over the six months after the disaster. 30 months later many problems were still evident, particularly smoking and particularly in those who had been bereaved.

FOCUS ON APPLICATION...
treating post-traumatic stress disorder

This was first recognised in DSM III (the American Psychiatric Association's Manual of Mental Disorders) in 1980 and comprises three groups of symptoms:

1 the presence of *re-experience phenomena,* which are images, flashbacks, recollections and dreams of the event that are difficult to control;

2 *avoidance* or *numbing phenomena,* which include avoiding thinking about or participating in activities that could be linked with the event and a reduction in emotional responses in general;

3 symptoms of *increased arousal,* such as insomnia, poor concentration, agitation and tension.

Given the range of symptoms, it is clear that different treatment strategies will be appropriate to different aspects of the disorder. Hodgkinson and Stewart (1991) suggest four main approaches could be useful,. First,

there is a need for a full exploration in the course of counselling or psychotherapy of the traumatic memories associated with the event concerned. Second, cognitive therapy may be used to correct the irrational beliefs or negative thinking that has resulted from attempts to cope. Anger management techniques may be included the tendency to irritable outbursts that is often found. Third, relaxation training or medication may be required to reduce arousal levels. Techniques such as systematic desensitisation may be used to lessen the impact of disturbing activities or objects (this therapy aims to reduce the fear response by replacing it with relaxation). Finally, it is important to encourage normal social activities and relationships, which may require marital counselling or family therapy, as well as desensitising people to any situations that they have come to avoid.

In general, the effects of stress are increased if the individual is injured, witnesses the death or injury of others, has been bereaved, suffered separation, relocation, financial loss or damage, environmental disruption or was in great personal danger with threat to life. According to Erikson (1976) many of the symptoms arise from the destruction of the community and consequent feelings of lack of belonging. There are three theoretical explanations of the effects that can be considered:

1 *Behavioural constraint* approaches emphasise the fact that people are forced to change their behaviour, for example by leaving their homes. Services are disrupted, inducing feelings of helplessness and loss of freedom; bereavement may increase the extent of the enforced changes.

2   *Ecological explanations* emphasise the sudden loss of community members, which leads to understaffing. Those that remain have to take on multiple roles, which is in itself stressful (known as role strain).

3   *Conservation of resources* explanations (Hobfoll, 1989) attribute stress to the loss of important resources, defining resources as anything that helps people to achieve goals, whether social, psychological or material. The conference for the study of the effects of Hurricane Hugo confirmed that this was the strongest predictor of postdisaster outcomes (Freedy et al., 1992). A model can be seen in Figure 7.8.

Technological catastrophes

These are manmade accidents resulting from human error or technological failures and they differ from natural disasters in several ways. They may be of short duration (e.g. train crashes or power failures) or long term (e.g. nuclear accidents)without having a clear low point. They are often associated with considerable uncertainty about the degree of harm or damage caused and greater feelings of loss of control, since we tend to feel that, because it is our creation, technology is safe and controllable compared with the forces of nature (Davidson et al., 1982). When it goes wrong, this conviction can be severely shaken, just as burglary shakes our confidence in the security of our home. Visible destruction may not be so apparent and there is generally very little warning, if any, prior to the event. Social relationships are often impaired afterwards, since people may have differences of opinion about the causes and consequences of the event. Cuthbertson and Nigg (1987) have demonstrated this in studies of episodes of asbestos contamination and pesticide spraying. Research into the aftermath of the Three Mile Island nuclear accident shows that some residents are worried about the nuclear contamination, while others are not, hence the community is divided. Perception of risk also varies, as shown by Sjoberg and Drottz-Sjoberg (1991) in their study of Swedish nuclear power plant workers; those with least knowledge about radiation and its effects perceived greater risks from radiation exposure at work. In Sellafield, Britain, Lee, Macdonald and Coote (1993) found large individual differences, with a tendency for people to become more cautious with increasing age.

Causes of catastrophes such as the King's Cross underground fire and the capsize of the Zeebrugge ferry, the Herald of Free Enterprise (both in 1987), have also been researched by psychologists. It is hoped that by examining the kinds of errors that people make, future catastrophes can be averted. For example, Riggio (1990, cited in Reason, 1990) has categorised these errors into errors of omission (not carrying out a task), errors of commission (acting incorrectly), timing errors (doing things too quickly or too slowly) and

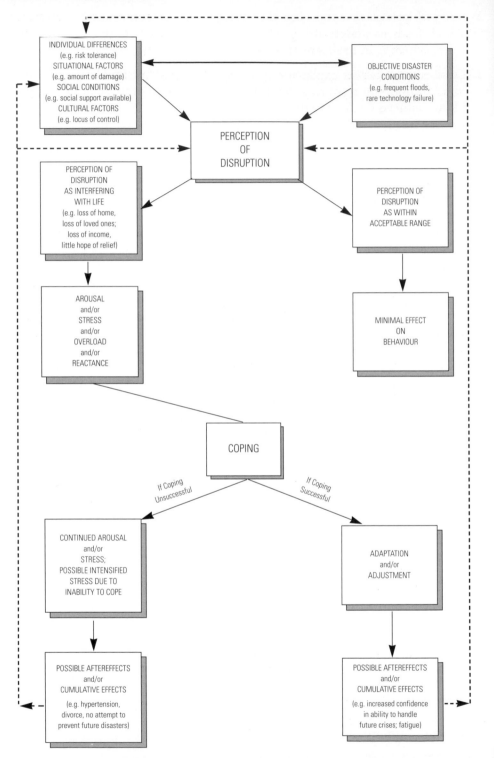

FIGURE 7.8 *A model of factors involved in response to disasters (adapted from Bell et al., 1996)*

sequence errors (doing things in the wrong order). An analysis of the errors made in the Zeebrugge ferry disaster by Reason (1990) is presented in Box 7.6. Notice that, in common with other case studies he has presented, most

---

Box 7.6 Herald of Free Enterprise

Chain of events and active failures	Contributing conditions and latent failures
Herald is docked at No. 12 berth in Zeebrugge's inner harbour and is loading passengers and vehicles before making the crossing to Dover.	This berth is not capable of loading both car decks (E and G) at the same time, having only a single ramp. Due to high water spring tides, the ramp could not be elevated sufficiently to reach E deck. To achieve this, it was necessary to trim the shop nosedown by filling trim ballast tanks Nos. 14 and 3. Normal practice was to start filling No. 14 tank 2 hours before arrival. *(System failure)*
At 1805 on 6 March 1987, the Herald goes astern from the berth, turns to starboard and proceeds to sea with both her inner and outer bow doors fully open.	The most immediate cause is that the assistant bosun (whose job it was to close the doors) was asleep in his cabin, having just been relieved from maintenance and cleaning duties. *(Supervisory failure and unsuitable rostering)* The bosun, his immediate superior, was the last man to leave G deck. He noticed that the bow doors were still open, but did not close them, since he did not see that as part of his duties. *(Management failure)*
Chief officer checks that there are no passengers on G deck, and thinks he sees assistant bosun going to close doors (though testimony is confused on this point).	The chief officer, responsible for ensuring door closure, was also required (by company orders) to be on the bridge 15 minutes before sailing time. *(Management failure)* Because of delays at Dover, there was great pressure on crews to sail early. Memo from operations manager: 'put pressure on your first officer if you don't think he's moving fast enough...sailing late out of Zeebrugge isn't on. It's 15 minutes early for us.' *(Management failure)* Company standing orders (ambiguously worded) appear to call for 'negative reporting' only. If not told otherwise, the master should assume that all is well. Chief officer did not make a report, nor did the master ask him for one. *(Management failure)*
On leaving harbour, master increases speed. Water enters open bow doors and floods into G deck. At around 1827, Herald capsizes to port.	Despite repeated requests from the masters to the management, no bow door indicators were available on the bridge and the master was unaware that he had sailed with bow doors open. Estimated cost of indicators was £400–500. *(Management failure)* Ship had chronic list to port.

(Management and technical failure)
Scuppers inadequate to void water from flooded G deck.
(Design and maintenance failure)
Top-heavy design of the Herald and other 'ro ro' ships in its class was inherently unsafe.
(Design failure)

Source: Reason (1990)

of the failures could be attributed to management failure rather than errors made by individual operatives.

Effects of catastrophes are initially similar to those observed for natural disasters, as detailed by Fritz and Marks (1954) in their study of a plane crash at an air show. The long-term effects are less well researched. Adler (1943) studied the long-term effects of a nightclub fire which killed 491 people. One year later, over half of the survivors showed psychiatric symptoms such as anxiety, guilt and nightmares. 75% of those who had no symptoms appeared to have lost consciousness during the fire, compared with 50% of those who had symptoms, indicating that losing consciousness may be protective, perhaps because it reduces the opportunity to view the fear and horror associated with the event. Similarly, Leopold and Dillon (1963) studied survivors of a collision at sea and found that 75% of survivors showed psychiatric distress and work-related problems four years later. As in PTSD, intrusive thoughts and memories are particularly problematic. A study of witnesses to a shooting at a school suggested that such people, because they do not wish to be reminded of the event, are less likely to seek the help that many of them need.

According to Hodgkinson and Stewart (1991), survivors typically report five central experiences:

1 the *death imprint* (images and flashbacks related to their encounter with death);

2 *survivor guilt* (questioning why they were singled out to survive when others died). An example of this is given in Box 7.7;

3 *psychic numbing* (appearing to be calm and unaffected);

4 *nurturance conflicts* (distrusting those who offer help);

5 *quest for meaning* (this extends from asking why the disaster occurred to why the individual escaped).

Potentially the worst catastrophes of all are those involving nuclear power plants and two of these will be discussed here. The installation at Three Mile Island in Pennsylvania, USA, suffered problems in 1979, caused by a combination of equipment failures and errors which led to reactor damage. This in turn led to leakage of radioactive water and gas, along with fears of explosion and meltdown of the reactor, so the population in the vicinity was evacuated. Fifteen months after the accident, there was still the threat of radiation leaks and controlled release of gas. Immediately after the event, residents showed an increase in psychological distress (Bromet, 1980); six years later, Davidson and Baum (1986) reported that stress effects were still evident, e.g. in increased levels of arousal, sleep disorders and fewer immune cells. Effects were found in residents within a five-mile radius and were reduced in those people who had greater levels of social support. The worst nuclear accident to date occurred at Chernobyl, in the Russian Ukraine, in 1986. This lasted longer than Three Mile Island, involved more radiation being released and affected a greater number of people. Acute stress was observed, as above, and chronic stress could be observed up to 20 months after the event (Koscheyev et al., 1993).

Box 7.7 Survivor guilt

One survivor of the Zeebrugge ferry disaster was a lorry driver who was on the ferry's vehicle deck when the ship capsized. His lorry ended up in the middle of a stack of articulated vehicles balanced on each other's sides. Frozen with fear, he heard his vehicle groaning under the weight of two lorries above and knew that he would die. He then remembered that his trailer was a refrigerated container and hence was strengthened – he had a little time before he was crushed. He smashed his suitcase through the window, climbed over the bonnet of his truck and into the water, which now flooded half of the hold. He swam towards the exit but as he did, he heard screams of trapped lorry drivers – 'God help us, God help us'. He swam on, climbed out onto the side of the ship and was one of the first to smash portholes, let down ropes into the ship and begin the rescue. Several hours later he was removed to a tug, frozen with cold, his hands lacerated. He could have humanly done no more than he did, yet he does not remember these actions – he only remembers the unanswered screams of the trapped men in the hold from which he escaped. 'They were drivers, like me, and I did nothing to help them.' Three years later he committed suicide.

Source: Hodgkinson and Stewart (1991)

EXTREME ENVIRONMENTS

These are defined as environments where survival would be impossible without special equipment (Suedfeld, 1987). They generally involve ambient stimulation well beyond the normal range and beyond our physical capacity to cope, together with social and sensory isolation due to the special clothing required. Two obvious examples are Antarctica and outer space.

Antarctica has been researched by the Polar Psychology Project, which has explored the effects of overwintering at research stations, involving conditions of extreme cold, long periods of darkness, reduced sensory input and social isolation. Cornelius (1991) has documented the following stressors: absence of windows, plants and animals; lack of sunlight and a partner of the opposite sex; loss of privacy and freedom to travel; a featureless landscape; low humidity; low air pressure which causes breathing difficulties; temperatures of −25°C to -80°C; and the formation of social cliques which isolate outsiders. The effects include weight gain, insomnia, loss of sense of time and reduced powers of memory and concentration (Blair, 1991). Barabasz (1991b) adds to these psychosomatic illness, depression, irritability, hostility and an increase in daydreaming and hypnotic susceptibility.

There are, however, individual differences in response and positive effects have also been demonstrated, such as a decrease in dependency, an increased capacity to form intimate relationships and an increase in self-esteem in those who manage to last the course (Palinkas, 1991b). Better adaptation is generally shown by those who are high in need for achievement, have an internal locus of control and are socially compatible, but all participants experience some degree of 're-entry shock' on returning home (Harris, 1991).

There are also changes in social behaviour: groups tend to communicate and co-operate less and have less regard for each other; the effects are less when there is a clear leader and division of labour (Barabasz, 1991a). An unusual effect reported by polar explorers is the sensed presence of another person (Suedfeld and Mocellin, 1987). This ranges from a vague feeling that another person is there to claims of seeing them helping with the situation. It usually occurs in low-temperature environments which are very monotonous, allowing parallels to be drawn with biblical references to people appearing to wanderers in the desert.

Outer space is a similarly confined environment; one of the favourite leisure activities of Soviet cosmonauts is reported to be looking out of the spaceship windows at the earth (Clearwater and Coss, 1991). Videos and pictures of natural scenery are popular things to take on the trip. Painting interiors so that the floor is dark and the ceiling light has been found to reduce motion sickness and increase feelings of comfort. A key problem is weightlessness, which reduces cardiovascular activity and leads to muscle atrophy, making work difficult (Levine, 1991). The organs of balance in the ear are also disrupted, leading to *space adaptation syndrome*. This involves sickness and loss of appetite which may last for five days. Stress is additionally caused by machinery noise and fear of equipment failure (Levine, 1991).

THEORIES OF STRESS

It follows from our discussion so far that the effects of the environment on human behaviour can be considerable. In the search for theoretical explanations, it has become obvious that no single approach is adequate, rather, several need to be used in combination or interchangeably, depending on the circumstances. Six different theories will be discussed here, in order to summarise the area: ecological psychology; arousal; stimulus load; adaptation level; behavioural constraint; and stress models. In an attempt to integrate these approaches, Bell et al. (1996) have produced a model of response to environmental stimulation, shown in Figure 7.9. The wide range of environments and individuals means that all the models may be appropriate on different occasions.

Ecological psychology models (Barker, 1990) argue that each behaviour setting affects the behaviour of large numbers of people, producing an *extraindividual behaviour pattern*, so the setting helps to predict the nature of the behaviour that will occur in it; consider a classroom setting, for example. Efficient functioning depends on optimum levels of staffing: understaffing produces stress because more roles have to be taken on by each individual; overstaffing produces stress because there are too many people using that environment (as in the example given earlier of traffic jams in Yosemite national park). Staffing levels, then, are an important determinant of functioning; for example, Barker and Gump (1964) found that pupils show more involvement if schools are not overstaffed. This approach has been found to predict group behaviour better than that of individuals.

Arousal theory looks at the physiological basis of stress. Stimulation from the environment increases activity in the reticular formation, which is the arousal centre of the brain (Hebb, 1972) and this in turn leads to increased cortical activity, heart rate, blood pressure, respiration and possibly physical activation. According to the Yerkes–Dodson Law, we all have an optimum level of arousal and will seek environmental conditions that promote this. Any deviation will be experienced as stressful and will lead to impaired performance.

Environmental load approaches are based on research into information processing. For example, Broadbent (1954) showed that we have a limited capacity for processing information and when we are overloaded we have to select the most relevant for attention. Unpredictable or uncontrollable items require more of our capacity and automatic tasks less attention. Our capacity also varies according to our current state of motivation and arousal (Kahneman, 1973). When there is overload, i.e. too many demands for attention, or demands over too long a period, stress may be experienced. Milgram (1970) suggested that in cities this can lead to *norms of uninvolvement*, a withdrawal from social interaction and reduced helpfulness to others. Similarly, Foa (1971) has

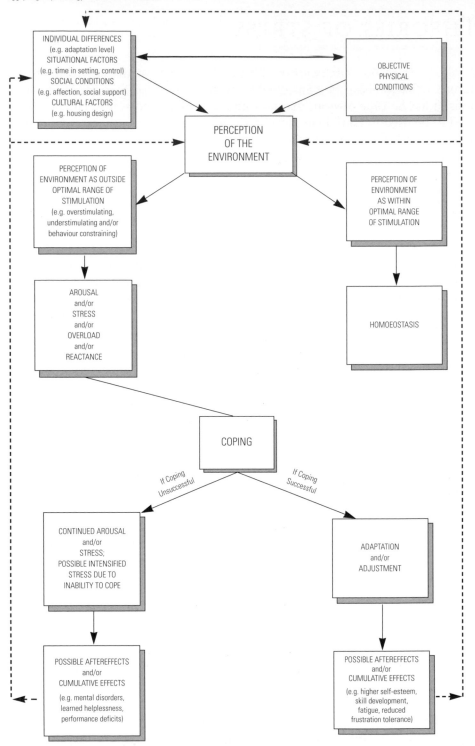

FIGURE 7.9 How different theories contribute to our understanding of stress (adapted from Bell et al., 1996)

argued that cities are good environments for the exchange of 'universalistic' goods, such as money, jobs and information, but not 'personalistic' ones such as communication, intimacy and love. In cities, depersonalisation of relationships, through the use of telephones to communicate and secretaries as social barriers, has become the norm. Kaplan and Kaplan (1989) have proposed that an important function of leisure activities in natural environments is to restore normal functioning after periods of prolonged concentration, which result in *directed attention fatigue*.

Understimulation approaches are the opposite of the above. Zubek (1969) found that deprivation of stimulation can lead to anxiety, as shown in studies of the Antarctic. Solitude is generally found to be aversive (Brown, 1992). The repetition and similarity of much urban stimulation has been associated by some with understimulation and boredom (Parr, 1966), possibly leading to vandalism. Rural environments are thought to be much more varied. However, Suedfeld et al. (1990) found that REST (restricted environment stimulation therapy), which involves spending periods on a waterbed in a dark, soundproof chamber, was helpful in reducing stress, which appears to be contradictory. This may be because the REST users were all volunteers and felt that they were controlling their stimulation levels by taking part. The next theory offers an alternative explanation.

Adaptation level theory (Wohlwill, 1974) argues that, regardless of the type of stimulation, what we want is an optimum level. This applies to sensory stimulation, social stimulation and movement and to the intensity, diversity and predictability of those stimuli. Each person's optimum level will differ according to past experience (consider the different responses of rural and urban dwellers to crowds, for example) and familiarity, known as the *adaptation level*, so there are also changes with time. Environments that differ dramatically from our adaptation level will have greater effects on us. As well as adapting, we can cope with the uncomfortable environment by adjusting it to our needs (Sonnenfeld, 1966). If we move to a warmer climate, for example, we will adapt to the temperature change eventually but initially we are more likely to adjust by turning on a fan or removing clothes. We will either adapt or adjust, depending on which is easiest.

Behaviour constraint approaches (Proshansky et al., 1970) emphasise the extent to which different environments can interfere with what we want to do and necessitate changes in behaviour. Our initial response will be psychological reactance (Brehm, 1966) – doing the opposite of what we feel pressurised into doing – as a way of regaining control. Avoidance of eye contact when in too close proximity to others can be seen as an example of this. If this strategy fails, learned helplessness could result (Seligman, 1975), where we stop trying and show depression and other maladaptive responses.

There are several different types of control we can exert over the environment. Averill (1973) mentions three: behavioural (responses such as complaining);

cognitive (processing information in such a way that its meaning is changed, e.g. deciding that a disaster is not likely to happen, despite warnings to the contrary); and decisional (exercising our choice of options). In general, the more in control we feel the better, but some individuals actually feel better if they can relinquish control to others, as shown by Rodin (1986) in studies of the elderly.

Environmental stress approaches (Baum et al., 1981) consider physiological and psychological reactions to stressors (aversive stimuli), incorporating arousal, environmental load, adaptation and behavioural constraint approaches. A model is given in Figure 7.10. Appraisal of the environment can be affected by individual variables such as experience and stimulus variables such as

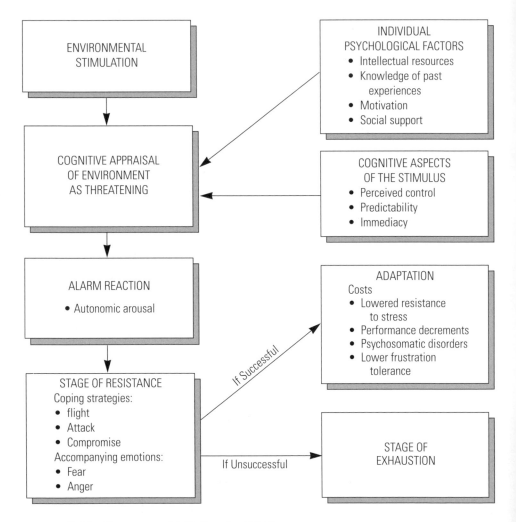

FIGURE 7.10 *The stress model (Bell et al., 1996)*

predictability. If it is seen as threatening, an alarm reaction is produced, leading to resistance; eventually, there is either successful adaptation and coping, or unsuccessful responses which lead to exhaustion and maladaptive behaviours. The difficulties in this model are predicting what individuals will perceive as stressful and how they will respond given the options available.

CHAPTER SUMMARY

To summarise this chapter, we have seen how we respond, physically and psychologically, to stress and we have considered what makes stimuli stressful in general. Both ambient and cataclysmic stressors have been explored and models of the nature of stress proposed. In the next chapter we will move on to examine the other side of the coin – how people affect the environment.

chapter eight

HOW PEOPLE AFFECT THE ENVIRONMENT

CHAPTER OVERVIEW

It is clear from the preceding discussion that the relationship between people and the environment is not unidirectional. The natural environment affects how we feel and behave, we act on this environment to try and adapt it to our own needs, these actions then alter the environment and in turn our behavioural response to it and so the cycle continues. In this chapter, we will be focusing on the way in which we affect the environment and the consequences of this. Then we will go on to look at attempts to intervene in this process and the effectiveness of these attempts.

ENVIRONMENTAL PROBLEMS

Modern awareness of 'green' issues has been traced back to the publication in 1962 of Rachel Carson's pioneering book on pesticides, called *Silent Spring*. This made the point that human actions have reached the stage where they no longer simply affect localised areas, such as landfill sites and open-cast mining, but are poised to disrupt natural systems on a global scale. The underlying reason for this is that the earth's population now numbers more than 5.6 billion and is expected to double, reaching 10 billion by 2050 (Wright, 1994). This rate of growth means that the population is increasing globally by over 10,000 people *per hour*, the equivalent of Austria in a month, Canada in 14 weeks and Mexico in a year (Miller, 1990). All these people must be fed, clothed, housed, educated, transported and employed; all these activities make demands on the Earth's resources, not all of which are readily renewable. Add to this the technology we have developed, which in turn requires resources such as steel, coal and oil for its manufacture and yet more resources, such as those required to produce electricity and petrol, for its operation. It then enables us to extract and utilise even more raw material – excavators can be used for mining and other machinery for logging, for example.

This has two effects: on the one hand, it increases use of resources; on the other, it increases conflict over resources, this latter being at least partially responsible for the Gulf War, for example. Both of these can be environmentally damaging. Using resources as quickly as we do means that some are in danger of being totally depleted. Soil erosion due to intensive agricultural practices, overfishing the oceans and excessive logging are all examples of resource depletion. The fundamental changes that take place in these areas mean that habitats are being destroyed and species (both plant and animal, human and non-human) that used to inhabit those areas are no longer able to. This reduction in *biodiversity* (since many species are faced with extinction when their habitats disappear) is not only aesthetically regrettable, it is potentially dangerous because it limits the range of genetic material available and hence the ability of existing species to evolve in appropriate ways to deal with changing environmental demands.

The way in which resources are extracted, processed and utilised also leads to a range of problems such as pollution and its consequences. One consequence is the *greenhouse effect*, whereby combustion of fossil fuels such as wood and coal in homes, factories and motor vehicles has led to general global warming, altering rainfall and storm patterns, affecting sea levels and necessitating changes in agricultural practices. Although the effects have been disputed (see Chapter 3), a recent report by Karl et al. (1997) notes that the global average temperature has increased by 0.5° Celsius over the last century and it will increase by a further 1–3.5°C by the year 2100. The consequences are complex and will depend on factors such as the continued burning of fossil fuels and further deforestation, but the following seem likely.

- Increase in overall rainfall and more intense downpours leading to more flooding.

- Greater increases in rainfall can be expected at higher latitudes; lower latitudes may show decreases.

- Soils will become drier in many places despite this (e.g. North America, Southern Europe), which will affect crops, groundwater reserves and building foundations.

- The minimum temperature will increase more than the maximum, leading to longer frost-free seasons, which will also affect crops and the growth of perennial plants which rely on a dormant season.

Another consequence is *depletion of the ozone layer* which shields the earth from ultraviolet radiation; this is the result of the release of chlorofluorocarbons (CFCs) from refrigeration plants and aerosol sprays. This in turn could interfere with crop growth and affect the functioning of the immune system; it has already been linked with an increase in skin cancer (Miller, 1990). A more recent cause for concern is *disruption of the nitrogen cycle*. Use of nitrogen in fertilisers makes more nitrogen available in general, which is readily dispersed from cropped fields into other areas, producing rapid plant growth and disrupting the ecosystem. In addition, other nutrients in soil may become less available to plants as a result of the presence of extra nitrogen. Nitrogen also filters into drinking water supplies and may subsequently affect humans.

The second major effect of increased demand is *conflict over resources*. It is well known in social psychology that competition between groups of people, such as that created by limited resources, leads to conflict (Sherif et al., 1961) and in the case of environmental resources this is exacerbated by the fact that industrialised nations frequently obtain their resources from non-industrialised 'third world' countries, where the standard of living is lower. Regions like the Middle East (oil producers) and Central and South America (which have large areas of forest and mineral deposits) are good examples of areas where frequent wars and revolutions are depleting the very resources that are partly responsible for the conflicts. Consider, for example, the burning of Kuwaiti oil wells during the Gulf War. War itself is a major environmental disaster and nuclear war is of course the ultimate, rendering the environment uninhabitable for many years.

Responses to problems

According to Heilbroner (1974), the external challenges posed by overpopulation, environmental problems and wars are compounded by what he describes as internal challenges. The first of these is the nature of our economic and political systems, which put expansion and growth above everything else (the reasons for these could, of course, ultimately be psychological in nature). The second he views as part of human nature and this is the unwillingness to make personal sacrifices and change our behaviour. Therefore he predicted that within 30 years we would reach a point where growth was no longer sustainable and social upheaval would become likely unless governments took steps to prevent it. Democratic governments would be less well placed to do this than the more centralised socialist governments. (Interestingly, the number of centralised socialist governments has fallen considerably since Heilbroner's book was written – Cuba is perhaps the best remaining example.) In order to survive, society will have to develop into a postindustrialised form, where standards of living are similar to those existing before the Industrial Revolution (Figure 8.1).

Environmental ethics

The implication of the foregoing is that only by facing our internal challenges will we avoid social upheaval and its consequences. Part of this is the requirement that we take an ethical stance over environmental issues. We have already seen in Chapter 6 that, possibly based on religious teachings, people

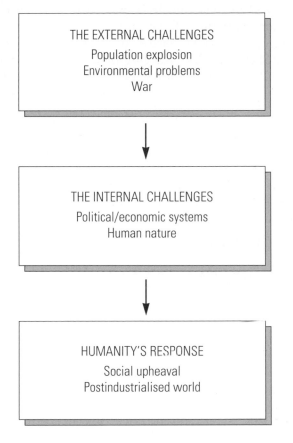

FIGURE 8.1 *Heilbroner's view of the future*

view the environment as a resource from which they are set apart and have to defeat. Chiras (1985) refers to this as the 'frontier mentality' and sees it as the basis for our exploitation of the environment. Preferable to this would be a holistic view (e.g. Russell, 1982), which sees humans as the nervous system of the organism formed by the earth and its inhabitants. The Gaia hypothesis (Lovelock, 1979) conceptualises the earth as a giant self-regulating system; if the body is killed, the brain will not survive it.

The role of environmental psychology

Many of the attempted solutions to environmental problems are technological, for example the use of wind power and solar energy. By comparison, relatively little has been done to change people's behaviour, which is somewhat surprising, since advances in technology are of little use if people won't use them or continue to be wasteful and destructive! A model similar to that used to illustrate the stress process can be employed here (Figure 8.2), showing that perception (or appraisal) of the situation and acceptance of personal responsibility (or control) are key factors in determining response to environmental problems. Many feel that changing behaviours would mean a reduced quality of life, but the fact that similar people living in identical homes can differ by 2–3 times in the amount of energy consumed (Socolow, 1978) suggests that this need not be the case.

In the following sections we will look at perceptions about environmental damage, the issues of 'the commons' and the 'social trap', strategies for changing environment-related behaviours and research on specific problems such as aesthetics (littering and vandalism), health (pollution and the greenhouse effect) and resource management (conservation and recycling).

PERCEPTION OF
ENVIRONMENTAL DAMAGE

This is an important area of study because these perceptions influence people's willingness to behave in environmentally responsible or irresponsible ways. Hardin (1968a) considers that humans have a genetic predisposition to underestimate risks, including those posed by environmental damage and will therefore fail to take any precautions against them. Although a total denial of risks would be maladaptive, a moderate amount could be adaptive in reducing fear levels that would otherwise prevent us from exploring and experimenting. The problem is that in modern society even a moderate denial (e.g. of small, easily perceptible changes) could be disastrous. Along similar lines, Ornstein and Ehrlich (1989) propose that we are genetically predisposed not to perceive or respond to gradual environmental deterioration. Our minds focus better on immediate danger, since that is what was most useful to our ancestors. Slow change is not what our 'Stone Age minds' are tuned in to.

A different kind of obstacle is suggested by Forrester (1969), who makes the point that humans have difficulty managing social, economic, political and environmental systems because they are too complex for the human mind to grasp. In this view, environmental problems are caused by a mismatch between environmental systems and the human and institutional systems that are 'managing' them.

Another problem with risk assessment in general is that it involves analysis of *costs* and *benefits*; if benefits outweigh costs, then the risk is considered acceptable but the estimation of costs and benefits can in itself be difficult. Transport, for example, has benefits as well as risks. A study by Baird (1986) found that at a hearing for an arsenic-emitting copper smelter, risks were

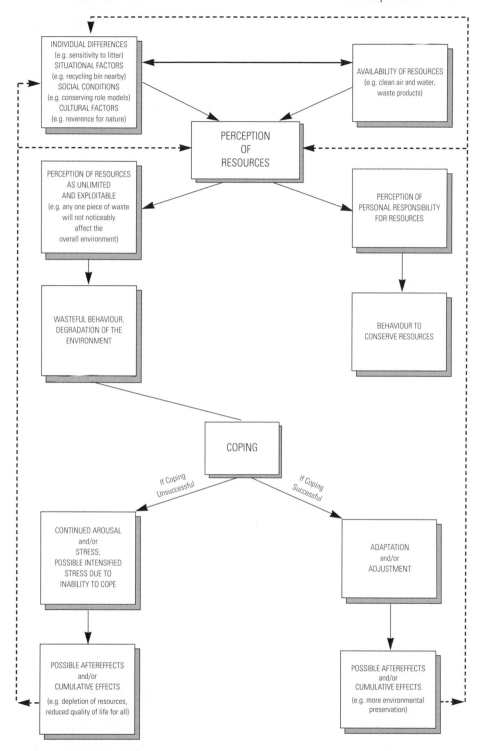

FIGURE 8.2 *A model of behaviour change related to conservation (adapted from Bell et al., 1996)*

weighed up against perceived benefits for residents (such as employment). In some cases the situation is complex: recycling newspapers might save trees but carries risks of water pollution from the inks used; plastic nappies may not be recyclable and may take up landfill space, but they require half as much energy and water to produce as cloth nappies and generate half the air and one-seventh of the water pollution during manufacture. On the basis of the above, then, we would not expect people to be able to perceive the risks of environmental damage accurately. Research has in fact shown both under- and overestimates compared to those of experts.

Risks tend to be perceived as lower if the activities concerned are voluntary, individual, easily reduced, carry a low risk for posterity, are not global in their effects and have negative consequences that will not be evident for some time, e.g. swimming, use of food preservatives and power mowers, littering and using the car instead of public transport. Perceived risks tend to be higher if the activities concerned are uncontrollable, catastrophic and likely to affect posterity, e.g. nuclear power. High-risk estimates are associated with greater knowledge of steps that can be taken to reduce the risk, as shown by Cvetkovich and Earle's (1988) study of water contamination. This study also showed that confidence in the ability of experts to control the problem was a significant determinant of perceived risk.

Three theories have been proposed to explain why people underestimate risks. First, Slovic et al. (1978), based on a study of seatbelt use (or lack of it!) proposed that for many the *effort* and inconvenience of buckling up and the restrictions on movement, outweigh the perceived safety advantages of the seat belt (the chances of being killed in a motoring accident being estimated to be 1 in 3.5 million for a single trip and 1 in 100,000 for being seriously injured, so the likelihood overall is small).

Secondly, Taylor and Brown (1988) consider that *perceived control* is the major factor. They argue that people generally overestimate their own skills and ability to control the world and are generally overoptimistic about the future; this illusion is necessary for mental health. Certainly, perceived control has been found to be important for physical health (Weinstein, 1989) and De Joy (1989) has shown people to be unreasonably optimistic about their chances of not having car accidents involving factors that they consider to be under their control, such as losing control at high speed.

The third approach is *stress theory* (Lazarus, 1966), which proposes that when environmental threats are perceived as being uncontrollable, people cope by trying to deny their existence. Thus, Vaughan (1993) found that pesticide-exposed agricultural workers were less likely to take preventive action to minimise their risks when they thought that no other jobs were available to them, indicating denial of the problem. This can be related to learned helplessness, described by Seligman (1975) as giving up trying when in a no-win situation.

Overestimation can be explained with reference to several well-known cognitive biases or heuristics, examples of which are given in Box 8.1

Box 8.1   Cognitive bias in risk estimation

The first bias is the *availability heuristic* (Tversky and Kahneman, 1973). This points out that the ease of recall of past events influences our judgement of the probability of future events. Direct experience of the event in the past therefore means that we will be on the look-out for it in the future. Where an event has not happened before (such as ozone depletion) we do not expect it to cause problems. A problem that is not clearly visible, such as air pollution or radiation, is also less likely to concern us. This is known as the *prisoner-of-experience phenomenon* (Kates, 1962).

When it comes to policy decisions, policymakers are also subject to biases. They take into account both actual and perceived risks when making their decisions. If perceived risk exceeds actual and they act on this, there could be overprotection; in the reverse case, there could be underprotection. Where perceived and actual risks differ dramatically, conflict is more likely. For example, McClelland et al. (1990) found that there were large discrepancies between homeowners' and experts' views of the risks associated with a landfill site. This could result from differences in knowledge, vested interest, conflict of values and mistrust of 'experts' (Deitz et al., 1989). Clearly, then, the possibility of damage to the environment and its inhabitants as a result of human activity, is not well estimated by most people and since policymakers are influenced by the public as much as by expert opinion, this does not bode well. Several theories suggest that both parties may be subject to biases simply because they are human. Note, however, that even many computer models are struggling with the complexity of the problem (Meadows, 1985).

THE COMMONS AND THE SOCIAL TRAP

Before we can go on to look at possible interventions, two further issues need to be considered which affect the way that people are likely to respond to environmental problems. Hardin (1968b) first noted what he called the *tragedy of the commons*. The 'commons' originally referred to public land areas where anyone from the village could graze livestock. This type of shared pasture first appeared in England in the 1100s and became universal by the 1400s, but has been found in many other countries as well (Levine, 1986). The problem raised by Hardin was that if each individual using the pasture were motivated purely by self-interest, each would aim to consume as much of the resource as possible, especially since the impact made by that individual would be small. However, if everyone took this view and the population increased as well, resources would soon be exhausted. Therefore there is a conflict between individual and group interests, often referred to as the *commons dilemma* (Dawes, 1973).

The relevance of this to present-day environmental problems is clear and perhaps the best example is the fishing industry. An abundance of fish has led to a great demand for them from the ever-increasing population and a growth in the fishing industry (which was able to provide many with a good living). Eventually, this has resulted in exhaustion of stocks to the point where quota systems have had to be introduced to restrict catches and fish under a certain size cannot be landed. According to Brown (1985), 13 out of 19 commercially important fish species had been overfished to the point of decline or collapse by the early 1980s. Publically owned forests and wilderness areas and mineral deposits on the sea bed are other examples. A reverse process can be seen with air pollution, where the 'common' is the air and people are putting things into it instead of removing them. Pollution of water supplies is another example of this. The River Danube, which passes through nine countries, acts as a resource (e.g. for hydroelectric power) but also as a waste disposal system. Although the waste from one individual country may not be harmful, by the time it reaches its delta at the sea it is heavily polluted. Again, individual use could be accommodated, but group usage results in abuse. Both pollution and depletion of resources, then, are part of the commons dilemma.

Platt (1973) refers to the commons dilemma as a type of *social trap*; he describes three of these, all of which are relevant to environmental problems and are outlined in Box 8.2.

Box 8.2 Social traps

First, there is the *individual good–collective bad trap*, which refers to the commons issue; destructive behaviour by one individual has little effect, but when carried out by a group it can be disastrous. Second, there is the *self-trap*, by which Platt means that for an individual the immediate consequences of the behaviour concerned may be reinforcing (pleasurable), while the costs are not apparent until some time later and may not even be obvious. Motoring is a good example; individuals enjoy it and it is only recently that the consequences have become apparent. Third, there is the *missing hero situation*, which is the failure to carry out appropriate behaviours such as campaigning against pollution. In this case, the behaviour itself may not be pleasant to carry out (e.g. picking up other people's litter) and the rewards are long term rather than immediate, which makes them less desirable.

Platt suggests that to deal with these we must rearrange the rewards and costs of carrying out such behaviours and suggests four ways of doing this.

1 Making negative consequences more immediate, e.g. having tolls on motorways to reduce car use.

2 Reinforcing desirable behaviours, e.g. by giving financial rewards for recycling and creating bus lanes and lanes for pool (shared) cars.

3 Changing long-term consequences so that they become more positive, e.g. encouraging the use of alternative energy sources and insulation in homes and introducing lead-free petrol and electric-powered cars.

4 Use of social pressure. If individuals are encouraged to make a public commitment to change or if social norms are changed, group pressure will bring about more compliance with desired behaviours. This can be seen in recent antismoking and antilittering campaigns. Without individual commitment people are more likely to show diffusion of responsibility and act selfishly (Latané and Darley, 1968), leaving it to others to change.

The above suggestions are based on the pessimistic view that rewards and punishments are the major determinants of behaviour. In fact, altruistic motives and ethical choices are often important as well, as found by Hopper and Nielsen (1991) in a study of recycling behaviour. Nevertheless, laboratory simulations have shown that reward for co-operation and punishment for selfishness can help to preserve the commons (Kline et al., 1984) and that those who are trusting and co-operative initially also manage the commons better (Parks, 1994). Being scrutinised by others also reduces the tendency to exploit the commons (Jerdee and Rosen, 1974). Dividing the commons into private territories helps to increase conservation (Edney and Bell, 1983), although this is not always feasible (e.g. the air) or desirable (e.g. national parks). It does have some applications, as in the 'adopt-a-highway' campaigns in some parts of America, where local groups take responsibility for keeping a section of road clear of rubbish.

Related to this issue is work by Chiras (1985) on value priorities, which shows that humans tend to give immediate individual goals higher priority than future, collective goals. Thus farmers questioned about soil conservation put profit before being environmentally responsible (Lynne and Rola, 1988). Chiras has shown that values relate primarily to the self and to the present (as shown in Figure 8.3); this, then, is what needs to be changed.

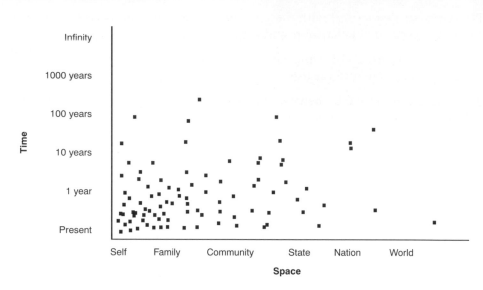

FIGURE 8.3 *What people value and when they value it (from Veitch and Arkkelin, 1995)*

STRATEGIES FOR INTERVENTION

Prevention of problems is regarded as more effective than cure (Blumberg and Gottlieb, 1989); if the example of household waste is considered, then clearly it is better to reduce packaging and to recycle than it is to work out how to dispose of the 25 lb of solid waste that is generated by a typical American in a week (Carless, 1992). Bell et al. (1996) suggest the following general goals:

■ reduce demands for energy, water and other resources (conservation);

■ reuse wherever possible (e.g. bottles);

■ recycle what cannot be reused (e.g. paper, which makes up 39% of municipal waste in America, according to Carless, (1992));

■ dispose safely of what remains.

Strategies used can be either *antecedent* (aiming to prevent or induce behaviour) or *consequent* (giving pleasant or unpleasant consequences for behaviour in order to induce or prevent recurrence). The latter group are based on Skinner's (1958) principle of operant conditioning, whereby giving a reward (or positive reinforcer) following a behaviour will strengthen it and make it more likely to be repeated (Figure 8.4). Thus the use of car pools can be increased by offering rewards for car sharing (Everett et al., 1974). The behaviour is likely to occur if the benefits outweigh the disadvantages, e.g. offering radios to men volunteering for sterilisation in India. Punishment, the giving of an unpleasant stimulus after the undesirable behaviour, will weaken it; this can be seen in the use of fines for littering and in penalties for childbearing in China. On the whole, positive reinforcement works better, is more cost-effective and more socially acceptable than punishment strategies (Geller, 1987).

CONSEQUENCES OF BEHAVIOUR

	Pleasant	**Unpleasant**
Give	Give 1 pence for each can put in bank Organise competitions for most litter collected around a school	Make litterers pick up rubbish dropped by others Force smokers to smoke outside in the rain and cold
Remove	Fines for littering Limit annual mileage for each car drive	No charges for company car parking for ride sharers Reduce water rates if target drop in consumption is achieved

RESPONSE

FIGURE 8.4 *Four types of reinforcement-based strategies for promoting the preservation of the environment*

Ophuls (1977) has identified four types of strategy for promoting prosocial behaviour in order to overcome the problem of the social trap. These are the use of: government laws and incentives to encourage prosocial behaviour; moral, religious or ethical appeals; educational programmes and information aimed at producing attitude change; social groups and communities to encourage prosocial behaviour. We will consider each of these in turn.

Laws and incentives, e.g. controls over emissions from cars, fines for polluters, grants for loft insulation, make it in the individual's own interests to behave in socially desirable ways. Included in this category is the use of prompts or cues to remind people about environmentally desirable behaviour. Notices about littering or switching off lights, for example, can be quite effective (Geller, 1980). It is important that they are polite and give specific instructions about what to do. In general, incentives can work, but it isn't always clear in advance which ones will be best or which ones can be evaded; carpool lane users have been spotted in some areas with dummies in their cars, for example! Another problem is that attitudes may remain the same even if behaviours change, particularly where the incentives are financial.

Ethical appeals have centred around several movements which have developed philosophical or religious arguments that justify changes in behaviour. Deep ecology is one of these, derived from the work of the Norwegian philosopher Naess (1989) and developed further by Devall (1988). This suggests that what is needed is a worldview different from that of most Western countries, less materialistic and human-centred. Another example is Inglehart's (1990) argument that Western countries are undergoing a shift in values. Based on public opinion surveys from 1970 to 1988, it appears that people are less materialistic and more interested in other goals such as developing their powers of self-expression, improving their self-esteem and creating aesthetic-ally pleasing environments, collectively known as postmaterialism. By the year 2000 there will be equal numbers of materialists and postmaterialists, compared with a ratio of 4:1 in the early 1970s. Although this change may not change behaviours in itself, it could have an important part to play in the overall impact of other attempts at intervention, for example by stimulating governments to introduce new schemes and laws.

Finally in this section, we should mention ecofeminism. Shiva (1989) argues that the dominant Western male paradigm emphasises domination and exploitation, as well as subjugation of the female. Sexism and environmental problems therefore have a common source. Women are symbolic of nature ('mother Earth'), therefore both must be dominated and seen as inferior. The solution to both environmental and women's problems is therefore to adopt the feminine worldview.

Educational programmes are frequently antecedent strategies, since they aim to prevent the problem behaviour occurring in the first place. Campaigns in the form of advertisements, school-based programmes, leafletting, etc. are employed in the hope of reaching a large number of people with minimum outlay and that by providing information their attitudes and hence their behaviours will change. The problem is that, as we have noted before, the link between attitudes and behaviour is not strong (Fishbein and Ajzen, 1975). For example, Bickman (1972) reported that 94% of students agreed that everyone should pick up litter when they see it, but in a practical test 99% walked straight past it! It is important to ensure that the severity of the problem is emphasised, as well as the importance of immediate action. Specific actions that people can take should also be outlined. Samuelson and Biek (1991) carried out an energy conservation attitude survey and found that the issue of consumer health, the size of the national problem and beliefs about the role of the individual consumer were all important determinants of behaviour, which emphasises the complexity of trying to induce changes.

Such attempts will be most likely to succeed when barriers to action are low, for example when actions are inexpensive and readily available. Recycling, for example, will be carried out if it is made more convenient by arranging for kerbside pick-ups; some energy conservation measures may be inappropriate for people who do not own their own property or who cannot afford the changes suggested, such as double glazing. Information is generally most acceptable if it is tied into behaviour through feedback, for example by monitoring the daily rate of energy consumption in a household. Video demonstrations about what to do are useful, provided they employ appropriate models for the target audience (Winett et al., 1982); teenage litterers, for example, are unlikely to be influenced by the Prime Minister but may respond to a high-status model of their own age, such as a Spice Girl. Messages also need to be appropriately framed. For example, Yates (1982) found that telling people how much energy or money they are wasting is more effective than telling them how much they could save, when trying to encourage them to insulate their homes. Kahneman and Tversky (1979) attribute this to a greater sensitivity to the prospect of losing something than to the prospect of gaining something of the same value.

Tightening the links between attitudes and behaviour by the use of prompts and cues is also useful. For example, Geller et al., (1982) found that reminders to put out recyclable materials for collection had a significant effect in middle and upper income neighbourhoods, although there was no noticeable effect in lower income neighbourhoods. Personal public commitment also tightens these links; again, Pardini and Katzev (1984) found it made a big difference to the amount of paper recycled, as shown in Table 8.1.

Table 8.1 Effects of public commitment on participation and paper collected in an experimental recycling programme

Condition	Number of households	Frequency of participation		Pounds of paper collected	
		First 2 weeks	Second 2 weeks	First 2 weeks	Second 2 weeks
Information	9	3	4	70	57
Minimal public commitment	9	10	4	210	54
Strong public commitment	9	13	11	247	166

In general, such campaigns must be carefully designed in accordance with psychological principles derived from research and take care to address the link between attitudes and behaviour. They may work best when combined with other strategies and have important long-term effects (often ignored when they are being evaluated) because they influence community norms and political behaviour. A good example of this from the area of health psychology is the long-term impact of the anti-smoking campaigns.

Social groups and communities can also be involved in changes more directly. For example, small groups, such as fishing communities, who are directly involved with some aspect of the environment have been encouraged to develop their own system for resource management. Thus Levine (1986) has pointed out that in the English agricultural commons, overuse was prevented by a practice called stinting, which restricted each user to only a limited number of animals each year. This was enforced by the social mechanisms of

---

Box 8.3   Conditions conducive to successful community resource management

1 Resource is controllable locally
   a) Definable boundaries (land is more controllable than water; water is more control-lable than air)
   b) Resources stay within their boundaries (plants are more controllable than animals; lake fish more than ocean fish)
   c) Local management rules can be enforced (higher level governments recognise rights of local control, help enforce local rules)
   d) Change in the resource can be adequately monitored.
2 Local resource dependence
   a) Perceptible threat of resource depletion
   b) Difficulty of finding substitutes for local resources
   c) Difficulty or expense attached to leaving area
3 Presence of community
   a) Stable, usually small population
   b) Thick network of social interactions
   c) Shared norms ('social capital'), especially norms for upholding agreements
   d) Resource users have sufficient 'local knowledge' of the resource to devise fair and effective rules
   [(a) facilitates (b), and both (a) and (b) facilitate (c). All three tend to make it easy to share information and resolve conflicts informally.]
4 Appropriate rules and procedures
   a) Participatory selection and modification of rules
   b) Group controls monitoring and enforcement processes and personnel
   c) Rules emphasise exclusion of outsiders, restraint of insiders
   d) Congruence of rules with resource
   e) Rules contain built-in incentives for compliance
   f) Graduated, easy to administer penalties

Source: Gardner and Stern (1996)

---

the community and by the fact that it was mutually agreed. Such measures are most likely to work when the resource concerned has clear boundaries, the community is stable, cohesive and reliant on the resource and when effective rules are developed for resource management, together with incentives for compliance (Box 8.3). An example of a successful scheme is that developed by the lobster fishers of Maine (Acheson, 1987), who have clearly defined and defended territories designed to prevent overfishing.

Overall, Gardner and Stern (1996) conclude that programmes that combine different types of intervention – incentives, education and community management – tend to be more effective. The most likely explanation for this is that there are a variety of different reasons why people do not behave in environmentally responsible ways and no one approach will deal with them all.

PRACTICAL APPLICATIONS

These will be divided into three main areas – aesthetics, health and resource management – both antecedent and consequent strategies being discussed for each.

Aesthetics

Aesthetics covers behaviours which, while not necessarily causing major damage, make the environment unsightly, i.e. littering and vandalism. Damage can, of course, result from these behaviours – for example, discarded plastic beer can ties can strangle water birds which become entangled with them, and newly planted trees can be uprooted in acts of destructive vandalism – but generally speaking their major impact is aesthetic.

Littering

Littering can be defined as depositing waste in the wrong place. A considerable proportion of the ton of solid waste generated every year by each person in the USA has been estimated to end up as litter (Forester, 1988). The presence of litter in an area promotes further littering (Finnie, 1973), although in some recreational areas such as campsites, people are more likely to pick up litter left by others (Geller et al., 1982). In general, people are very unlikely to pick up litter dropped by others (Geller et al., 1977). Young people tend to litter more than older people, males more than females, rural residents more than urban and people alone are more likely to litter than those who are with others (Osborne and Powers, 1980). Birdwatchers, hikers and canoeists are least likely to litter and hunters, fishermen, campers, motorboaters and waterskiers are most likely to litter of all the outdoor pursuit groups studied by Heberlein (1971).

Box 8.4   How littering can be prevented

Antecedent interventions have used prompts such as signs, which are effective (though on a relatively small scale), polite signs in proximity to litter bins being found to be especially effective (Geller et al., 1982). Observation of models is another useful prompt (Cialdini, 1977), as is the presence of litter bins (Finnie, 1973), which have been found to reduce littering by 15% in the street and 30% on the highways. The more bins there are, the greater the effect and the more colourful they are, the greater the effect (15% as opposed to 3% for less colourful bins). Baltes and Hayward (1976) found that giving football fans plastic bags as they entered the stadium led to a reduction in littering; the bags provided a convenient form of storage until the litter could be disposed of properly.

Consequent strategies aim to encourage people to pick up existing litter; these have generally been more effective than the antecedent strategies. Reinforcement is used, frequently coupled with prompts. Although costly to operate, these are more effective than educational campaigns (Cone and Hayes, 1980). One interesting example is the 'litter lottery', whereby invisibly marked items are scattered amongst the litter and prizes are given to those who pick them up and deposit them in the appropriate place (Bacon-Prue et al., 1980). Similarly, Burgess et al. (1971) found that giving out litter bags in a cinema led to a 30% increase in correctly placed litter; the rate of litter pick-up increased to 95% if a free cinema ticket was offered in return for a full bag.

Vandalism

Vandalism is defined as 'the wilful or malicious destruction, injury, disfigurement or defacement of any public or private property' (Uniform Crime Reporting Handbook, 1978). The difference between this and many of the other areas which we will be considering is that it is intentional. Fisher et al. (1984) estimate the annual costs in the USA to have been 1–4 billion dollars in 1976. Different types of vandalism can be distinguished (Bell et al., 1996):

- *acquisitive* vandalism, carried out for personal gain, includes looting and theft;

- *tactical ideological* vandalism is that which is done to draw attention to an issue, e.g. Greenpeace blocking the waste water outlets from a nuclear reprocessing plant, as shown in Figure 8.5;

- *vindictive* vandalism is carried out to get revenge or to be aggressive, e.g. daubing a racist slogan on the door of a shop;

- *play* vandalism is carried out to alleviate boredom, e.g. some examples of graffiti;

- *malicious* vandalism is carried out to release anger and frustration, e.g. 'keying' cars (scratching the paintwork with a sharp object such as a key).

FIGURE 8.5 *Greenpeace blocking nuclear waste outlets; an example of tactical ideological vandalism*

This suggests that there are a variety of motives for vandalism, ranging from financial gain to territorial behaviour. A theory has been proposed by Fisher and Baron (1982), which suggests that vandalism is a way for people who feel unfairly treated to restore the balance when all else has failed. This suggests that the important elements are perception of the environment as being unsatisfactory and a feeling of lack of control, so that change cannot be brought about in any other way.

Some environments are more likely than others to be vandalised: it is more common in cities than in small towns (Zimbardo, 1969); in ugly places that have already been vandalised (Pablant and Baxter, 1975), such as picnic tables in rest areas which already have names carved into them (Samdahl and Christensen, 1985); and in areas that are not obviously under the control of others, i.e. are not defensible space (Newman, 1972). Objects that break in satisfying ways, such as parking meters, are more likely to be vandalised than hardened objects such as concrete litter bins.

Techniques aimed at discouraging vandalism include improved street lighting and increased facilities for surveillance (Magill, 1976). The presence of an authority figure can act as a deterrent, hence Samdahl and Christensen (1985) found less vandalism when a picnic area was supervised. Cleaning up the area quickly helps to discourage further attempts (Molloy and Labahn, 1993), as does the offering of rewards for information leading to the arrest and conviction of graffiti 'artists'. Fisher and Baron's model suggests that increasing perceived control over the environment or decreasing perceived inequality should lead to a reduction in vandalism, but no studies are available on this to date.

Health

Health issues are mainly to do with pollution and its related problems of transport and the use of agrochemicals; in practical terms, of course, these are inseparable from a consideration of the way that we use resources.

Pollution affects air, water and soil, so everyone is potentially at risk. The air is affected by exhaust fumes from cars and lorries, factory emissions, cigarette smoke, etc. Water supplies may be polluted by pesticide and fertiliser run-off, sewage, industrial wastes and oil spills. The land is affected by burial of wastes in landfill sites and the use of agrochemicals. Radiation is a form of pollution that can pervade everything and does not decay for many years. Miller (1990) reported that one-third of Americans will get some form of cancer and the World Health Organisation claim that 80–90% of cancers are traceable to environmental factors. As well as serious chronic effects such as cancer, lung and heart disease, genetic defects and nervous disorders such as Gulf War syndrome, there are short-term acute effects such as sickness, dizziness, headaches, skin complaints, convulsions and even death. Domestic and wild animals also suffer; for example, farm animals may be exposed to radiation if kept in the vicinity of nuclear power plants and both fish and sea birds suffer from pollution such as oil spillages. Vegetation can be destroyed (e.g. by acid rain) or encouraged to grow excessively (e.g. by fertiliser run-off), both of which will disrupt the existing ecosystems.

Air pollution has been one of the most researched areas; it includes carbon monoxide and other gases, soot, dust, asbestos, lead and radioactive substances, as documented in Chapter 3. Links have been made with respiratory and cardiovascular problems (Coffin and Stokinger, 1977) and 140,000 deaths a year are thought to result from air pollution in the USA (Mendelsohn and Orcutt, 1979). At low levels, negative moods, poor reaction times and inability to concentrate have been reported (Bullinger, 1989). Smog has been shown to be linked with an increase in the number of disturbances reported to the police (Rotton and Frey, 1985). Unfortunately, because it is invisible, it is difficult to convince people that it is a problem.

One problem that has been mentioned only briefly in earlier chapters is that of *radon gas*. This is a natural radioactive gas found in soil and rocks, which is sufficiently diluted in air to be insignificant in most natural situations. However, if it penetrates buildings, which it can via gaps and cracks in the floor and walls, it can become trapped and higher concentrations can result. Hence the nature of our buildings and the need for insulation, create a problem. It is the biggest single contributor to radiation exposure in the UK population, accounting for 50% of the radiation dose that a person in this country will receive in a lifetime (National Radiation Protection Board, 1996), as shown in Figure 8.6. Some areas of the country appear to have higher natural levels than others, as shown in Figure 3.5 (see page 63), but it can also show considerable variation from one house to another within an area and within a given house at different times of the day (Figure 8.7). The effects of radon are described in Box 8.5.

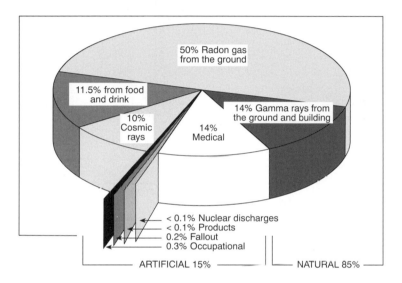

FIGURE 8.6 Radon's contribution to radiation exposure

Box 8.5   Research into the effects of radon gas

The gas is dangerous because inhalation of particles formed as it decays can lead to lung cancer; it is the second largest cause of lung cancer, after smoking. Lubin and Boice (1997), comparing 4000 cancer cases with 6000 controls, found an increased risk of cancer with an increase in the indoor radon levels. Some occupations, such as mining, are particularly at risk because of the nature of the working environment (Muirhead and Kendall, 1996). It can also enter drinking water supplies and hence affect the gastro-intestinal tract; although in this country public supplies appear not to be significantly affected (Henshaw et al., 1993), some private supplies and foreign supplies may not be so safe. It is a sufficient problem for the government to have included it in the *Health of the Nation* strategy (1996), which sets targets for indoor radon levels as well as air quality, noise pollution and levels of lead in drinking water. It can be controlled by sealing gaps in floors and walls and improving ventilation.

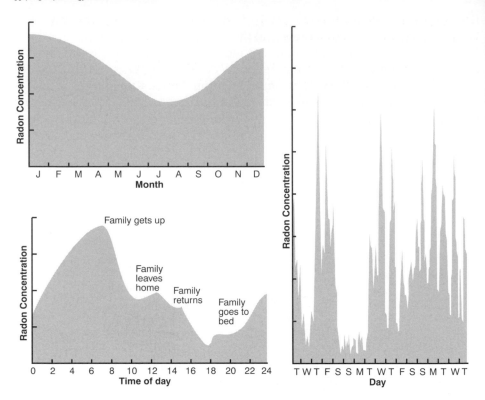

FIGURE 8.7 *How radon levels in a house vary during the day, over a fortnight, and over a year*

Transport

A significant contributor to air pollution is transport, which accounts for 50% of urban air pollution. The primary emission from car exhausts is carbon monoxide, which leads to decrements in attention and learning, judgement of time, reaction time, manual dexterity and vigilance (Evans and Jacobs, 1981).

It has already been established in previous chapters that the rewards for car use as opposed to public transport are considerable. Everett and Watson (1987) have attempted to redress the balance by introducing a scheme in Seattle whereby purchase of a monthly season ticket for the bus carried the additional rewards of unlimited travel and discounts in various places in the city. This led to a 37% increase in sales of bus passes, but it was not established whether it had also reduced car use. Bus lanes and park-and-ride schemes are other systems that have been used to make public transport more appealing. Some companies have used incentives such as priority parking for ride sharers and have offered matching services within the company. This has led to an increase in the number of sharers from 22% to 55% (Geller et al., 1982). However, in 1990 only 13% of people overall shared rides, compared with

5% who used public transport and 73% who drove alone; this last is an increase compared to the 64% recorded in 1980 (Davis and Strang, 1993).

The explanation offered for this by Gardner and Stern (1996) is that Americans have plenty of incentives to drive alone, in the form of cheap petrol, good road connections and an ideal of owning a cheap house in the suburbs; such obstacles to change can only be removed slowly. Other obstacles are present in the form of the vested interests of the motor and oil industries. For these reasons, legislation has been found to be the best measure. Manufacturers of cars in America have been required to redesign them to reduce emissions. Between 1976 and 1981 the permitted levels of hydrocarbon, carbon monoxide and nitrous oxide emissions were reduced by 73%, 77% and 68% (Stern and Gardner, 1981b). This has had more impact than any attempts to encourage people to share cars or reduce their level of use.

Agrochemicals

Another big contributor to pollution is the use of agrochemicals such as pesticides and fertilisers. According to the Pesticides Trust (1996) 60 different pesticide active ingredients have been recognised as carcinogenic to some degree and 118 pesticides have been found to disrupt hormonal balance. The WHO has estimated that there are 3 million acute severe pesticide poisonings and 20,000 accidental deaths every year; in agriculture, 14% of all injuries and 10% of fatalities are caused by pesticides. Of course, these chemicals affect not only humans but also the flora and fauna of the natural environment.

The best known of these are the organophosphates (OPs), which were first developed for use as insecticides as a byproduct of nerve gas research in Germany in World War Two (Minton and Murray, 1988). These are the most toxic to vertebrates of all the pesticides and are most widely used in insecticides (111 different varieties are in use and in the UK, one-third of all applications for licences in 1994 were for OPs), some being used as herbicides and fungicides as well. As well as their agricultural uses, they are used in catering and in the house in fly papers and sprays, ant and wasp destroyers, mothballs, antilice shampoos and flea collars for pets. Their best known applications are as sheep dip and to protect soldiers against insects in the Gulf War. They work by preventing the breakdown of the neurotransmitter acetylcholine, through inactivating the enzyme acetylcholinesterase. This leads to a build-up of acetylcholine, which interferes with nervous transmission. Research into the effects of this is outlined in Box 8.6.

Although OPs break down quickly after use, this is not the case with all agrochemicals. Others remain active and can take decades to penetrate drinking water supplies. For example, Meadows et al. (1992) report on a soil disinfectant widely used in Holland in the 1960s which will reach a concentration that is 50 times the permitted maximum by the year 2000. Thus damage can be 'locked in' to the system and by the time we are aware of it, it may be too late.

Box 8.6 The effects of OPs

In humans, the main effects are sweating, salivation, nausea, diarrhoea, abdominal pains, muscle weakness, headaches and muscle tremors, possibly leading to respiratory failure and death. Delayed neuropathy (nerve damage) can lead to burning and tingling sensations and paralysis of the lower limbs. Psychological effects include poor concentration, confusion, anxiety, depression, slurred speech, insomnia, nightmares, emotional instability and toxic psychosis (Blondell and Dobzy, 1997).

Chronic effects have been documented in studies of sheep dippers and Gulf War veterans. Sheep dippers have often been exposed to relatively low doses over long periods. There is some conflict in findings, but Stephens et al. (1995) have reported that dippers who had been exposed but had not complained of symptoms nevertheless took longer than non-exposed quarry workers to carry out tasks requiring information processing and sustained attention. They may also show an increase in depression (Davies, 1995). Parron et al. (1996) found in Spain that suicide rates were higher in areas of greater OP use and that introduction of OPs was associated with an increase in suicide rates. A parallel can be seen in the high suicide rates in Scottish and Welsh sheep farmers (although of course there may be other explanations too, such as financial problems). Other possible effects include reduced cardiac functioning and an increased risk of osteoporosis.

Gulf War veterans have also been studied; Haley et al. (1997) found in a study of 3695 soldiers that those who had been in the Gulf showed a higher incidence of medical and psychiatric problems than those who had not. They found evidence of neuromyoarthropathy (joint and muscle pains, muscle weakness and tiredness) in soldiers exposed to sprays containing antinerve gas agents; others who had worn pet-type flea collars to protect them against insects showed distractability, depression, insomnia, fatigue, slurred speech, confused thinking, headaches and poor memory.

Once a problem is known to exist, solutions can be applied on either a 'downstream' (cure) or an 'upstream' (prevention) basis. It may not always be possible to use the preferable upstream methods, but an example applied to pesticide use is shown in Figure 8.8 (Fischhoff et al., 1978). The upstream solutions here include the development of a rapidly degrading pesticide, using more organic methods of pest control or changing consumer tolerance for pest-damaged food. Traditionally, treatment of visible effects using downstream solutions has been more popular, although some of these, such as blocking pesticide run-off or prevention and treatment of the cancer, are not feasible.

Resource management

Resources can be examined from three different viewpoints: conservation of energy; conservation of water; disposal of waste.

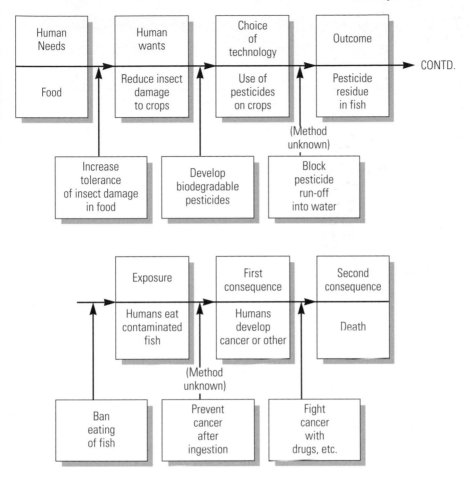

FIGURE 8.8 *Pesticide causal sequence* (from Fischhoff, B. et al., 1978)

Conservation of energy is of considerable importance, since it is mainly our huge demands for energy that are responsible for high pollution levels (e.g. the waste from power stations) and for the depletion of resources such as coal and other fossil fuels. Energy use can be divided into household/individual use, for private residences and cars for example, and industrial use. Stern (1992b) has shown that about one-third of consumption is household/individual, one-third industrial and the last one-third is commercial/service and other users. Most attention has been focused on household/individual use, which has been further broken down (Stern and Gardner, 1981) as shown in Table 8.2. Energy use for motoring is very wasteful; apart from the pollution issue discussed in a previous section, automobiles are inefficient to operate and also make considerable demands on energy and resources in their manufacture.

Table 8.2 Estimated percentage of total individual/household sector energy consumed for different end uses in the US (figures are for 1970–1975)

End use	%
Transportation:	
Auto	41.7
Other	5.3
Subtotal	47.0
In home use:	
Space heat	29.2
Water heat	7.7
Refrigeration and freezing	4.1
Lighting	3.0
Cooking	2.7
Air conditioning	2.4
Drying	.9
Other	3.0
Subtotal	53.0

Source: Stern and Gardner (1981)

Planes are the least efficient means of transport (Hirst, 1973), being 60 times more costly than trains for moving freight and three times more costly for moving passengers.

In the home, a great deal of energy is wasted because of the uniform approach to house design, irrespective of the climate and location of the house. Better use could generally be made of insulation, shade in summer to reduce heat and sun in winter to increase it. Heating, cooking, refrigeration, lighting and appliances all consume energy and more modern appliances frequently require more energy; colour televisions, for example, need more than black and white sets and incandescent lights more than fluorescent. Choosing appliances on the basis of their energy efficiency would, however, lead to great savings. Neely (1972) estimated that in 1970, if the most efficient refrigerators had been chosen by all 6. 6 million purchasers in that year, 17 million tons of coal could have been saved in reduced electricity needs and 26,000 acres could have been saved from strip-mining, as well as 690,000 tons of sulphur dioxide emissions being prevented.

Over half of the industrial use of energy is in three industries – metals, chemicals and the energy industry itself. One important consideration that could reduce consumption is the choice of materials in manufacturing; glass takes less energy to produce than steel, which in turn takes less than aluminium. Reuse and recycling could reduce demands still further. Commercial use includes the energy required to heat and cool offices; high-rise blocks require more energy input, especially when constructed using a great deal of glass, which makes heating and cooling costly.

The environmental costs of all this are high especially when we take into account extraction, processing and transport. Some resources, such as mercury, gold and tin are almost depleted. The inevitable disasters can have drastic consequences, as can be seen in the Exxon Valdez oil tanker disaster which eliminated a significant proportion of marine life in Prince William Sound in Alaska. Accidents, however, represent only one-fifth of the total spillage (SCEP, 1970); most occurs as a result of normal operations such as cleaning out tanks, production procedures at offshore oil rigs and losses and releases of pollutants from refineries. In 1970 the National Wildlife Federation reported that one refinery alone dumped up to 2½ tons of lead per day into the Mississippi River.

A final consideration is that of electromagnetic fields. These are created by overhead power lines, electricity substations, microwave sources, VDUs, household appliances and mobile telephones. Evidence exists that suggests links between exposure and childhood leukaemia, as well as other cancers and depression, possibly as a result of impaired immune system functioning. Mobile phones are a particular cause for concern at present due to their popularity and the fact that they produce pulses of microwave radiation which can heat cells in the user's head. However, Sienkiewicz and Chadwick (1996) consider that there are no significant long-term effects from use unless overheating occurs, in which case there is a possibility of damage to nerves and blood vessels behind the ear.

Both antecedent and consequent strategies have been applied to energy conservation. Antecedent strategies attempt to change attitudes and give advice about how to behave, as shown in Table 8.3. This includes giving information on how to change energy demands, including curtailing use and making adjustments such as using more energy-efficient equipment; the latter is generally better but involves spending money at the outset, which is not always possible. Curtailment needs to be maintained over a long period, but adjustment just has to be done once and is less likely than curtailment to interfere with the person's lifestyle by, for example, requiring that heating is turned down in winter. In some countries, such as Sweden, where energy efficiency is becoming essential now that nuclear power is being phased out, buildings are already energy efficient due to their strict building regulations, so further improvements must rely on curtailment. Curtailment of use can include using less energy, not throwing away thing that are still usable (such as paper bags), reusing products (such as yoghurt pots for seedling plants), making things more repairable or recyclable, avoiding throwaway items (e.g. disposable barbecues) and excess packaging (responsible for 9% of the food budget costs for most families, according to Veitch and Arkkelin, 1996). Kempton et al., (1985) found that the general public think of energy conservation in terms of curtailment (e.g. turning lights off and thermostats down) but over-

Table 8.3 Estimated percentage of current total individual/household energy consumption that can be saved by 30 different conservation behaviours (in the US) (figures are for the early 1980s)

End use	Curtailment	% energy saved	increased efficiency	% energy saved
	Transportation			
Automobile:				
	Car-pool to work with one to two others	4–6	Buy more fuel-efficient auto (27.5 vs 14 mpg)	20
	Cut shopping trips to one-half of current mileage	2	Get frequent tune-ups	2
	Alter driving habits with mpg or vacuum feedback	2 (or more)	Maintain correct tyre inflation	1
	Inside the home			
Space heat:				
	Set back thermostat from 72° F. to 68° F. days, 65° F. nights	4	Insulate and weatherise house	10
			Install more efficient heating equipment	8
Water heat:				
	Set back thermostat by 20° F.	1	Install more efficient unit	2
Refrigeration/freezing:				
	Decide on items you want in advance and open/close quickly	0.5	Buy more efficient unit	1.6
	Thaw frozen foods in refrigerator before cooking	0.1	Clean refrigerator coils frequently	0.1
Lighting:				
	Do not leave porch light on all night	1.0	Change one-half of all incandescent bulbs to fluorescent	1.0
	Replace all hall and ceiling fixtures with 40-watt bulbs	0.1	Clean bulbs and fixtures regularly	0.3

Table 8.3 *Continued*

End use	Curtailment	% energy saved	increased efficiency	% energy saved
Cooking:				
	Do not use self-cleaning feature of oven	0.2	Buy more efficient unit	0.9
	Use right-size pots and do not open oven door to check food	0.2		
Air conditioning:				
	Set back (up) thermostat from 73–78° F.	0.6	Buy more efficient unit	0.7
			Insulate and weatherise home (see above under 'Space heat')	0.8
Drying:				
	Do not use dryer six months of the year	0.5	Buy more efficient unit	0.2
Miscellaneous:				
	Do not use garbage disposal unit	less than 0.1	Fix all dripping hot water taps	0.1
			Replace leaking refrigerator door seal	0.1

Source: Stern and Gardner (1981)

look efficiency-increasing measures such as double glazing windows and replacing central heating. They also overestimate how much would be saved by curtailment, compared to the estimates of experts, and underestimate the savings produced by energy-efficient behaviours. This is explained in terms of visibility (it can be seen when lights are on or off, for example, but the efficiency of a machine cannot be seen) and in terms of frequency (lights are turned on and off frequently and act as a reminder, whereas a new boiler is a rare occurrence).

One example of the efficiency approach is reported by Howard et al. (1993), where 2000 incandescent light bulbs in a university dormitory were replaced with more efficient fluorescent bulbs, saving 2.3 dollars each per month; the university is now in the process of replacing a further 8000 bulbs. Included here is the use of alternative energy sources such as solar and wind power, which are environmentally preferable because they are renewable. Most research has been carried out into solar systems, which can be divided into active and passive. Active systems use solar panels to collect the sun's energy and transform it into heat, which is then pumped into the living area or stored. The panels contain a black metal plate or have water running through to absorb heat and are generally placed on the house roof but can be ground mounted. Passive systems have no solar panels, but use the building itself to collect solar energy, for example by using skylights, south-facing windows, conservatories and greenhouses to collect heat and thermal storage in the floors and walls to retain it. The difficulty is that it requires a long-term investment, taking up to five years to pay off compared to the 2–3 years most people are prepared to wait for dividends (Veitch and Arkkelin, 1995).

Educational strategies, such as those shown in Figure 8.9, have not been found to be very effective; Heberlein (1975), looking at the effects of measures such as providing booklets of tips and information about the costs of not conserving, found that none was effective. Geller (1981) found that workshops had an effect on attitudes but that there was no evidence of a carry-over into behaviour. Stevens et al. (1979) found interventions that were directly linked to experience were more successful. Students who were taught how to monitor home energy consumption and carry out an energy audit at home changed their behaviour and this change was transmitted to their parents as well. Public commitment also helps, so if participants are told that their names and the results obtained will be published, more change is obtained (Pallack et al., 1980). This, of course, raises ethical problems. Modelling desired behaviours on video has been shown to reduce overall electricity use by 14% (Winnett et al., 1982) and prompts next to light switches are also effective (Winnett, 1978).

Consequent strategies use reward and punishment, usually by providing incentives and fines. They appear to work well with large corporations, but are less effective with individuals, whose behaviour may be decided on a less rational basis. Stern and Gardner (1981), for example, found that doubling the cost of energy only leads to a 10% reduction in use and has the added drawback that it penalises the poor. Financial rewards for reduced use are effective (Cone and Hayes, 1980) but may not be financially viable. Shifting energy use to non-peak hours can also be done. Use of feedback (both individual and group) is helpful, especially if it is done in inexpensive ways such as self-monitoring of meters (Winnett et al., 1982).

Conservation of water could relieve the pressure on reservoirs and underground aquifers by reducing the use of fresh water in residences, industry and agriculture. Geller et al. (1982) found that installation of water conserving devices reduced consumption, but feedback and educational interventions had no effect (Thompson and Stoutmeyer, 1991). Upper middle-class participants were found not to respond to any intervention, whilst lower-class participants responded to appeals emphasising the need for individual action and the long-term consequences more than appeals based on economics.

ENERGY SPECIAL

One third of all the energy produced nationally is consumed in the home, and up to 25% of this is lost to the outside world because of poorly-insulated homes and old or inefficient boilers and electrical appliances.

The borough council is now taking action to deal with the local problem and suggest ways of improving energy efficiency in domestic properties. The action is being taken in response to the global warming alerts issued at the 1992 and 1997 Earth Summits and the Home Energy Conservation Act introduced last year.

However little you do to improve the energy efficiency of your home, it will contribute to reducing the overall wastage that is occurring at present, and at little or no cost. There are also direct benefits to you, such as a warmer home, added value to your house and reduced heating bills.

THE FOLLOWING SUGGESTIONS WILL COST YOU NOTHING:-

DO -

- Reduce the central heating thermostat to the lowest comfortable level
- Ensure that the room or hot water cylinder thermostats are correctly set (maximum 21°C for rooms and 60°C for hot water)
- Turn off/programme heating to be off when not required (remember to keep some heating on low in winter to prevent pipes from freezing)
- Programme heating to turn off well before going to bed
- On a sunny but cold day, open internal doors to allow the air heated by the sun to circulate
- Close curtains and tuck them behind radiators at dusk to retain heat within the home
- Cover boiling saucepans to reduce heat waste

DON'T -

- Leave fridge/freezer doors open for longer than necessary
- Let the ice build up in your fridge/freezer - defrost regularly
- Leave windows open when the heating is switched on
- Overfill kettles or saucepans - use only sufficient water for the purpose
- Leave unused lights or electrical appliances switched on - televisions on 'standby' use nearly as much electricity as when switched on
- Use a partly-loaded washing machine - wait for a full load or use the half-load or economy programme

THE FOLLOWING SUGGESTIONS INVOLVE SOME DIY WORK AND WILL COST YOU SOME MONEY BUT WILL HELP SAVE MONEY IN THE LONG RUN:-

- Draughtproof windows and doors - save on average between £15 and £25 a year in fuel bills
- Increase loft insulation to 150mm and lag pipework - save as much as 25% of lost heat
- Upgrade your hot water tank insulation by using a well-fitting 80mm jacket
- Fix aluminium foil behind radiators on external walls to reflect heat
- Fill gaps between floorboards and skirting boards on ground floors to stop draughts
- Fit thermostatic radiator/drain valves to control temperatures in each room
- Draughtproof windows in winter with cling film, polythene or another DIY product
- Pressure cookers are fast and economical and slow cookers use little electricity
- Mend dripping taps - hot taps waste water _and_ energy
- Replace lights with low energy compact fluorescent lights - if every home in Britain used one low-energy light bulb, it would save the energy of an entire power station
- Install cavity wall insulation - annual savings of between £75 and £100 are possible
- A shower uses only 40% of the hot water needed for a bath

'AFFORDABLE HEATING' LEAFLETS FOR TENANTS AND HOMEOWNERS ARE AVAILABLE FROM THE ENVIRONMENTAL HEALTH DEPARTMENT.

FIGURE 8.9 *One local authority's leaflet advising householders how to save energy*

Waste is a conservation problem even if unwanted items are thrown away appropriately rather than just being littered. They are manufactured or derived from natural resources, therefore they contribute to resource depletion. There is also the problem of where to put them, the traditional solutions being landfill sites and dumping at sea. Management strategies include down-stream and upstream solutions. Prevention is preferable to discarding, with reuse (putting them to different uses, e.g. using old tyres for silage clamps), recycling (where material is recovered and used for its original purpose, as in bottle banks and bottle deposit systems), reclamation (where material is remanufactured, e.g. making plastic drinks bottles into insulation materials) and source reduction in between. De Young (1993) found that pamphlets advocating source reduction (e.g. avoiding overpackaged products) on both economic and environmental grounds led to greater conservation behaviour. In general, consumer behaviour is the same for reuse, reclamation and re-cycling, so they will be considered as a whole. For example, making paper from recycled materials instead of wood takes less energy and reduces air and water pollution and the amount of solid waste generated from paper mills.

FOCUS ON APPLICATION...
increasing recycling behaviours

Antecedent strategies have looked at the effects of commitment; for example, Wang and Katzev (1990) evaluated retirement home residents who had pledged to participate in a four-week recycling project and found that there was a 47% increase in recycling which was maintained for at least another four weeks. Another form of commitment is goal setting. McCaul and Kopp (1982) found a 37% increase in recycling in college students who had been set goals. The foot-in-the-door technique can also be employed, whereby people are initially asked to comply with a small request, such as saving cans for a week; this leads to more compliance with a larger request made later (Arbuthnot et al., 1976) and was found to be associated with greater use of a recycling centre 18 months later.

Consequent strategies include the use of incentives; Jacobs and Bailey (1982) found that offering one cent per pound of papers left at the kerbside for recycling increased the rate of recycling from 3–4% to 9% of house-holders. Providing information on the benefits of recycling led to an increase in the rate to 8% and offering a chance to participate in a lottery increased the rate to 14%. Despite this, the cost of administering the programme rendered it uneconomic. Geller et al., (1973) found that having prompts in stores was effective in promoting sales of returnable bottles. The 'bottle bills' that have made deposits mandatory in nine states in the USA since 1991 have led to 90% being returned, provided that the deposit is at least five cents (Knapp, 1982). Feedback is also helpful, as shown by Katzev and Mishima (1992) who found that posting daily notices in a college recycling centre about the number of pounds of waste collected on the previous day produced a 77% increase in the amount collected over a weekly period.

Finally, it is even possible to reduce the amount discarded. In Seattle, for example, a pay-per-can system charges according to the amount of rubbish put out for collection. Cohn (1992) reported that for the average household in the early 1980s this was 3½ cans per week; by 1992 this had reduced to just one can per week. Illegal dumping does not seem to have increased, as was feared. People either buy more recyclable products or do the 'Seattle stomp' (dancing on rubbish to pack it down!), both of which reduce pressure on landfill sites.

One good example of an intervention that has used a range of approaches is in St Paul, Minnesota, where local groups have instituted a recycling programme that involves community organisation and participation, incentive schemes, education and information and political action to change the existing waste disposal system (Gardner and Stern, 1996).

IMPLICATIONS

Finally, we need to mention the implications of these environmental issues; these are economic, political and legal. From the *economic* standpoint, existing measures of the standard of living in terms of gross national product (the total national output of goods and services) is missing the point. What must be taken into consideration, as has been demonstrated in other spheres such as health and work, is quality of life. Existing economic theories are also incompatible with the new environmental ethics, since they assume that unlimited resources are available and that people value immediate returns more than possible returns in the future (Heyne, 1976), known as a high rate of time preference. The frontier ethic also has a high *rate of time preference*. Conservation, on the other hand, requires a low rate of time preference. Economics must be prepared to shift to a steady state (e.g. Peters, 1990), relying on conservation, recycling and population control, instead of insisting on maximum growth and base its values on the quality of the environment.

Second, we must consider the *political* implications of these problems. The lack of consensus from both the public and governments about the correct direction to take in future makes legislation difficult to enact and enforce. Financial constraints make many environmental issues low priority for many governments, compared to the problems of poverty, health and education, which are more visible and more urgent. Crisis politics is not ideal for long-term planning.

Finally, there are *legal* implications to consider, since environmental issues often demonstrate that there is a conflict between the rights of individuals, business corporations, the community at large and the environment. Examples of key concepts that cause difficulties are nuisance (arising from unreasonable, unwarranted or unlawful activity that results in injury to the public or to an individual) and negligence (acting in an unreasonable manner that leads to property damage). Both are difficult to prove – what is 'reasonable', when considering pollution control, for example?

CHAPTER SUMMARY

To summarise, we have looked at the ways in which our behaviour is damaging the environment and at how this in turn has an impact on our physical and psychological health. The relevance of environmental psychology in assessing some of these problems and in devising interventions to bring about changes in behaviour has hopefully been made clear. Examples of practical applications to such areas as aesthetics, health and conservation have been used to illustrate the possibilities and the implications for some other disciplines have been mentioned to stress the fact that holistic approaches are essential if such efforts are to succeed. In the final chapter, further areas for development will be suggested – as if there isn't already enough to do!

chapter nine

FUTURE APPLICATIONS

It has not been possible in a book of this length to consider the complexity of our relationship with the environment, but hopefully you have come to realise that there are a great many issues involved and a great deal of research that needs to be carried out. We know that the nature of the environment affects our cognition; that we select and interpret information and form images of our environment that will differ from objective reality. We know that our functioning is affected by basic physical aspects of the environment, such as light, noise and air quality; it is also affected by the other people around us and we desire our own space as much as we desire control over noise. The environment we build for ourselves has to take these needs into account if it is to serve us well and the design, both interior and exterior, of residences, institutions and cities can make a great deal of difference to our ability to function in them. The natural environment must also be considered, as it is something that we are drawn to and derive mental and physical benefits from. For this to continue, it needs to be managed properly to make sure that it is available to us in the future.

On the negative side, although the environment can be stimulating, it can also be stressful. When we feel that it is beyond our control or dangerous or when disasters occur, we can suffer physical and psychological damage. The environment in turn can be damaged by our behaviour and interventions such as pollution control, conservation and recycling are essential elements of modern environmental psychology.

What of the future? There are several areas which are likely to need attention from environmental psychologists, some of which have already been touched on. For example, the growth of computing has altered the way that we work and will continue to do so. The office may disappear altogether and people may increasingly work from their homes, which has implications for the design of residences, town planning and transportation systems. Transportation too is an area where environmental psychologists can assist with what is now a pressing problem, requiring government intervention of some kind. Increased leisure promotes outdoor recreation and this in turn requires the careful planning and management of recreation areas. Tourism and contact with other cultures would be a smoother process if training were available to teach the appropriate social skills for successful interpersonal encounters in those cultures, referred to by Furnham and Bochner (1996) as 'culture-based social skills training' or SST.

In addition to the above, Sommer (1987)has addressed the issue of a 'research agenda for the 21st century', taking as his theme the urgent global problems that need to be dealt with as priorities and it is these that we will consider next.

First, Sommer refers to *pollution*, particularly where it is an international problem. For example, French nuclear tests in the Pacific affect air quality in Europe; destruction of the Amazonian rainforest affects the air quality in North America; acid rain in eastern Canada originates in the USA. Next comes the issue of *population*, which again has become an international problem because of the number of refugees and migrant workers. Carrying capacities for different regions need to be established before any logical systems of control can be introduced. Demographic changes in the population, such as the ever-increasing number of elderly people, also have implications for the planning of institutions and housing.

Third, but perhaps most significant of all, is the issue of *war and peace*. Often resulting from territorial disputes about boundaries, it is fundamental to any form of environmental planning, as the massive destruction in Bosnia and Kuwait has made clear in recent years. Likewise, our ability to live in *harmony with other species* requires some cultivation. The present reduction in biodiversity is tending to lead to the survival of only those plant and animal species, such as nettles and urban foxes, that can tolerate us and the environments that we create. The establishment of reserves and the careful planning of zoos and visitor centres, is one area requiring attention here. Another is research into the effects on both parties of active involvement with other species, such as occurs in gardening and the adoption of animals as pets. *Resource conservation* has already been mentioned, mainly in the context of research into changing the behaviour of individuals. An obvious area for development is the examination of how institutions operate and how policies are developed; this could then be applied to changing agricultural practices and the way that water authorities operate, for example.

Finally, there is an increasing need for research into *space travel and settlement*. Research on extreme environments such as polar stations and submarines provides some relevant information, since they also involve isolation, confinement and risk (Earls, 1969). Findings include exotic environment syndrome (Harrison and Connors, 1984) where, as a result of the monotony and limited facilities, people show mood changes, reduced alertness, intellectual impairment, reduced motivation and an increase in illness. These, then, must be addressed initially; as space travel becomes easier and settlement becomes more likely, these problems will be superseded by issues of territory, adaptation to bleak landscapes and how best to protect the new environment from the human presence.

One crucial point raised by all of this is the change in emphasis, in recent years particularly, from the effect of the environment on people to the effect of people on the environment. Sommer refers to the *advocacy* issue, meaning the argument about whether it is possible to be neutral or value-free. This can be applied to ethical decisions about the way in which research is carried out and to the way in which the knowledge gained is applied. It does seem that we will shortly have to stop being purely descriptive in our approach and start to make (and act on – see Figure 9.1!) recommendations based on ethical decisions about what is right. When we do, perhaps it is worth remembering that we can create the environment that we want but we need to make sure that we want the environment that we create. Above all else, we are active participants in our environment.

FIGURE 9.1 *Practising what you preach: the need to strengthen the link between attitudes and behaviour*

REFERENCES

Abey-Wickrama, I., A'Brook, M., Gattoni, F. and Herridge, C.F. (1969) Mental hospital admissions and aircraft noise. *Lancet*, 2, 1275–1277.

Acheson, J.M.(1987). The lobster fiefs revisited: economic and ecological effects of territoriality in the Maine lobster industry. In McCay, B. and Acheson, J. (eds) *The question of the commons*. Tucson, AZ: University of Arizona Press.

Acking, C.A. and Kuller, R. (1972). The perception of an interior as a function of its color. *Ergonomics*, 15, 645–654.

Acredolo, L.P. (1982). The familiarity factor in spatial research. In Cohen, R. (ed) *Children's Conception of Spatial Relationships*. San Francisco: Jossey-Bass.

Acredolo, L.P., Pick. H.L. and Olsen, M.G. (1975) Environmental differentiation and familiarity as determinants of children's memory for spatial location. *Developmental Psychology*, 11, 495–501.

Adler, A. (1943) Neuropsychiatric complications in victims of Boston's Coconut Grove Disaster. *Journal of the American Medical Association*, 17, 1098–1101.

Aiello, J.R. (1977) A further look at equilibrium theory: visual interaction as a function of interpersonal distance. *Environmental Psychology and Nonverbal Behavior*, 1, 122–140.

Aiello, J.R. (1987) Human spatial behavior. In Stokols, D. and Altman I. (eds) *Handbook of Environmental Psychology*. New York: Wiley.

Aiello, J.R. and Thompson, D.E. (1980) Personal space, crowding and spatial behavior in a cultural context. In Altman, I., Wohlwill, J.F. and Rapoport, A. (eds) *Human Behavior and Environment* (vol 4). New York: Plenum

Aiello, J.R. Thompson, D. E. and Baum, A. (1981) The symbiotic relationship between social psychology and environmental psychology: implications from crowding, personal space and intimacy regulation research. In Harvey, J.H. (ed) *Cognition, Social Behavior and the Environment*. Hillside, NJ: Erlbaum.

Allen, G.L. (1981) A developmental perspective on the effects of 'subdividing' macrospatial experience. *Journal of Experimental Psychology*, 7, 120–132.

Allport, F.H. (1955) *Theories of Perception and the Concept of Structure*. New York: Wiley.

Allport, G.W. and Odbert, H.S.(1935) Attitudes. In Murchison, C.M. (ed) *Handbook of Social Psychology*. Clark University Press.

Altman, I. (1975) *Environment and Social Behavior: Privacy, Personal Space, Territory and Crowding*. Pacific Grove, CA: Brooks/Cole.

Altman, I. and Chemers, M.M. (1980) *Culture and Environment*. Pacific Grove, CA: Brooks/Cole.

Altman, I. and Gauvain, M. (1981) A cross-cultural and dialectical analysis of homes. In Liben, L., Patterson, A. and Newcombe, N. (eds) *Spatial Representation Across the Life Span*. New York: Academic Press.

Altman, I. and Low, S.M. (eds) (1992) *Place attachment. Human Behavior and Environment: Advances in Theory and Research* (vol 12). New York: Plenum.

Altman, I. and Taylor, D.A. (1973) *Social Penetration: The Development of Interpersonal Relationships*. New York: Holt, Rinehart and Winston.

Altman, I., Nelson, P.A. and Lett, E.E. (1972) The ecology of home environments. *Catalog of Selected Documents in Psychology* (No. 150).

Ames, A. (1952) in Ittelson, W.H. *The Ames Demonstrations in Perception*. Princeton: Oxford University Press.

Anderson, C.A. and Anderson, D.C. (1984) Ambient temperature and violent crime: tests of the linear and curvilinear hypotheses. *Journal of Personality and Social Psychology*, 46, 91–97.

Angyal, A. (1941). *Foundations for a Science of Personality*. New York: Commonwealth Fund.

Anooshian, A.J. and Wilson, K.L. (1977) Distance distortions in memory for spatial locations. *Child Development*, 48, 1704–1707.

Appleton, J. (1984) Prospects and refuges revisited. *Landscape Journal*, 8, 91–103.

Appleyard, D. (1970) Styles and methods of structuring a city. *Environment and Behavior*, 2, 101–117.

Appleyard, D. and Lintell, M. (1972) The environmental quality of city streets: the residents' viewpoint. *Journal of the American Institute of Planners*, 38, 84–101.

Arbuthnot, J. (1977) The roles of attitudinal and personality variables in the prediction of environmental behavior and knowledge. *Environment and Behavior*, 9, 217–232.

Arbuthnot, J., Tedeschi, R., Wayner, M., Turner, J., Kressel, S. and Rush, R. (1976) The induction of sustained recycle behavior through the foot- in -the- door technique. *Journal of Environmental Systems*, 6, 355–358.

Archea, J. (1977) The place of architectural factors in behavioural theories of privacy. *Journal of Social Issues*, 33(3), 116–137.

Ardrey, R. (1966) *The Territorial Imperative*. New York: Dell.

Argyle, M. and Dean, J. (1965) Eye-contact, distance and affiliation. *Sociometry*, 28, 289–304.

Aronow, W.S., Harris, C.N., Isbell, M.W., Rokaw, M.D. and Imparto, B. (1972) Effect of freeway travel on angina pectoris. *Annals of Internal Medecine*, 77, 669–676.

Assael, M., Pfeifer, Y. and Sulman, F.G. (1974) Influence of artificial air ionization on the human electroencephalogram. *International Journal of Biometeorology*, 18, 306–312.

Attarzadeh, F. (1983) Seasonal variation in stature and body weight. *International Journal of Orthodonics*, 21(4), 3–12.

Austin, W.T. (1982) Portrait of a courtroom: social and ecological impressions of the adversary process. *Criminal Justice and Behaviour*, 9, 286–302.

Averill, J.R. (1973) Personal control over aversive stimuli and its relationship to stress. *Psychological Bulletin*, 80, 286–303.

Bacon-Prue, A., Blount, R., Pickering, D. and Drabman, R. (1980) An evaluation of three litter control procedures – trash receptacles, paid workers and the marked item technique. *Journal of Applied Behavior Analysis*, 13, 165–170.

Baird, B.N. (1986) Tolerance for environmental health risks: the influence of knowledge, benefits, voluntariness and environmental attitudes. *Risk Analysis*, 6(4), 425–435

Balling, J.D., and Falk, J.H. (1982) Development of visual preference for natural environments. *Environment and Behavior*, 14, 5–28.

Baltes, M.M. and Hayward, S.C. (1976) Application and evaluation of strategies to reduce pollution: behavior control of littering in a football stadium. *Journal of Applied Psychology*, 61, 501–506.

Bandura, A. (1969) *Principles of Behavior Modification*. New York: Rinehart and Winston.

Banzinger, G. and Owens, K. (1978) Geophysical variables and behavior: II. Weather factors as predictors of local social indicators of maladaptation in two non-urban areas. *Psychological Reports*, 43, 427–434.

Barabasz, A.F. (1991a) A review of Antarctic behavioral research. In Harrison, A.A., Clearwater, Y.A. and McKay, C.P. (eds) *From Antarctica to Outer Space: Life in Isolation and Confinement*. New York: Springer-Verlag.

Barabasz, A.F. (1991b) Effects of isolation on states of consciousness. In Harrison, A.A., Clearwater, Y.A. and McKay, C.P. (eds) *From Antarctica to Outer Space: Life in Isolation and Confinement*. New York: Springer-Verlag.

Barker, R. and Wright, H. (1955) *Midwest and Its Children: The Psychological Ecology of an American Town*. New York: Harper and Row.

Barker, R.G. (1968) *Ecological Psychology: Concepts and Methods for Studying the Environment of Human Behavior*. Stanford, CA: Stanford University Press.

Barker, R.G. (1990) Settings of a professional lifetime. In Altman, I. and Christensen, K. (eds) *Environment and Behavior Studies: Emergence of Intellectual Traditions*. New York: Plenum.

Baron, R.A. (1976) The reduction of human aggression: a field study of the influence of incompatible reactions. *Journal of Applied Social Psychology*, 6, 260–274.

Baron, R.A. (1978) Invasions of personal space and helping: mediating effects of invader's apparent need. *Journal of Experimental Social Psychology*, 14, 304–312.

Baron, R.A. (1987) Effects of negative ions in interpersonal attraction: evidence for intensification. *Journal of Personality and Social Psychology*, 52, 547–553.

Baron, R.A., Russell, G.W. and Arms, R.L. (1985) Negative ions and behavior: impact on mood, memory and aggression among Type A and Type B persons. *Journal of Personality and Social Psychology*, 48, 746–754.

Bastlin Normoyle, J. and Foley, J.M. (1988) The defensible space model of fear and elderly public housing residents. *Environment and Behavior*, 20(1), 50–74.

Baum, A. and Davis, G.E. (1976) Spatial and social aspects of crowding perception. *Environment and Behavior*, 8, 527–544.

Baum, A. and Jonides, J. (1977) Cognitive maps: comparative judgements of imagined vs. perceived distance. Paper presented at the meeting of the Psychonomic Society, Washington, DC.

Baum, A. and Paulus, P.B. (1987) Crowding. In Stokols, D. and Altman, I. (eds) *Handbook of Environmental Psychology*, (vol 1). New York: Wiley.

Baum, A. and Valins, S. (1977) *Architecture and Social Behavior: Psychological Studies of Social Density*. Hillside, NJ: Erlbaum.

Baum, A., Aiello, J. and Calesnick, L.E. (1978) Crowding and personal control: Social density and the development of learned helplessness. *Journal of Personality and Social Psychology*, 36, 1000–1011.

Baum, A., Fisher, J.D. and Solomon, S. (1981) Type of information, familiarity and the reduction of crowding stress. *Journal of Personality and Social Psychology*, 40, 11–23.

Baum, A., Singer, J.E., and Baum, C. (1982) Stress and the environment. In Evans, G.W. (ed), *Environmental Stress*. New York: Cambridge University Press.

Baum, A., Fleming, R. and Singer, J.E. (1983) Coping with technological disaster. *Journal of Social Issues*, 39, 117–138.

Beard, R.R. and Wertheim, G.A. (1967) Behavioral impairment associated with small doses of carbon monoxide. *American Journal of Public Health*, 57, 2012–2022.

Becker, F.D. and Mayo, C. (1971) Delineating personal distance and territoriality. *Environment and Behavior*, 3, 375–381.

Belk, R.W. (1992) Attachment to possessions. In Altman, I. and Low, S.M. (eds) *Place Attachment*. New York: Plenum.

Bell, P.A. and Baron, R.A. (1977) Aggression and ambient temperature: the facilitating and debilitating effects of hot and cold environments. *Bulletin of the Psychonomic Society*, 9, 443–445.

Bell, P.A. and Greene, T.C. (1982) Thermal stress: physiological, comfort, performance and social effects of hot and cold environments. In Evans, G.W. (ed), *Environmental Stress*. New York: Cambridge University Press.

Bell, P.A., Fisher, J.D., Baum, A. and Greene, T.E. (1990) *Environmental Psychology*. Fort Worth, TX: Holt, Rinehart and Winston.

Bell, P.A., Greene, T.C., Fisher, J. D. and Baum, A. (1996) *Environmental Psychology*. Fort Worth, TX: Harcourt Brace.

Bem, D.J. (1970) *Beliefs, Attitudes and Human Affairs*. Belmont, CA: Brooks/Cole.

Benson, H. (1975) *The Relaxation Response*. New York: Morrow.

Berlyne, D.E. (1960) *Conflict, Arousal and Curiosity*. New York: McGraw-Hill.

Berlyne, D.E. (1974) *Studies in the New Experimental Aesthetics: Steps Toward an Objective Psychology of Aesthetic Appreciation*. New York: Halsted.

Bernaldez, F.G., Gallardo, D., and Abello, R.P. (1987) Children's landscape preferences: from rejection to attraction. *Journal of Environmental Psychology*, 7, 169–176.

Berry, P.C. (1961) Effects of colored illumination upon perceived temperature. *Journal of Applied Psychology*, 45, 248–250.

Bickman, L. (1972) Environmental attitudes and actions. *Journal of Social Psychology*, 87, 323–324.

Bitgood, S., Patterson, D., and Benefield, A. (1988) Exhibit design and visitor behavior: empirical relationships. *Environment and Behavior*, 20, 474–491.

Black, J.C. (1968) Uses made of spaces in owner-occupied homes. Unpublished doctoral dissertation, University of Utah, Salt Lake City.

Blair, S.M. (1991) The Antarctic experience. In Harrison, A.A, Clearwater, Y.A. and McKay, C.P. (eds) *From Antarctica to Outer Space: Life in Isolation and Confinement*. New York: Springer-Verlag.

Block, L.K. and Stokes, G.S. (1989) Perfomance and satisfaction in private versus nonprivate work settings. *Environment and Behavior*, 21, 277–297.

Blondell, J. and Dobzy, V. (1997) *Review of Chlorpyrifos Poisoning Data. Special Review,* Washington, DC: EPA.

Blumberg, L. and Gottlieb, R. (1989) *War on Waste: Can America Win Its Battle with Garbage?* Washington, DC: Island Press.

Bolt, Beranek and Newman, Inc. (1982) Cited in Raloff, J. Occupational noise: the subtle pollutant. *Science News*, 121(21), 347–350.

Booth, A. (1976) *Urban Crowding and Its Consequences.* New York: Praeger.

Borsky, P.N. (1969) Effects of noise on community behavior. In Ward, W.D. and Fricke, J.E. (eds) *Noise as a Public Health Hazard.* Washington, DC: American Speech and Hearing Association.

Boschetti, M.A. (1987) Memories of childhood homes: some contributions of environmental autobiography to interior design education and research. *Journal of Interior Design Education and Research*, 13, 27–36.

Bowman, U. (1964) Alaska earthquake. *American Journal of Psychology*, 121, 313–317.

Box, S., Hale, C. and Andrews, G. (1988) Explaining fear of crime. *British Journal of Criminology*, 28(3), 340–356.

Bradley, J.S. (1992) Disturbance caused by residential air conditioner noise. *Journal of the Acoustical Society of America*, 93, 1978–1986.

Brehm, J.W. (1966) *A Theory of Psychological Reactance.* New York: Academic Press.

Breisacher, P. (1971) Neuropsychological effects of air pollution. *American Behavioral Scientist*, 14, 837–864.

Briere, J., Downes, A. and Spensley, J. (1983) Summer in the city: urban weather conditions and psychiatric emergency room visits. *Journal of Abnormal Psychology*, 92, 77–80.

Broadbent, D.E. (1954) Some effects of noise on visual performance. *Quarterly Journal of Experimental Psychology*, 6, 1–5.

Broadbent, D. (1972) Individual differences in annoyance by noise. *Sound*, 6, 56–61.

Bromet, E. (1980) *Preliminary Report on the Mental Health of Three Mile Island Residents.* Pittsburg, PA: Western Psychiatric Institute, University of Pittsburg.

Bromet, E., Ryan, C. and Parkinson, D. (1986) Psychosocial correlates of occupational lead exposure. In Lebovits, A.H. Baum, A. and Singer, J. (eds) *Advances in Experimental Psychology* (vol 6). Hillside, NJ: Erlbaum.

Brower, S. (1977) *The Design of Neighbourhood Parks.* Baltimore: City Planning Commission.

Brower, S., Dockett, K. and Taylor, R. (1983) Residents' perceptions of territorial features and perceived local threat. *Environment and Behavior*, 15, 419–437.

Brown, B.B. (1987) Territoriality. In Stokols, D. and Altman, I. (eds) *Handbook of Environmental Psychology* (vol 1). New York: Wiley.

Brown, B.B. (1992) The ecology of privacy and mood in a shared living group. *Journal of Experimental Psychology*, 12, 5–20.

Brown, B.B. and Altman, I. (1983) Territoriality, defensible space, and residential burglary: an environmental analysis. *Journal of Environmental Psychology*, 3, 203–220.

Brown, B.B. and Harris, P.B. (1989) Residential burglary victimization: reactions to the invasion of a primary territory. *Journal of Environmental Psychology*, 9, 119–132.

Brown, G.G. and Nixon, R. (1979) Exposure to polybrominated biphenyls: some effects on personality and cognitive functioning. *Journal of the American Medical Association*, 242, 523–527.

Brown, L. (1985) Maintaining world fisheries. In Brown, L. et al. (eds) *State of the World.* New York: W.W. Norton.

Brown, L.T., Ruder, V.G., Ruder, J.H. and Young, S.D. (1974) Stimulation seeking and the change seeker index. *Journal of Consulting and Clinical Psychology*, 42, 311.

Brown, P.J. Hautaluoma, J.E. and McPhail, S. (1977) Colorado deer hunting experiences. In Transactions of the 42nd North American Wildlife and Natural Resources Conference. Washington, DC: Wildlife Management Institute.

Brunswik, E. (1956) *Perception and the Representative Design of Psychological Experiments.* Berkeley: University of California Press.

Brunswik, E. (1969) The conceptual framework of psychology. In Neurath, O. Carnap, R. and Morris, C. (eds) *Foundation* of the Unity of Science: Toward an International Encyclopaedia of Unified Science. Chicago: University of Chicago Press.

Bryant, K.J. (1982) Personality correlates of sense of direction and geographical orientation. Journal of Personality and Social Psychology, 43, 1318–1324.

Buckalew, L.W. and Rizzuto, A.P. (1984) Negative air ion effects on human performance and physiological condition. Aviation, Space, and Environmental Medicine, 55(8), 731–734.

Bull, A.J., Burbage, S.E., Crandall, J.E. et al. (1972). Effects of noise and intolerance of ambiguity on attraction for similar and dissimilar others. Journal of Social Psychology, 88, 151–152.

Bullinger, M. (1989) Psychological effects of air pollution on healthy residents – a time-series approach. Journal of Environmental Psychology, 9, 103–118.

Bunston, T. and Breton, M. (1992) Homes and homeless women. Journal of Environmental Psychology, 12, 149–162.

Bunting, T.E. and Cousins, L.R. (1983) Development and applications of the Children's Environmental Response Inventory. Journal of Environmental Education, 15, 3–10.

Burch, G.E. and De Pasquale, N.P. (1962) Hot Climates, Man and his Heart. Springfield, IL: Chas. C. Thomas.

Burgess, R.L., Clark, R.N. and Hendee, J.C. (1971) An experimental analysis of anti-litter procedures. Journal of Applied Behavioral Analysis, 4, 71–75.

Burke, J. (1985) The Day the Universe Changed. Boston: Little, Brown.

Burns, T. (1964) Nonverbal communication. Discovery, 31–35.

Burton, I., Kates, R.W., and White, G.F. (1978) The Environment as Hazard. New York: Oxford University Press.

Butler, D.L. and Steuerwald, B.L. (1991) Effects of view and room size on window size preferences made in models. Environment and Behavior, 23, 334–358.

Buttel, F.H., Murdock, S.H., Leistritz, F.L. and Hamm, R.R. (1987) Rural environments. In Zube, E. and Moore, G.T. (eds) Advances in Environment, Behavior, and Design (vol 1). New York: Plenum.

Byrne, D. and Clore, G. (1970) A reinforcement model of evaluative

responses. Personality: An International Journal, 1, 103–108.

Byrne, R.W. (1979) Memory for urban geography. Quarterly Journal of Experimental Psychology, 31, 147–154.

Calhoun, J.B. (1962) Population density and social pathology. Scientific American, 206, 139–148.

Campbell, A.C., Munce, S. and Galea, J. (1982) American gangs and British subcultures: a comparison. International Journal of Offender Therapy and Comparative Criminology, 26, 76–89.

Campbell, S. (1984) A new zoo? Zoonooz, 55, 4–7.

Cannon, W.B. (1929) Bodily Changes in Pain, Hunger, Fear and Rage. New York: Appleton-Century-Crofts.

Canter, D. (1972) Psychology for Architects. London: Applied Sciences.

Carless, (1992) Taking Out the Trash. Washington, DC: Island Press.

Carpman, J.R., Grant, M.A. and Simmons, D.A. (1984) Wayfinding in the hospital environment: the impact of various floor numbering alternatives. Journal of Environmental Systems, 13, 353–364.

Cass, R.C. and Hershberger, R.G. (1973) Further toward a set of semantic scales to measure the meaning of designed environments. Paper presented at the annual meeting of the Environmental Design Research Association, Blacksburg, Virginia.

Castell, R. (1970) Effect of familiar and unfamiliar environments on proximity behaviour of young children. Journal of Experimental Child Psychology, 9, 342–347.

Charlesworth, W.R. (1976) Human intelligence as adaptation: an ethological approach. In Resnick, L.B. (ed) The Nature of Intelligence. Hillside, NJ: Erlbaum.

Charry, J.M. and Hawkinshire, F.B.W. (1981) Effects of atmospheric electricity on some substrates of disordered social behavior. Journal of Personality and Social Psychology, 41, 185–197.

Chavis, D.M., Hogge, J.H., McMillan, D.W. and Wandersman, A. (1986) Sense of community through Brunswik's lens: a first look. Journal of Community Psychology, 14, 24–40.

Cheek, W.H. and Burch, W.R. (1976). The Social Organisation of Leisure in Human Society.

New York: Harper and Row.

Cherek, D.R. (1985) Effects of acute exposure to increased levels of background industrial noise on cigarette smoking behavior. *International Archives of Occupational and Environmental Health*, 56, 23–30.

Cherulnik, P.D. (1993) *Applications of Environment-Behavior Research: Case Studies and Analysis*. New York: Cambridge University Press.

Chiras, D.D. (1985) *Environmental Science: A Famework for Decision Making*. Menlo Park, CA: Benjamin/Cummings.

Christian, J.J., Flyger, V. and Davis, D.E. (1960) Factors in the mass mortality of a herd of sika deer, Cervus nippon. *Chesapeake Science*, 1, 79–95.

Cialdini, R. (1977) Littering as a function of extant litter. Unpublished manuscript, Arizona State University

Cicchetti, C.J. (1972) A multivariate statistical analysis of wilderness users in the United States. In Krutilla, J.V. (ed), *Natural Environments: Studies in Theoretical and Applied Analysis*. Baltimore: Johns Hopkins University Press.

Clearwater, Y.A. and Coss, R.G. (1991) Functional aesthetics to enhance well-being in isolated and confined settings. In Harrison, A.A., Clearwater, Y.A. and McKay, C.P. (eds), *From Antarctica to Outer Space: Life in Isolation and Confinement*. New York: Springer-Verlag.

Coates, J. (1991) Crowds threaten U. S. park system. *Chicago Tribune*, 1, 14.

Cochran, C.D., Hale, W.D. and Hissam, C.P. (1984) Personal space requirements in indoor versus outdoor locations. *Journal of Personality*, 111, 137–140

Coffin, D. and Stokinger, H. (1977) Biological effects of air pollutants. In Stern, A.C. (ed), *Air Pollution* (vol 3). New York: Academic Press.

Cohen, A. (1969) *Effects of Noise on Psychological State. Noise as a Public Health Hazard.* Washington, DC: American Speech and Hearing Association

Cohen, S.A. (1978) Environmental load and the allocation of attention. In Baum, A., Singer, J.E. and Valins, S. (eds), *Advances in Environmental Psychology* (vol 1). Hillsdale, NJ: Erlbaum.

Cohen, S.A. (1980) Aftereffects of stress on

human performance and social behavior: A review of research and theory. *Psychological Bulletin*, 88, 82–108.

Cohen, S. A. and Wills, T.A. (1985) Stress, social support, and the buffering hypothesis. *Psychological Bulletin*, 98, 310–357.

Cohen, S.A., Glass, D.C. and Singer, J.E. (1973) Apartment noise, auditory discrimination, and reading ability in children. *Journal of Experimental Social Psychology*, 9, 407–422.

Cohen, S.A., Glass, D.C. and Phillips, S. (1977) Environment and health. In Freeman, H.E., Levine, S. and Reeder, L.G. (eds), *Handbook of Medical Sociology*. Englewood cliffs, NJ: Prentice-Hall.

Cohen, S.A., Evans, G.W., Stokols, D. and Krantz, D.S. (1986) *Behavior, Health, and Environmental Stress*. New York: Plenum.

Cohn, D. (1992) Per-can fees catch on as area's trash mounts. *Washington Post*, March 11.

Cohn, E.G. (1993) The prediction of police calls for service: the influence of weather and temporal variables on rape and domestic violence. *Journal of Environmental Psychology*, 13, 71–83.

Collins, B.L. (1975) Windows and people: a literature survey. Psychological reaction to environments with and without windows. *NSB Building Science Series*, 70, 88.

Colman, R., Frankel, F., Ritvo, E. and Freeman, B. (1976) The effects of fluorescent and incandescent illumination upon repetitive behaviour in autistic children. *Journal of Autism and Childhood Schizophrenia*, 6, 157–162.

Cone, J.D. and Hayes, S.C. (1980) *Environmental Problems/Behavioral Solutions*. Pacific Grove, CA: Brooks/Cole.

Contrada, R.J. (1989) Type A behavior, personality hardiness and cardiovascular responses to stress. *Journal of Personality and Social Psychology*, 57, 895–903.

Cook, C.C. (1988) Components of neighborhood satisfaction: responses from urban and suburban single-parent women. *Environment and Behavior*, 20, 115–149

Cook, M. (1970) Experimentation on orientation and proxemics. *Human Relations*, 23, 61–76.

Cooper, C. (1972) The house as symbol.

Design and Environment, 14, 178–182.

Cornelius, P.E. (1991) Life in Antarctica. In Harrison, A.A., Clearwater, Y.A. and McKay, C.P. (eds) From *Antarctica to Outer Space: Life in Isolation and Confinement*. New York: Springer-Verlag.

Cornell, E.H. and Hay, D.H. (1984) Childen's acquisition of a route via different media. *Environment and Behavior*, 16, 627–642.

Couclelis, H., Golledge, R.G. Gale, N. and Tobler, W. (1987) Exploring the anchor-point hypothesis of spatial cognition, *Journal of Environmental Psychology*, 7, 99–122.

Cox, T. (1975) The nature and management of stress. *New Behaviour*, 25, 493–495.

Cox, V.C., Paulus, P.B., McCain, G. and Karlovac, M. (1982) The relationship between crowding and health. In Baum, A. and Singer, J.E. (eds), *Advances in Environmental Psychology* (vol 4). Hillsdale, NJ: Erlbaum.

Cox, V.C., Paulus, P.B. and McCain, G. (1984) Prison crowding research: the relevance for prison housing standards and a general approach regarding crowding phenomena. *American Psychologist*, 39, 1148–1160.

Craik, K.H. and Zube, E.H. (1976) *Perceiving Environmental Quality: Research and Applications*. New York: Plenum.

Crompton, J. (1979) Motivations for pleasure vacation. *Annals of Tourism Research*, 6, 408–424.

Csikszentmihalyi, M. and Kleiber, D.A. (1991) Leisure and self-actualization. In Driver, B.L., Brown, P.J. and Peterson, G.L. (eds), *Benefits of Leisure*. State college, PA: Venture Publishing.

Cunningham, M.R. (1979) Weather, mood and helping behavior: quasi experiments with the sunshine Samaritan. *Journal of Personality and Social Psychology*, 37, 1947–1956.

Cuthbertson, B.H. and Nigg, J.M. (1987) Technological disaster and the nontherapeutic community: a question of true victimization. *Environmenty and Behavior*, 19, 462–483.

Cvetkovich, G. and Earle, T. (1988) Judgement and hazard adaptation: a longitudinal study of responses to risks of water contamination. 11th Conference on Subjective Probability, Utility and

Decision Making, 1987. *Acta Psychologica*, 68, 343–353.

Cvetkovich, G., and Earle, T.C. (1995) Classifying hazardous events. *Journal of Environmental Psychology*, 5, 5–35.

Dabbs, J.M. and Stokes, N.A. (1975) Beauty is power: the use of space on the sidewalk. *Sociometry*, 38, 551–557.

Dann, G. (1977) anomie, ego enhancement and tourism. *Annals of Tourism Research*, 4, 184–194.

Davidson, L.M. and Baum, A. (1986) Chronic stress and post traumatic stress disorders. *Journal of Consulting and Clinical Psychology*, 54, 303–308.

Davidson, L.M., Baum, A. and Collins, D.L. (1982) Stress and control-related problems at Three Mile Island. *Journal of Applied Social Psychology*, 12, 349–359.

Davies, D.R. (1995) Organophosphates, affective disorders and suicide. *Journal of Nutritional and Environmental Medicine*, 5, 367–374.

Davis, S.C. and Strang, S.G. (1993) *Transportation Energy Data Book: Edition 13*. ORNL-6743. Oak Ridge, TN: Oak Ridge National Laboratory.

Dawes, R.M. (1973) The commons dilemma game: an N-peson mixed-motive game with a dominating strategy for defection. *ORI Research Bulletin*, 13, 1–12.

Dean, L.M., Willis, F.N. and Hewitt, J. (1975) Initial interaction distance among individuals equal and unequal in military rank. *Journal of Personality and Social Psychology*, 32, 294–299.

De Groot, I. (1967) Trends in public attitudes toward air pollution. *Journal of the Air Pollution Control Association*, 17, 679–681.

Deitz, T., Stern, P.C. and Rycroft, R.W. (1989) Definitions of conflict and the legitimation of resources: The case of environmentla risk. *Sociological Forum*, 4(1), 47–70.

De Jonge, D. (1962) Images of urban areas. *Journal of American Institute of Planners*, 28, 266–276.

De Joy, D. (1989) The optimism bias and traffic accident risk perception. *Accident Analysis and Prevention*, 21, 333–340.

Deregowski, J.B. (1980) *Illusions, Patterns and Pictures: A Cross-cultural Perspective*. London: Academic Press.

Derwin, C.W. and Piper, J.B. (1988) The African Rock Kopje Exhibit: evaluation and interpretive elements. *Environment and Behavior*, 20, 435–451.

DeSanctis, M., Halcomb, C.G. and Fedoravicius, A.S. (1981) Meteorological determinants of human behaviour: a holistic environmental perspective with special reference to air ionization and electrical field effects. Unpublished manuscript, Texas Technical University, Lubbock, TX.

Devall, B. (1988) *Simple in Means, Rich in Ends: Practicing Deep Ecology*. Salt Lake City: Peregrine Smith.

Devlin, A.S. (1980) Housing for the elderly: cognitive considerations. *Environment and Behavior*, 12, 451–466.

Dexter, E. (1904). School deportment and weather. *Educational Review*, 19, 160–168.

DeYoung, R. (1993) Changing behaviour and making it stick. *Environment and Behavior*, 25, 485–505.

Dorfman, P.W. (1979) Measurement and meaning of recreation satisfaction. *Environment and Behavior*, 11, 485–510.

Dosey, M. and Meisels, M. (1969) personal space and self-protection. *Journal of Personality and Social Psychology*, 11, 93–97.

Downs, R.M. and Stea, D. (1977) Cognitive maps and social behavior: process and products. In Downs, R.M. and Stea, D. (eds) *Image and Environment: Cognitive Mapping and Spatial Behavior*. Chicago: Aldine.

Downs, R.M. and Stea, D. (1973) *Maps in Minds: Reflections on Cognitive Mapping*. New York: Harper and Row.

Driver, B.L. and Knopf, R.C. (1976) Temporary escape: one product of sport fisheries management. *Fisheries*, 1, 21–29.

Driver, B.L. and Knopf, R.C. (1977) Personality, outdoor recreation and expected consequences. *Environment and Behavior*, 9, 169–193.

Dubos, R. (1965) *Man Adapting*. New Haven, CT: Yale University Press.

Duke, M.P. and Nowicki, S. (1972) A new measure and social-learning model for interpersonal distance. *Journal of Experimental Research in Personality*, 6, 119–132.

Earls, J.H. (1969) Human adjustment to an exotic environment: the nuclear submarine. *Archives of General Psychiatry*, 20, 117–123.

Ebbesen, E.B., Kjos, G.L. and Konecni, V.J. (1976) Spatial ecology: its effects on the choice of friends and enemies. *Journal of Experimental Social Psychology*, 12, 505–518.

Edney, J.J. (1972) Property, possession and permanence: a field study in human territoriality. *Journal of Applied Social Psychology*, 2, 275–282.

Edney, J.J. (1975) Territoriality and control: a field experiment. *Journal of Personality and Social Psychology*, 31, 1108–1115.

Edney, J.J. and Bell, P.A. (1983) The commons dilemma: comparing altruism, the Golden Rule, perfect equality of outcomes, and territoriality. *Social Science Journal*, 20, 23–33.

Edwards, D.J.A. (1972) Approaching the unfamiliar: a study of human interaction distances. *Journal of Behavioral Sciences*, 1, 249–250.

Eibl-Eiblesfeldt, I. (1988) The biological foundations of aesthetics. In Rentschler, I. Herzberger, B. and Epstein, D. (eds) *Beauty and the Brain: Biological Aspects of Aesthetics*. Boston: Birkhauser-Verlag.

Emlen, S.T. (1975) The stellar-orientation system of a migratory bird. *Scientific American*, 233, 102–111.

Environmental Protection Agency (1972) *Report to the President and Congress on Noise*. Washington, DC: US Government Printing Office.

Epstein, Y.M. (1982) Crowding stress and human behaviour. In Evans, G.W. (ed) *Environmental Stress*. New York: Cambridge University Press.

Erikson, K.T. (1976) Loss of communality at Buffalo Creek. *American Journal of Psychiatry*, 133, 302–305.

Espe, H. (1981) Differences in the perception of National Socialist and Classicist architecture. *Journal of Environmental Psychology*, 1, 33–42.

Esser, A.H. (1968) Dominance hierarchy and clinical course of psychiatrically hospitalised boys. *Child Development*, 39, 147–157.

Esser, A.H. (1976) Discussion of papers presented in the symposium 'Theoretical and empirical issues with regard to privacy, territoriality, personal space and crowding'. *Environment and Behavior*, 8, 117–125.

Evans, G.W. (1979) Behavioral and

physiological consequences of crowding in humans. *Journal of Applied Social Psychology*, 9, 27–46.

Evans, G.W. (1980) Environmental cognition. *Psychological Bulletin*, 88, 259–287.

Evans, G.W. and Cohen, S.A. (1987) Environmental stress. In Stokols, D. and Altman, I. (eds) Handbook of Environmental Psychology (vol 1). New York: Wiley.

Evans, G.W. and Howard, R.B. (1973) Personal space. *Psychological Bulletin*, 80, 334–344.

Evans, G.W. and Jacobs, S.V. (1981) Air pollution and human behavior. *Journal of Social Issues*, 37, 95–125.

Evans, G.W., Jacobs, S.V. and Frager, N. (1979) Human adaptation to photochemical smog. Paper presened to American Psychological Association, New York.

Evans, G.W., Fellow, J., Zorn, M. and Doty, K. (1980) Cognitive mapping and architecture. *Journal of Applied Psychology*, 65, 474–478.

Evans, G.W., Smith, C. and Pezdek, K. (1982a) Cognitive maps and urban form. *American Planning Association Journal*, 48, 232–244.

Evans, G.W., Jacobs, S.V. and Frager, N. (1982b) Behavioral responses to air pollution. In Baum, A. and Singer, J. (eds) *Advances in Environmental Psychology* (vol 4). Hillsdale, NJ: Erlbaum.

Evans, G.W., Jacobs, S.V., Dooley, D. and Catalano, R. (1987) The interaction of stressful life events and chronic strains on community mental health. *American Journal of Community Psychology*, 15, 23–34.

Evans, G.W., Hygge, S. and Bullinger, M. (1993) Psychology and the environment. Unpublished manuscript, Cornell University.

Everett, P. and Watson, B. (1987) Psychological contributions to transportation. In Stokols, D. and Altman, I. (eds) *Handbook of Environmental Psychology*. New York: Wiley.

Everett, P.B., Hayward, S.C. and Meyers, A.W. (1974) The effects of a token reinforcement procedure on bus ridership. *Journal of Applied Behavior Analysis*, 7, 1–9.

Eysenck, H.J. and Rachman, S. (1965) *The Cause and Care of Neurosis*. London: RKP.

Eyusenck, M.W. (1975) Intereactive effects of noise, activation level and dominance in memory latencies. *Journal of Experimental Psychology*, 104, 143–148.

Falkenberg, V. and Kirk, R.E. (1977) Effects of ionized air on early acquisition of Sidman aviodance behavior in rats. *Psychological Reports*, 41, 1071–1074.

Fantz, R.L. (1961) The origin of form perception. *Scientific American*, 204, 66–72.

Faulkner, R. and Faulkner, S. (1975) *Inside Today's Home*. New York: Holt, Rinehart and Winston.

Fazio, R.H. (1990) Multiple processes by which attitudes guide behavior: the MODE model as an integrative framework. In Zanna, M.P. (ed) *Advances in Experimental Social Psychology*. San Diego, CA: Academic Press.

Fazio, R.H., Chen, J., McDonel, E.C. and Sherman, S.J. (1982) Attitude accessibility and the strength of the object-evaluation association. *Journal of Experimental Social Psychology*, 18, 339–357.

Fechner, G.T. (1966) *Elements of Psychophysics*. New York: Holt, Rinehart and Winston.

Feimer, N.R. (1981) Personality and sociodemographic variables as sources of variation in environmental perception. In Proshansky, H.M. (ed) *Environmental Cognition*. Symposium at the meeting of the American Psychological Association (ERIC Document Reproduction Service No. ED 211 393).

Festinger, L.A. (1957) *A Theory of Cognitive Dissonance*. Stanford, CA: Stanford University Press.

Festinger, L.A., Schacter, S. and BAck, K. (1950) *Social Pressures in Informal Groups*. New York: Harper and Row.

Finnie, W.C. (1973) Field experiments and litter control. *Environment and Behavior*, 5, 123–143.

Firestone, I.J., Lichtman, C.M. and Evans, J.R. (1980) Privacy and solidarity: effects of nursing home accommodation on environmental perception and sociability preferences. *International Journal of Aging and Human Development*, 11, 229–241.

Fischhoff, B., Slovic, P. and Lichtenstein, S. (1978) Fault trees: sensitivity of estimated failure probabilities to problem representation. *Journal of Experimental Psychology: Human Perception and Performance*, 4(2), 330–344.

Fishbein, M. and Ajzen, I. (1975) *Belief, Attitude, Intention and Behavior*. Reading, MA: Addison-Wesley.

Fisher, J.D. and Baron, R.M. (1982) An equity-based model of vandalism. *Population and Environment*, 5, 182–200.

Fisher, J.D. and Byrne, D. (1975) Too close for comfort: sex differences in response to invasions of personal space. *Journal of Personality and Social Psychology*, 32, 15–21.

Fisher, J.D., Bell, P.A. and Baum, A. (1984) *Environmental Psychology*. New York: Holt, Rinehart and Winston.

Fletcher, D. (1983) Effects of classroom lighting on the behaviour of exceptional children. *Exceptional Education Quarterly*, 4, 75–89.

Flin, R., Mearns, K., Gordon, R. and Fleming, M. (1996) Risk perception by offshore workers on UK oil and gas platforms. *Safety Science*, 22.

Foa, U.G. (1971) Interpersonal and economic resources. *Science*, 171, 345–351.

Forester, W.S. (1988) Solid waste: There's a lot more coming. Environmentla Protection Agency Journal, 14, 11–12.

Forrester, J.W. (1969) *Urban Dynamics*. Cambridge, MA: MIT Press.

Freedman, J.L. (1975) *Crowding and Behavior*. New York: Viking Press.

Freedy, J.R., Shaw, D.L., Jarrell, M.P. and Masters, C.R. (1992) Towards an understanding of the psychological impact of natural disasters: an application of the conservation of resources stress model. *Journal of Traumatic Stress*, 5, 441–454.

Fridgen, J.D. (1984) Environmental psychology and tourism. *Annals of Tourism Research*, 11, 19–39.

Fried, M. (1982) Residential attachment: sources of residential and community satisfaction. *Journal of Social Issues*, 38(3), 107–119.

Frisancho, A.R. (1979) *Human Adaptation*. St Louis: Mosby.

Fritz, C.E. and Marks, E.S. (1954) The NORC studies of human behavior in disaster. *Journal of Social Issues*, 10, 26–41.

Froelicher, V.F. and Froelicher, E.S. (1991) Cardiovascular benefits of physical activity. In Driver, B.L., Brown, P.J. and Peterson, G.L. (eds) *Benefits of Leisure*. State College, PA: Venture Publishing.

Furnham, A. (1984) Tourism and culture shock. *Annals of Tourism Research*, 11, 41–57.

Furnham, A. (1985) Why do people save? Attitudes to, and habits of, saving money in Britain. *Journal of Applied Social Psychology*, 15, 354–373.

Furnham, A. and Bochner, S. (1986) *Culture Shock*. London: Routledge.

Galanter, E. (1962) Contemporary psychophysics. In Brown, R. et al. (eds) *New Directions in Psychology*. New York: Holt, Rinehart and Winston.

Gallant, S.J., Hamilton, J.A., Popiel, D.A. and Morokoff, P.J. (1991) Daily moods and symptoms: effects of awareness of study focus, gender, menstrual cycle phase, and day of the week. *Health Psychology*, 10, 180–189.

Galle, O.R., Gove, W.R. and McPherson, J.M. (1972) Population density and pathology: what are the relationships for man? *Science*, 176, 23–30.

Galster, G. and Hesser, G. (1981) Residential satisfaction: compositonal and contextual correlates. *Environment and Behavior*, 13, 735–759.

Garabino, J. (1980) Some thoughts on school size and its effects on adolescent development. *Journal of Youth and Adolescence*, 9, 19–31.

Gardner, G.T. and Stern, P.C. (1996) *Environmental Problems and Human Behavior*. Needham Heights, MA: Allyn and Bacon.

Gärling, T., Böök, A., Lindberg, E. and Nilsson, T. (1981) Memory for the spatial layout of the everyday physical environment: Factors affecting the rate of acquisition. *Journal of Environmental Psychology*, 1, 263–277.

Gärling, T., Böök, A., Lindberg, E. (1984) Cognifive mapping of large-scale environments: the interrelation between action plans, acquisition and orientation. *Environment and Behavior*, 16, 3–34.

Geen, R.G. and O'Neal, E.C. (1969) Activation of cue-elicited aggression by general arousal. *Journal of Personality and Social Psychology*, 11, 289–292.

Geller, E.S. (1980) Applications of behavioral analysis for litter control. In Glenwick, D. and Jason, L. (eds) *Behavioral Community Psychology: Progress and Prospects.* New York: Praeger.

Geller, E.S. (1981) Evaluating energy conservation programs: is verbal report enough? *Journal of Consumer Research,* 8, 331–335.

Geller, E.S., Farris, J. and Post, D. (1973) Promoting a consumer behaviour for pollution control. *Journal of Applied Behaviour Analysis,* 6, 367–376.

Geller, E.S., Mann, M. and Brasted, W. (1977) Trash can design: a determinant of litter-related behavior. Paper presented to American Psychological Association, San Francisco.

Geller, E.S., Winett, R.A. and Everett, P.B. (1982) *Preserving the Environment: New Strategies for Behavior Change.* New York: Pergamon.

Gergen, K.J., Gergen, M.M., and Barton, W.H. (1973) Deviance in the dark. *Psychology Today,* 7, 129–130.

Giannini, A.J., Castellani, S. and Dvoredsky, A.C. (1983) Anxiety state: relationship to atmospheric cations and serotonin. *Journal of Clinical Psychiatry,* 44(7), 262–264.

Gibbs, M.S. (1986) Psychopathological consequences of exposure to toxins in the water supply. In Lebovits, A.H., Baum, A. and Singer, J. (eds) *Advances in Environmental Psychology.* Hillsdale, NJ: Erlbaum.

Gibson, J.J. (1960) Perception. In *Encyclopaedia of Science and Technology.* New York: McGraw-Hill.

Gibson, J.J. (1966) *The Senses Considered as Perceptual Systems.* Boston: Houghton Mifflin.

Gifford, R. (1980) Environmental dispositions and the evaluation of architectural interiors. *Journal of Research in Personality,* 14, 386–399.

Gifford, R. (1987) *Environmental Psychology.* Needham Heights, MA: Allyn and Bacon.

Gifford, R., and Price, J. (1979) Personal space in nursery school children. *Canadian Journal of Behavioural Science,* 11, 318–326.

Gifford, R., Hay, R. and Boros, K. (1982) Individual differences in environmental attitudes. *Journal of Environmental Education,* 14 (2), 19–23.

Glass, D.E. and Singer, J.E. (1972) *Urban Stress.* New York: Academic Press.

Glass, G.V., Cahen, L.S., Smith, M.L. and Filby, N.N. (1982) *School Class Size: Research and Policy.* Beverly Hills: Sage.

Goffman, E. (1959) *The Presentation of Self in Everyday Life.* New York: Doubleday.

Gold, J.R. (1982) Territoriality and human spatial behavior. *Progress in Human Geography,* 6, 44–67.

Gold, J.R., and Burgess, J. (eds.) (1982) *Valued Environments.* London: George Allen and Unwin.

Goldsmith, J.R. (1968) Effects of air pollution on human health. In Stern, A.C. (ed) *Air Pollution* (vol 1). New York: Academic Press.

Goldstein, K. (1942) Some experimental observations concerning the influence of colours on the functions of the organism. *Occupational Therapy,* 21, 147–151.

Goransen, R.E. and King, D. (1970) *Rioting and Daily Temperature: Analysis of the US Riot in 1967.* Toronto: York University.

Gould, J.L. (1982) *Ethology: The Mechanisms and Evolution of Behaviour.* New York: W.W. Norton.

Gove, W.R. and Hughes, M. (1983) *Crowing in the Household.* New York: Academic Press.

Greenbaum, P.E. and Greenbaum, S.D. (1981) Territorial personalisation: Group identity and social interaction in a Slavic-American neighborhood. *Environment and Behavior,* 13, 574–589.

Greene, T.C. and Bell, P.A. (1980) Additional considerations concerning the effects of 'warm' and 'cool' colors on energy conservation. *Ergonomics,* 23, 949–954.

Griffit, W. (1970) Environmental effects on interpersonal affective behavior: ambient effective temperature and attraction. *Journal of Personality and Social Psychology,* 15, 240–244.

Griffit, W. and Veitch, R. (1971) Hot and crowded: influence of population density and temperature on interpersonal affective behavior. *Journal of Personality and Social Psychology,* 17, 92–99.

Guardo, C.J., and Meisels, M. (1971) Child-parent spatial patterns under praise and reproof. *Developmental Psychology,* 5, 365.

Gump, P.V. (1987) School and classroom environments. In Stokols, D. and Altman, I. (eds), *Handbook of Environmental Psychology* (vol 1) New York: Wiley.

216

Haley, R.W., Kurt, T.L., et al. (1997) Is there a Gulf War syndrome? *Journal of the American Medical Association*, 3, 215–222.

Hall, E.T. (1959) *The Silent Language*. New York: Doubleday.

Hall, E.T. (1966) *The Hidden Dimension*. New York: Doubleday.

Halpern, D. (1995) *Mental Health and the Built Environment*. London: Taylor and Francis.

Hammitt, W.E. (1982) Cognitive dimensions of wilderness solitude. *Environment and Behavior*, 14, 478–493.

Hancock, P.A. (1986) Sustained attention under thermal stress. *Psychological Bulletin*, 99, 263–281.

Hansell, C.W. (1961) An attempt to define ionization of the air. Proceedings of the International Conference on Ionization of the Air. Philadelphia: Franklin Institute, I-J, 1–10.

Hardin, G. (1968a) Denial and the gift of history. In Hardin, G. (ed) *Population, Evolution and Birth Control*. San Francisco: W.H. Freeman.

Hardin, G. (1968b) The tragedy of the commons. *Science*, 162, 1243–1248.

Harris, P.R. (1991) Personnel deployment systems: managing people in polar and outer space settings. In Harrison, A.A., Clearwater, Y.A. and McKay, C.P. (eds) *From Antarctica to Outer Space: Life in Isolation and Confinement*. New York: Springer-Verlag.

Harrison, A.A. and Connors, M.M. (1984) Groups in exotic environments. In Berkowitz, L. (ed) *Advances in Experimental Social Psychology*. New York: Academic Press.

Hart, C.H. and Sheehan, R. (1986) Preschoolers' play behavior in outdoor environments: effects of traditional and contemporary playgrounds. *Amercian Education Research Journal*, 23, 669–678.

Hart, R.A. and Moore, G.T. (1973) The development of spatial cognition: a review. In Downes, R.M. and Stea, D. (eds) *Image and Environment: Cognitive Mapping and Spatial Behavior*. Chicago: Aldine.

Hartig, T., Mang, M. and Evans, G.W. (1991) Restorative effects of natural environment experience. *Environment and Behavior*, 23, 3–26.

Hassell, M.J. and Peatross, F.D. (1990) Exploring connections between women's changing roles and house forms.

Environment and Behavior, 22, 3–26.

Hawkins, L.H. (1981) The influence of air ions, temperature and humidity on subjective wellbeing and comfort. *Journal of Environmental Psychology*, 1, 279–292.

Hawkins, L.H. and Barker, T. (1978) Air ions and human performance. *Ergonomics*, 21, 273–278.

Hayduk, L.A. (1981) The permeability of personal space. *Canadian Journal of Behavioral Science*, 13 274–287.

Hayduk, L.A. (1985) Personal space: the conceptual and measurement implications of structural equation models. *Canadian Journal of Behavioral Science*, 17, 140–149.

Hayward, D.G., Rothenberg, M. and Beasley, R.R. (1974) Children's play and urban playground environments: a comparison of traditional, contemporary and adventure playground types. *Environment and Behavior*, 6, 131–168.

Hebb, D.O. (1972) *Textbook of Psychology*. Philadelphia: W.B. Saunders.

Heberlein, T.A. (1971) Moral norms, threatened sanctions and littering behavior. Doctoral dissertation, University of Wisconsin-Madison.

Heberlein, T.A. (1975) Conservation information, the energy crisis and electricity consumption in an apartment complex. *Energy Systems and Policy*, 1, 105–117.

Hedge, A. (1984) Evidence of a relationship between office design and self-reports of ill-health among office workers in the United Kingdom. *Journal of Architectural and Planning Research*, 1, 163–174.

Hedge, A., Burge, P.S., Robertson, A.S., Wilson, S. and Harris-Bass, J. (1989) Work-related illness in offices: a proposed model of the sick building syndrome. *Environment International*, 15, 143–158.

Hedge, A., Mitchell, G.E. and McCarthy, J. (1993) Effects of furniture integrated breathing zone filtration system indoor air quality, Sick Building Syndrome, productivity, and absenteeism. *Indoor Air*, 3, 328–336.

Heerwagen, J.H. (1990) Affective functioning, 'light hunger', and room brightness preferences. *Environment and Behavior*, 22, 608–635.

Heft, H. and Wohlwill, J.F. (1987)

Environmental cognition in children. In Stokols, D. and Altman, I. (eds) *Handbook of Environmental Psychology*. New York: Wiley.

Heilbroner, R.L. (1974) *An Enquiry into the Human Prospect*. New York: W.W. Norton.

Helson, H. (1964) *Adaptation Level Theory*. New York: Harper and Row.

Hendee, J.C., Stankey, G.H. and Lucas, R.C. (1978) *Wilderness Management*. Washington, DC: US Government Printing Office.

Henshaw, D.L. et al. (1993) Radon in domestic water supplies in the UK. *Radiation Prot. Dosimetry*, 46, 285–289

Herzberg, F. (1966) *Work and the Nature of Man*. Cleveland: World Publishing.

Heyne, P. (1976) *The Economic Way of Thinking*. Chicago: University of Washington Science Research Assoc.

Hicks, P.E. (1977) *Introduction to Industrial Engineering and Management Science*. New York: McGraw-Hill.

Hildreth, A.M., Derogatis, L.R. and McCusker, K. (1971) Body buffer zone and violence: a reassessment and confirmation. *American Journal of Psychiatry*, 127, 1641–1645.

Hirst, E. (1973) *Energy Intensiveness of Passenger and Freight Transport Modes, 1950–1970*. ORNL Report NSF-EP-44. Oak Ridge, Tenn: Oak Ridge National Laboratory.

Hobfoll, S.E. (1989) Conservation of resources: a new attempt at conceptualising stress. *American Psychologist*, 44, 513–524.

Hodgkinson, P.E. and Stewart, M. (1991) *Coping with Catastrophe*. London: Routledge.

Holahan, C.J. (1972) Seating patterns and patient behavior in an experimental dayroom, *Journal of Abnormal Psychology*, 80, 115–124.

Holahan, C.J. (1977) Rural differences in judged appropriateness of altruistic responses: personal versus situational effects. *Sociometry*, 40, 378–382.

Holding, C.S. (1992) Clusters and reference point in cognitive representations of the environment. *Journal of Experimental Psychology*, 12, 45–56.

Hollander, J. and Yeostros, S. (1963) The effect of simultaneous variation of humidity and barometric pressure on arthritis. *Bulletin of the American Meteorological Society*, 44, 489–494.

Hollister, F.D. (1968) *Greater London Council: a Report on the Problems of Windowless Environments*. London: Hobbs.

Holman, E.A. and Silver, R.C. (1994) The relationship between place attachment and social relationships in coping with the southern California firestorms. Paper presented to American Psychological Association, Los Angeles, CA.

Holmes, T.H. and Rahe, R.H. (1967) The Social Readjustment Rating Scale. *Journal of Psychosomatic Research*, 11, 213–218.

Hopper, J.R. and Nielsen, J.M. (1991) Recycling as altruistic behavior: normative and behavioural strategies to expand participation in a community recycling program. *Environment and Behavior*, 23, 195–220.

Horowitz, M.J., Duff, D.F. and Stratton, L.O. (1964) Body-buffer zone. *Archives of General Psychiatry*, 11, 651–656.

Howard, D. (1948) *Territory and Bird Life*. London: Cellen.

Howard, G.S., Delgado, E., Miller, D. and Gubbins, S. (1993) Transforming values into actions: ecological preservation. *Counselling Psychologist*, 21, 582–596.

Howell, S.C. (1980) Environments as hypotheses in human aging research. In Poon, L. (ed) (1980) *Aging in the 1980s*. Washington: American Psychological Association.

Hull, R.B. and Revell, G.R.B. (1989) Cross-cultural comparison of landscape scenic beauty evaluations: a case study in Bali. *Journal of Environmentla Psychology*, 9, 177–191.

Hunter, A. and Baumer, T.L. (1982) Street traffic, social interaction, and fear of crime. *Sociological Inquiry*, 52(2), 122–131.

Imamoglu, V. (1973) The effect of furniture density on the subjective evaluation of spaciousness and estimation of size of rooms. In Kuller, R. (ed) *Architectural Psychology: Proceedings of the Lund Conference*. Stroudsberg, PA: Dowden, Hutchison and Ross.

Inglehart, R. (1990) *Culture Shift in Advanced Industrial Society*. Princeton, NJ: Princeton University Press.

Ising, H., Rebebtisch, E., Poustka, F. and Curio, I. (1990) Annoyance and health risk caused by military low-altitude flight noise. *International Archives of Occupational and Environmental Health*, 62, 357–363.

Iso-Ahola, S.E. (1986) A theory of substitutability of leisure behavior. *Leisure Science*, 8, 367–389.

Ittelson, W.H., Proshansky, H.M. and Rivlin, L.G. (1970) A study of bedroom use on two psychiatric wards. *Hospital and Community Psychiatry*, 21, 25–28.

Ittelson, W.H., Proshansky, H.M., Rivlin, L.G., and Winkel, G.H. (1974) *An Introduction to Environmental Psychology*. New York: Holt, Rinehart and Winston.

Jacobs, H.E. and Bailey, J.S. (1982) Evaluating participation in a residential program. *Journal of Environmental Systems*, 13, 245–254.

Jacobsen, F.M., Murphy, D.L. and Rosenthal, N.E. (1989) The role of serotonin in seasonal affective disorder and the antidepressant response to phototherapy. In Rosenthal, N.E. and Blehar, M.C. (eds) *Seasonal Affective Disorders and Phototherapy*. New York: Springer-Verlag.

Jemmott, J.B., Borysenko, M., McClelland, D.C., Chapman, R., Meyer, D. and Benson, H. (1983) Academic stress, power motivation, and decrease in salivary secretory immunoglobulin A secretion rate. *Lancet*, 1, 1400–1402.

Jerdee, T.H. and Rosen, B. (1974) The effects of opportunity to communicate and visibility of individual decisions on behavior in the common interest. *Journal of Applied Psychology*, 59, 712–716.

Jerkova, H. and Kremorova, B. (1970) Observation of the effect of noise on the general health of workers in large engineering factories;attempt at evaluation. *Pracovni Lekarstvi*, 17, 147–148.

Jermier, J.M., Gaines, J. and McIntosh, N.J. (1989) Reactions to physically dangerous work: a conceptual and empirical analysis. *Journal of Organisational Behaviour*, 10, 15–33.

Joiner, D. (1971) Office territory. *New Society*, 7, 660–663.

Kahneman, D. (1973) *Attention and Effort*. Englewood cliffs, NJ: Prentice-Hall.

Kahneman, D. and Tversky, A. (1979) Prospect theory: an analysis of decisions under risk. *Econometrica*, 47, 262–291.

Kaitilla, S. (1993) Satisfaction with public housing in Papua New Guinea: the case of West Taraka housing scheme. *Environment and Behavior*, 25, 514–545.

Kaniasty, K. and Norris, F. (1993) A test of the social support deterioration model in the context of natural disaster. *Journal of Personality and Social Psychology*, 64, 395–408.

Kanner, A., Coynes, J., Schaefer, C. and Lazarus, R. (1981) Comparison of two modes of stress measurement: daily hassles and uplifts versus major life events. *Journal of Behavioural Medicine*, 4, 1–39.

Kaplan, R. (1977a) Patterns of environmental preference. *Environment and Behavior*, 9, 195–215.

Kaplan, R. (1984) The impact of urban nature: a theoretical analysis. *Urban Ecology*, 8, 189–197.

Kaplan, R. and Kaplan, S. (1989) *The Experience of Nature: A Psychological Perspective*. New York: Cambridge University Press.

Kaplan, S. (1977b) Tranquillity and Challenge in the natural environment. In *Children, Nature and the Urban Environment*. Upper Darby, PA: US Dept of Agriculture, Forest Service, NE Forest Experiment Station.

Kaplan, S. and Kaplan, R. (1982) *Cognition and Environment*. New York: Praeger.

Kaplan, S. and Kaplan, R. (1989) The visual environment: public participation in design and planning. *Journal of Social Issues*, 45, 59–86.

Kaplan, P.P., Bladen, W.A. and Singh,G. (1980) Slum dwellers' and squatters' images of the city. *Environment and Behavior*, 12, 81–100.

Karl, T., Nicholls, N. and Gregory, J. (1997) The coming climate. *Scientific American*, May, 55–59.

Karlin, R.A., Katz, S., Epstein, Y.M. and Woolfolk, R.L. (1979) The use of therapeutic interventions to reduce crowding-related arousal: a preliminary investigation. *Environmental Psychology and Nonverbal Behavior*, 1, 30–40.

Karmel, L.J. (1965) Effects of windowless classroom environments on high school students. *Perceptual and Motor Skills*, 20, 277–278.

Kates, R. (1962) Hazard and choice perception in flood plain management. Chicago: University of Chicago, Dept of Geography research paper no. 78.

Kates, R.W. (1976) Experiencing the environment as hazard. In Proshansky,

H.M., Ittelson, W.H. and Rivlin, L.G. (eds) *Environmental Psychology: People and Their Physical Settings.* New York: Holt, Rinehart and Winston.

Katz, P. (1937) *Animals and Men.* New York: Longmans, Green.

Katzev, R. and Mishima, H.R. (1992) The use of posted feedback to promote recycling. *Psychological Reports, 71,* 259–264.

Kaufman, J. and Christensen, J. (eds) (1984) *IES Lighting Handbook.* New York: Illuminating Engineering Society of North America.

Kaye, S.M., and Murray, M.A. (1982) Evaluations of an architectural space as a function of variations in furniture arrangement, furniture density, and windows. *Human Factors, 24,* 609–618.

Kazantizis, G. (1967) Hypothermia. In Davis, C.N., Davis, P.R. and Taylor, F.H. (eds) *The Effects of Abnormal Physical Conditions at Work.* Edinburgh: Livingstone.

Keane, T.M. and Wolfe, J. (1990) Comorbidity in post-traumatic stress disorder: an analysis of community and clinical studies. *Journal of Applied Social Psychology, 20,* 1776–1788.

Keller, L.M., Bouchard, T.J., Arvey, R.D., Segal, N.L. and Davis, R.V. (1992) Work values: genetic and environmental influences. *Journal of Applied Psychology, 77,* 79–88.

Kempton, W., Harris, C., Keith, J., and Weihl, J. (1985) Do consumers know 'what works' in energy conservation? *Marriage and Family Review, 9,* 115–133.

Kennedy, S., Kiecolt-Glaser, J. and Glaser, R. (1990) Social support, stress and the immune system. In Sarason, B., Sarason, I. and Pierce, G. (eds) *Social Support: An Interactional View.* New York: Wiley.

Kevan, S.M. (1980) Perspectives on season of suicide: a review. *Social Science and Medicine, 14,* 369–378.

Kira, A. (1976) *The Bathroom.* New York: Viking.

Kline, L.M. Harrison, A., Bell, P.A., Edney, J.J. and Hill, E. (1984) Verbal reinforcement and feedback as solutions to a simulated commons dilemma. *Psychological Documents, 14,* 24.

Klitzman, S. and Stellman, J.M. (1989) The impact of the physical environment on the psychological well-being of office workers. *Social Science and Medicine, 29*(6), 733–742.

Knapp, D. (1982) *Resource Recovery: What Recycling can Do.* Berkeley, CA: Materials World Publishing.

Knopf, R.C. (1987) Human behavior, cognition and affect in the natural environment. In Stokols, D. and Altman, I. (eds) *Handbook of Environmental Psychology* (vol 1). New York: Wiley.

Knopf, R.C., Driver, B.L. and Bassett, J.R. (1973) Motivations for fishing. In Transactions of the 38th North American Wildlife and Natural Resources Conference. Washington, DC: Wildlife Management Institute.

Knowles, E.S. (1980) An affiliative conflict theory of personal and group spatial behavior. In Paulus, P.B. (ed) *Psychology of Group Influence.* Hillsdale, NJ: Erlbaum.

Knowles, E.S. (1983) Social physics and the effects of others: Tests of the effects of audience size and distance on social judgements and behavior. *Journal of Personality and Social Psychology, 45,* 1263–1279.

Kobasa, S.C. (1979) Stressful life events, personality and health: an enquiry into hardiness. *Journal of Personality and Social Psychology, 37,* 1–11.

Koffka, K. (1935) *Principles of Gestalt Psychology.* New York: Harcourt.

Kopnecni, V.J., Libuser, L., Morton, H. and Ebbesen, E.B. (1975) Effects of a violation of personal space on escape and helping responses. Journal of Experimental Social Psychology, 11, 288–299.

Koscheyev, V.S., Martens, V.K., Kosenov, A.A., LArtzev, M.A. and Leon, G.R. (1993) Psychological status of Chernobyl nuclear power plant operators after the natural disaster. *Journal of Traumatic Stress, 6,* 561–568.

Kryter, K.D. (1970) *The Effects of Noise on Man.* New York: Academic Press.

Kuethe, J.L. (1962) Social schemas and the reconstruction of social object displays from memory. *Journal of Abnormal and Social Psychology, 65,* 71–74.

Lambert, J.F. and Olivereau, J.M. (1980) Single-trial passive avoidance learning by rats treated with ionized air. *Psychological Reports, 47,* 1323–1330.

Lang, J. (1987) *Creating Architectural Theory: The Role of Behavioral Sciences in Environmental Design.* New York: Van Nostrand Reinhold

La Pière, R.T. (1934) Attitudes v. actions. *Social Forces*, 13, 230–237.

Larson, C.T. (1965) *The Effect of Windowless Classrooms on Elementary School Children.* Ann Arbor: Architectural Research Laboratory, University of Michigan.

Latané, B. and Darley, J.M. (1968) Group inhibitions of bystander intervention in emergencies. *Journal of Personality and Social Psychology*, 10, 215–221.

Laufer, R. and Wolfe, M. (1977) Privacy as a concept and as a social issue: a multidimensional development theory. *Journal of Social Issues*, 33, 22–42.

Lawson, B.R. and Walters, D. (1974) The effects of a new motorway on an established residential area. In Canter, D. and Lee, T. (eds) *Psychology and the Built Environment.* New York: Wiley.

Lawton, M.P. (1987) Housing for the elderly in the mid-1980's. In Lesnoff-Caravaglia, G. (ed) *Handbook of Applied Gerontology.* New York: Human Sciences Press.

Lazarus, R. (1966) *Psychological Stress and the Coping Process.* New York: McGraw-Hill.

Lebovits, A., Byrne, M. and Strain, J. (1986) The case of asbestos-exposed workers: a psychological evaluation. In Lebovits, A., Baum, A. and Singer, J. (eds) *Advances in Environmental Psychology* (vol 6). Hillsdale, NJ: Erlbaum.

Le Corbusier(1963) *Towards a New Architecture.* New York: Praeger.

Lee, T.R. (1978) A theory of socio-spatial schemata. In Kaplan, S. and Kaplan, R. (eds) *Humanscape: Environments for People.* North Scituate, MA: Duxbury.

Lee, T.R., Macdonald, S.M. and Coote, J.A. (1993) Perceptions of risk and attitudes to safety at a nuclear reprocessing plant. Paper presented at Society for Risk Assessment (Europe) Fourth Conference, Rome.

Leiber, A.L. (1978) *The Lunar Effect.* Garden City, New York: Anchor Press/Doubleday.

Leopold, R.L. and Dillon, H. (1963) Psychoanatomy of a disaster: a long term study of post-traumatic neurosis in survivors of a marine explosion. *American Journal of Psychiatry*, 119, 913–921.

Lepore, S.J., Evans, G.W. and Schneider, M.L. (1991) Dynamic role of social support in the link between chronic stress and psychological distress. *Journal of Personality and Social Psychology*, 61, 899–909.

Levine, A.S. (1991) Psychological effects of long-duration space missions and stress amelioration techniques. In Harrison, A.A., Clearwater, Y.A. and McKay, C.P. (eds) *From Antarctica to Outer Space: Life in Isolation and Confinement.* New York: Springer-Verlag.

Levine, B.L. (1986) The tragedy of the commons and the comedy of community: the commons in history. *Journal of Community Psychology*, 14, 81–99.

Levine, M. (1982) You-are-here maps: psychological considerations. *Environment and Behavior*, 14, 221–237.

Levy, L., and Herzog, A.W. (1974) Effects of population density and crowding on health and social adaptation in the Netherlands. *Journal of Health and Social Behaviour*, 4, 228–240.

Levy, R.L. (1983) Social support and compliance: a selective review and critique of treatment integrity and outcome measurement. *Social Science and Medicine*, 17(8), 1329–1338.

Lewin, K. (1951) Formalization and progress in psychology. In Cartwright, D. (ed) *Field Theory in Social Science.* New York: Harper.

Lime, D.W. (1986) River recreation and natural resource management: a focus on river running and boating. In the President's Commission on Americans Outdoors (ed) *A Literature Review.* Washington, DC: US Government Printing Office.

Link, J.M. and Pepler, R.D. (1970) Associated fluctuations in daily temperature, productivity and absenteeism. *ASHRAE Transactions*, 76(2), 326–377.

Little, B.R. (1976) Specialization and the varieties of human experience: empirical studies within the personality paradigm. In Wapner, S., Cohen, S.B. and Kaplan, B. (eds) *Experiencing the Environment.* New York: Plenum Press.

Litton, R.B. (1972) Aesthetic dimensions of the landscape. In Krutilla, J.V. (ed), *Natural Environments: Studies in Theoretical and Applied*

Analysis. Baltimore: Johns Hopkins University Press.

Lovelock, J.E. (1979) *Gaia: A New Look at Life on Earth*. Oxford: Oxford University Press.

Lowry, S. (1991) *Housing and Health*. London: British Medical Journal.

Lubin, J.H. and Boice, J.D. (1997) Lung cancer risk fron residential radon: a meta-analysis of eight epidemiological studies. *Journal of the National Cancer Institute*, 89, 49–57

Lucas, R.C. (1964) *The Recreational Capacity of the Quetico-Superior (Research Paper 5–15)*. Washington, DC: Lake State Forest Experiment Station, Forest Service, USDA.

Lynch, K. (1960) *The Image of the City*. Cambridge, MA: MIT Press.

Lynn, G.D. and Rola, L.R. (1988) Improving attitude-behavior prediction models with economic variables: farmer actions toward soil conservation. *Journal of Social Psychology*, 128(1), 19–28.

Magill, A.W. (1976) The message of vandalism. In *Vandalism and Outdoor Recreation*. Berkeley, CA: US Dept of Agriculture, Pacific Southwest Forest and Range Experiment Station.

Maguire, M. (1982) *Burglary in a Dwelling*. London: Heinemann.

Malandro, L.A., Barker, L, and Barker, D.A. (1989) *Nonverbal Communication*. New York: Random House.

Maloney, M.P. and Ward, M.P. (1973) Ecology: let's hear from the people. *American Psychologist*, 30, 787–790.

Mandell, L. and Marans, R. (1972) *Participation in Outdoor Recreation: A National Perspective*. Ann Arbor, MI: Institute for Social Research.

Marans, R.W. (1972) Outdoor recreation behavior in residential environments. In Wohlwill, J.F. and Carson, D.H. (eds) *Environment and the Social Sciences: Perspectives and Applications*. Washington, DC: American Psychological Association.

Marshall, M. (1972) Privacy and environment. *Human Ecology*, 1, 93–110.

Martin, J. and O'Reilly, J. (1988) Editor's introduction: contemporary environment-behavior research in zoological parks. *Environment and Behavior*, 20, 387–395.

Maslow, A. (1954) *Motivation and Personality*. New York: Harper and Row.

Maslow, A.H. and Mintz, N.C. (1956) Effects of aesthetic surrounding: I. initial effects of three aesthetic conditions upon perceiving 'energy' and 'well-being' in faces. *Journal of Psychology*, 41, 247–254.

Mathes, K.E. and Canon, L.K. (1975) Environmental noise level as a determinant of helping behavior. *Journal of Personality and Social Psychology*, 32, 571–577.

Matthews, M.H. (1985) Young children's representation of the environment: a comparison of techniques. *Journal of Experimental Psychology*, 5, 261–278.

McAndrew, F.T. (1992) The home advantage also operates in individual sports: a study of high school wrestlers. Paper presented to the Eastern Psychological Association, Boston, MA.

McAndrew, F.T. (1993) *Environmental Psychology*. Pacific Grove, CA: Brooks/Cole.

McCain, G., Cox, V.C. and Paulus, P.B. (1976) The relationship between illness complaints and degree of crowding in a prison environment. *Environment and Behavior*, 8, 283–290.

McCallum, R., Rusbult, C., Hong, G., Walden, T. and Schopler, J. (1979) Effect of resource availability and importance of behavior on the experience of crowding. *Journal of Personality and Social Psychology*, 37, 1304–1313.

McCarthy, D.O., Ouimet, M.E. and Dunn, J.M. (1992) The effects of noise stress on leukocyte function in rats. *Research in Nursing and Health*, 15, 131–137.

McCarthy, D.P. and Saegert, S. (1979) Residential density, social overload and social withdrawal. In Aiello, J.R. and Baum, A. (eds) *Residential Crowding and Design*. New York: Plenum.

McCaul, K.D. and Kopp, J.T. (1982) Effects of goal-setting and commitment on increasing metal recycling. *Journal of Applied Psychology*, 67, 377–379.

McClelland, G.H., Schultze, W.D. and Hurd, B. (1990) The effect of risk beliefs on property values: a case study of a hazardous waste site. *Risk Analysis*, 10 (4), 485–497.

McDonald, J.E. and Gifford, R. (1989) Territorial cues and defensible space theory: the burglar's point of view. *Journal of Environmental Psychology*, 9, 193–205.

McDonal, T.P. and Pellegrino, J.W. (1993) Psychological perspectives on spatial cognition. In Garling, T. and Golledge, R.G. (eds) *Behavior and Environment: Psychological and Geographical Approaches.* Amsterdam: Elsevier.

McElroy, J.C., Morrow, P.C. and Wall, L.C. (1983) Generalizing impact of object language to other audiences: peer response to office design. Psychological Reports, 53, 315–322.

McFarland, R.A. (1972) Psychophysiological implications of life at high altitude and including the role of oxygen in the process of aging. In Yousef, M.K., Horvath, S.M. and Bullard, R.W. (eds) *Physiological Adaptations: Desert and Moutnain.* New York: Academic Press.

McGilley, B.M. and Holmes, D.S. (1988) Aerobic fitness and response to psychological stress. *Journal of Research in Personality,* 22, 129–139.

McKechnie, G.E. (1974) ERI Manual: *Environmental Response Inventory.* Berkeley, CA: Consulting Psychologists' Press.

McKechnie, G.E. (1977) Simulation techniques in environmental psychology. In Stokols, D. (ed) *Perspectives on Environment and Behavior.* New York: Plenum.

Meadows, D.H. (1985) Charting the way the world works. *Technology Review,* Feb/Mar, 54–63.

Meadows, D.H., Meadows, D.L. and Randers, J. (1992) *Beyond the Limits: Confronting Global Collapse; Envisioning a Sustainable Future.* Post Mills, Vermont: Chelsea Green.

Mearns, K. and Flin, R. (1996) Risk perception in hazardous industries. *The Psychologist,* 9(9), 401–404.

Medalia, N.Z. (1964) Air pollution as a socio-environmental health problem: a survey report. *Journal of Health and Human Behavior,* 5, 154–165.

Mehrabian, A. (1976a) *Manual for the Questionnaire Measure of Stimulus Screening and Arousability.* Los Angeles: Albert Mehrabian.

Mehrabian, A. (1976b) *Public Places and Private Spaces.* New York: Basic Books.

Mehrabian, A. (1978) Characteristic individual reactions to preferred and unpreferred environments. *Journal of Personality,* 46, 717–731.

Mehrabian, A. and Russell, J.A. (1974) *An Approach to Environmental Psychology.* Cambridge, MA: MIT Press.

Mendell, M.J. and Smith, A.H. (1990) Consistent patterns of elevated symptoms in air-conditioned office buildings: a re-analysis of epidemiologic studies. American Journal of Public Health, 80, 1193–1199.

Mendelsohn, R. and Orcutt, G. (1979) An empirical analysis of air pollution dose-response curves. *Journal of Environmental Economics and Management,* 6, 85–106.

Mercer, G.W. and Benjamin, M.L.)1980) Spatial behavior of university undergraduates in double-occupancy residence rooms: an inventory of effects. *Journal of Applied Social Psychology,* 10, 32–44.

Michelson, W. (1977) *Environmental Choice, Human Behavior and Residential Satisfaction.* New York: Oxofrd University Press.

Middlemist, R.D., Knowles, E.S. and Matter, C.F. (1976) Personal space invasions in the lavatory: Suggestive evidence for arousal. *Journal of Personality and Social Psychology,* 33, 541–546.

Milgram, S. (1970) The experience of living in cities. *Science,* 167, 1461–1468.

Miller, G.T. (1990) *Living in the Environment.* Belmont, CA: Wadsworth

Miller, P.A. (1984) Visual preference and implications for coastal management: A perceptual study of the British Columbia shoreline. Unpublished doctoral dissertation, University of Michigan, Ann Arbor, Michigan.

Miller, S. and Nardini, K.M. (1977) Individual differences in the perception of crowding, *Environmental Psychology and Nonverbal Behavior,* 2, 3–13.

Miller, S.M. and Mangan, C.E. (1983) Interacting effects of information and coping style in adapting to gynecologic stress: should the doctor tell all? *Journal of Personality and Social Psychology,* 45, 223–236.

Minckley, B. (1968) A study of noise and its relationship to patient discomfort in the recovery room. Nursing Research, 17, 247–250.

Minton, N.A. and Murray, V.S.G. (1988) A review of organophosphate poisoning. *Medical Toxicology,* 3, 350–375.

Mitchell, M.Y., Force, J.E., Carroll, M.S. and McLaughlin, W.J. (1991) Forest places of the heart: incorporating special places into public management. *Journal of Forestry*, 4, 32–37.

Mitchell, R. (1971) Some social implications of high-density housing. American Sociology Review, 36, 18–29.

Moar, I. (1978) Mental triangulation and the nature of internal representations of space. Unpublished PhD thesis, University of Cambridge.

Molloy, J.T. and Labahn, T. (1993) 'Operation getup' targets taggers to curb gang-related graffiti. *The Police Chief*, 121–123.

Montello, D.R. (1988) Classroom seating location and its effect on course achievement, participation and attitudes. *Journal of Environmental Psychology*, 8, 149–157.

More, T.A. (1973) Attitudes of Massachusetts hunters. In Hendee, J.C. and Schoenfeld, C. (eds) *Human Dimensions in Wildlife Programs*. Rockville, MD: Mercury.

Morris, P.A. (1982) The effect of pilgrimage on anxiety, depression and religious attitude. *Psychological Medicine*, 12, 291–294.

Morris, T., Greer, S., Pettingale, K.W. and Watson, M. (1981) Patterns of expression of anger and their psychological correlates in women with breast cancer. *Journal of Psychosomatic Research*, 25, 11–117.

Mueller, D. (1980) Social networks: a promising direction for research on the relationship of the social environment to psychiatric disorder. *Social Science and Medicine*, 14(A), 147–161

Muirhead, C. and Kendall, G. (1996) Hazards of exposure to radon. *Radiological Protection Bulletin*, 181, 8–11.

Naess, A. (1989) *Ecology, Community and Lifestyle: An Outline of an Ecosophy*. Cambridge: Cambridge University Press.

Nakshian, J.S. (1964) The effects of red and green surroundings on behaviour. *Journal of General Psychology*, 70, 143–161.

Nasar, J.L. (1981) Responses to different spatial configurations. *Human Factors*, 23, 439–446.

Nasar, J.L. and Min, M.S. (1984) Modifiers of perceived spaciousness anc crowding: a cross-cultural study. Paper presented at the Annual Meeting of the American Psychological Association, Toronto, Ontario.

Nash, R. (1982) *Wilderness and the American Mind* (3rd edn). New Haven: Yale university Press.

Navarro, P.L., Simpson-Housley, P. and DeMan, A.F. (1987) Anxiety, locus of control and appriasal of air pollution. *Perceptual and Motor Skills*, 64, 811–814.

Needleman, H.L., Leviton, A. and Bellinger, D. (1982) Lead-associated intellectual deficit. *New England Journal of Medicine*, 306, 367.

Neely, J. (1972) Thesis in energy utilisation. Cambridge, MA: Harvard University Press.

Neisser, U. (1976) *Cognitive Psychology*. New York: Appleton-Century-Crofts.

Nelson, P.D. (1976) Psychologists isn habitability research. Paper presented to the American Psychological Association, Washington, DC.

Nesbitt, P.D. and Steven, G. (1974) Personal space and stimulus intensity at a Southern California amusement park. *Sociometry*, 37, 105–115.

Newman, O. (1972) *Defensible Space: Crime Prevention through Urban Design*. New York: Macmillan.

Newman, O. and Franck, K.A. (1982) The effects of building size on personal crime and fear of crime. Population and Environment, 5, 203–220.

Nickerson, R.S. (1968) A note on long-term recognition memory for pictorial material. *Psychonomic Science*, 11, 58.

Normoyle, J. and Lavrakas, P.J. (1984) Fear of crime in elderly women: perceptions of control, predictability and territoriality. *Personality and Social Psychology Bulletin*, 10, 191–202.

Oberg, K. (1960) Cultural shock: adjustment to new cultural environments. *Practical anthropology*, 7, 177–182.

O'Connell, B.J., Harper, R.S. and McAndrew, F.T. (1985) Grip strength as a function of exposure to red or green visual stimulation. *Perceptual and Motor Skills*, 61, 1157–1158.

O'Keefe, J. and Nadel, L. (1987) *The Hippocampus as a Cognitive Map*. Oxford: Clarendon Press.

Oldham, G.R. and Brass, D.J. (1979) Employee reactions to an open-plan office: a naturally occurring quasi-experiment. *Administrative Science Quarterly*, 24, 267–284.

Ophuls, W. (1977) *Ecology and the Politics of Scarcity*. San Francisco: Freeman.

O'Riordan, T. (1976) Attitudes, behaviour and environmental policy issues. In Altman, I. and Wohlwill, J.F. (eds) *Human Behavior and the Environment: Advances in Theory and Research* (vol 1). New York: Plenum.

Orleans, P. (1973) Differential cognition of urban residents: effects of social scale on mapping. In Downs, R.M. and Stea, D. (eds) *Image and Environment: Cognitive Mapping and Spatial Behavior*. Chicago: Aldine.

Orleans, P. and Schmidt, S. (1972). Mapping the city: environmental cognition of urban residents. In Mitchell, W. (ed) *EDRA* 3. Los Angeles: University of California.

Ornstein, R. and Ehrlich, P. (1989) *New World, New Mind: Moving Towards Conscious Evolution*. New York: Touchstone /Simon and Schuster.

Osborne, J.G. and Powers, R.B. (1980) Controlling the litter problem. In Martin, G.L. and Osborne, J.G. (eds) *Helping the Community: Behavioral Applications*. New York: Plenum.

Osmond, H. (1959) The relationship between architect and psychiatrist. In Goshen, C. (ed) *Psychiatric Architecture*. Washington, DC: American Psychiatric Association.

Oxley, D., Haggard, L.M., Werner, C.M. and Altman, I. (1986) Transactional qualities of neighbourhood social networks: a cast study of 'Christmas Street'. Environment and Behavior, 18, 640–677.

Pablant, P. and Baxter, J.C. (1975) Environmental correlates of school vandalism. *Journal of the American Institute of Planners*, 270–279.

Page, R.A. (1977) Noise and helping behavior. *Environment and Behavior*, 9, 559–572.

Page, R.A. (1978) Environmental influences on prosocial behavior: the effect of temperature. Paper presented to the Midwestern Psychological Association, Chicago.

Palinkas, L.A. (1991b) Effects of physical and social environments on the health and well-being of Antarctic winter-over personnel. *Environment and Behavior*, 23, 782–799.

Pallack, M.S., Cook, D.A. and Sullivan, J.J. (1980) Commitment and energy conservation. In Bickman, L. (ed) *Applied Social Psychology Annual*, 1, 235–253..

Palmer, J.F. and Zube, E.H. (1976) Numerical and perceptual landscape classification. In Zube, E.H. (ed) *Studies in Landscape Perception*. Amherst, MA: Institute for Man and Environment, University of Massachusetts.

Pardini, A.U. and Katzev, R.D. (1984) The effect of strength of commitment on newspaper recycling. *Journal of Environmental Systems*, 13, 245–254.

Parks, C.D. (1994) The predictive ability of social values in resource dilemmas and public goods games. Personality and Social PSychology Bulletin, 20, 431–438.

Parr, A.E. (1996) Psychological aspects of urbanology. *Journal of Social Issues*, 22, 39–45.

Parron, T., et al. (1996) Increased risk of suicide with exposure to pesticides in an intensive agriculture area: a 12 year retrospective study. Forensic Science International, 79, 53–63.

Parsons, H.M. (1972) The bedroom. *Human Factors*, 14, 421–450.

Paslawskyj, L. and Ivinskis, A. (1980) Dominance, agonistic and territorial behaviour in institutionalised mentally retarded patients. *Australian Journal of Development Disabilities*, 6, 17–24.

Passini, R. (1990) Spatial representations, a wayfinding perspective. *Journal of Environmental Psychology*, 4, 153–164.

Passini, R., Proulx, G. and Rainville, C. (1990) The spatio-cognitive abilities of the visually impaired population. Environment and Behavior, 22, 91–118.

Patri, P. (1971) Personal communication. Cited in Ittelson, W.H., Proshansky, H.M., Rivlin, L.G. and Winkel, G.H. (1974) *An Introduction to Environmental Psychology*. New York: Holt, Rinehart and Winston.

Oatsfall, M.R., Feimer, N.R., Buhyoff, G.J. and Wellman, J.D. (1984) The prediction of scenic beauty from landscape content and composition. *Journal of Environmental Psychology*, 4, 7–26.

Patterson, A.H. and Chiswick, N.R. (1981) The role of the social and physical environment in privacy maintenance among the Iban of Borneo. *Journal of Environmental Psychology*, 1, 131–139.

Patterson, M. (1973) Stability of nonverbal immediacy behaviours. Journal of *Experimental Social Psychology*, 9, 97–109.

Patterson, M.L. (1976) An arousal model of interpersonal intimacy. *Psychological Review*, 83, 235–245.

Patterson, M.L. and Sechrest, L.B. (1970) Interpersonal distance and impression formation. *Journal of Personality*, 38, 161–166.

Pearce, P.L. (1977) Mental souvenirs: a study of tourists and their city maps. *Australian Journal of Psychology*, 29, 203–210.

Pearce, P.L. (1981) Environmental shock: a study of tourists' reactions to two tropical islands. *Journal of Applied Social Psychology*, 11, 268–280.

Pearce, P.L. (1982) *The Social Psychology of Tourist Behaviour*. Oxford: Pergamon.

Pearson, J.L. and Ialongo, N.S. (1986) The relationship between spatial ability and environmental knowledge. *Journal of Environmental Psychology*, 6, 299–304.

Pedersen, D.M. (1982) Cross-validation of privacy factors. *Perceptual and Motor Skills*, 55, 57–58.

Pellegrini, R.J., Schauss, A.G. and Birk, T.J. (1980) Leg strength as a function of exposure to visual stimuli of different hues. *Bulletin of the Psychonomic Society*, 16, 111–112.

Penwarden, A.D. (1973) Acceptable wind speeds in towns. *Building Science*, 8, 259–267.

Peters, J.S. (1990) Integrating psychological and economic perspectives on energy consumption: the determinants of thermostat setting behaviour. *Dissertation Abstracts International*, 51(4-B), 2116–2117.

Phifer, J.F. (1990) Psychological distress and somatic symptoms after natural disasters: differential vulnerability among older adults. *Psychology and Aging*, 5(3), 412–420.

Pilkington, E. (1995) Work till you drop. *Guardian*, 23 May.

Pitt, D.G. and Zube, E.H. (1987) Management of natural environments. In Stokols, D. and Altman, I. (eds) *Handbook of Environmental Psychology* (vol 2). New York: Wiley.

Platt, J. (1973) Social traps. *American Psychologist*, 28, 641–651.

Ponomarenko, I.J. (1966) The effect of constant high-frequency noise on certain physiological functions in adolescents. *Hygiene and Sanitation*, 31, 188–193.

Ponte, L. (1981) How artificial light affects your health. *Reader's Digest*, 118, 131–134.

Porteus, J. (1977) *Environment and Behavior*. Reading, MA: Addison-Wesley.

Poulton, E.C. (1970) *The Environment and Human Efficiency*. Springfield, IL: Charles C. Thomas.

Prak, N.L. and van Wegen, H.B.R. (1975) The influence of cognitive factors on the perception of buildings. Paper presented at the Annual Meeting of the Environmental Design Research Association, Lawrence, Kansas. President's Commission on Americans Outdoors (1987) *Final Report*. Washington, DC: US Government Printing Office.

Profusek, P.J. and Rainey, D.W. (1987) Effects of Baker-Miller pink and red on state anxiety, grip strength and motor precision. *Perceptual and Motor Skills*, 65, 941–942.

Proshansky, H.M. (1978) The city and self-identity. *Environment and Behavior*, 10, 147–169.

Proshansky, H.M., Ittelson, W.H. and Rivlin, L.G. (eds) (1970) *Environmental Psychology: Man and his Physical Setting*. New York: Holt, Rinehart and Winston.

Provins, K.A. and Bell, C.R. (1970) Effects of heat stress on the performance of two tasks running concurrently. *Journal of Experimental Psychology*, 85, 40–44.

Pylyshyn, Z.W. (1981) The imagery debate: analogue media versus tacit knowledge. *Psychological Review*, 88, 16–45.

Quarantelli, E.L. and Dynes, R.R. (1972) When disaster strikes. *Psychology Today*, 5(9), 66–70.

Raloff, J. (1982) Occupational noise – the subtle pollutant. *Science News*, 121, 347–350.

Ray, O. (1978) *Drugs, Society and Human Behavior* (2nd edn). St Louis, MO: Mosby.

Reason, J. (1990) *Human Error*. Cambridge: Cambridge University Press.

Reddy, D.M., Baum, A., Fleming, R. and Aiello, J.R. (1981) Mediation of social density by coalition formation. *Journal of*

Applied Social Psychology, 11, 529–537.

Reynolds, R. (1974) Community and occupational influences in stress at Cape Kennedy: relationship to heart disease. In Eliot, R.S. (ed) Stress and The Heart. Mt Kisko, NY: Future.

Rice, B. (1982) The Hawthorne defect: persistence of a flawed theory. Psychology Today, 16(2), 70–74.

Rim, Y. (1975) Psychological test performance during climatic heat stress from desert winds. International Journal of Biometeorology, 19, 37–40.

Robinson, E.S. (1928) The Behavior of the Museum Visitor. Washington, DC: American Association of Museums.

Rodin, J. (1976) Crowding, perceived choice and response to controllable and uncontrollable outcomes. Journal of Experimental Social Psychology, 12, 564–578.

Rodin, J. (1986) Aging and health: effects of the sense of control. Science, 233, 1271–1276.

Roethlisberger, F.J. and Dickson, W.J. (1939) Management and the Worker. Cambridge, MA: Harvard University Press.

Rohe, W.M. (1982) The response to density in residential settings: the mediating effects of social and personal variable. Journal of Applied Social Psychology, 12, 292–303.

Rohe, W. and Patterson, A.H. (1974) The effects of varied levels of resources and density on behavior in a day care centre. Paper presented to the Environmental Design Research Association, Milwaukee, WI.

Ronco, P. (1972) Human factors applied to hospital patient care. Human Factors, 16, 314–322.

Rosen, S. (1970) Noise, hearing and cardiovascular function. In Welch, B.L. and Welch, A.S. (eds) Physiological Effects of Noise. New York: Plenum.

Rosenthal, N.E. and Blehar, M.C. (eds) (1989) Seasonal Affective Disorders and Phototherapy. New York: Guilford.

Ross, R.T. (1938) Studies in the psychology of the theatre. Psychological Record, 2, 127–190.

Rossman, B.B. and Ulehla, Z.J. (1977) Psychological reward values associated with wilderness use: a functional-reinforcement approach. Environment and

Behavior, 9, 41–66.

Rotter, J. (1966) Generalised expectancies for internal versus external control of reinforcement. Psychological Monographs, 80 (whole No. 609).

Rotton, J. (1983) Affective and cognitive consequences of malodorous pollution. Basic and Applied Social Psychology, 4, 171–191.

Rotton, J. and Frey, J. (1984) Psychological costs of air pollution: atmospheric conditions, seasonal trends and psychiatric emergencies. Population and Environment, 7, 3–16.

Rotton, J. and Frey, J. (1985) Air pollution, weather and violent crimes: concomitant time-series analysis of archival data. Journal of Personality and Social Psychology, 49, 1207–1220.

Rotton, J., Barry, T., Frey, J. and Soler, E. (1978) Air pollution and interpersonal attraction. Journal of Applied Social Psychology, 8, 57–71.

Rotton, J., Frey, J., Barry, T., Milligan, M. and Fitzpatrick, M. (1979) The air pollution experience and interpersonal aggression. Journal of Applied Social Psychology, 9, 397–412.

Ruback, R.B. and Pandey, J. (1991) Crowding, perceived control and relative power: an analysis of households in India. Journal of Applied Social Psychology, 21, 315–344.

Rubonis, A.V. and Bickman, L. (1991) Psychological impairment in the wake of disaster: the disaster–psychopathology relationship. Psychological Bulletin, 109, 384–399.

Russell, J.A. and Lanius, U.F. (1984) Adaptation levels and the affective appraisal of environments. Journal of Environmental Psychology, 4, 119–135.

Russell, J.A. and Mehrabian, A. (1977) Evidence for a three-factor theory of emotions. Journal of Research in Personality, 11, 273–294.

Russell, J.A. and Ward, L.M. (1982) Environmental psychology. Annual Review of Psychology, 33, 651–688.

Russell, P. (1982) The Global Brain. Los Angeles: Tarcher.

Saarinen, T.F. (1973) The use of projective techniques in geogrpahic research. In Ittelson, W.H. (ed) Environment and Cognition. New York: Seminar Press.

Sadalla, E.K. and Oxley, D. (1984) The perception of room size: the rectangularity illusion. *Environment and Behavior*, 16, 394–405.

Sadalla, E.K. and Sheets, V.S. (1993) Symbolism in building materials: self-preservation and cognitive components. *Environment and Behavior*, 25, 155–180.

Sadalla, E.K., Vershure, B. and Burroughs, J. (1987) Identity symbolism in housing. Environment and Behavior, 19, 569–587.

Saegert, S., Mackintosh, E. and West, S. (1975) Two studies of crowding in urban public spaces. Environment and Behavior, 7, 159–184.

Samdahl, D.M. and Christensen, H.H. (1985) Environmental cues and vandalism: an exploratory study of picnic table carving. *Environment and Behavior*, 17, 445–458.

Samuelson, C.D. and Biek, M. (1991) Attitudes towards energy conservation: a confirmatory factor analysis. *Journal of Applied Social Psychology*, 21, 549–568.

Sandman, P.M., Weinstein, N.D. and Klotz, M.L. (1987) Public response to the risk from geological radon. *Journal of Communication*, 37, 93–108.

Savinar, J. (1975) The effect of ceiling height on personal space. *Man-Environment Systems*, 5, 321–324.

Schaeffer, G.H. and Patterson, M.L. (1980) Intimacy, arousal and small group crowding. Journal of Personality and Social Psychology, 38, 283–290.

Schauss, A. (1979) Tranquillising effect of color reduces aggressive behavior and potential violence. *Journal of Orthomolecular Psychiatry*, 8, 218–221.

Scherer, S.E. (1974) Proxemic behavior of primary school children as a function of their socioeconomic class and subculture. *Journal of Personality and Social Psychology*, 29, 800–805.

Schiffenbauer, A.I., Brown, J.E., Perry, J.L., Shulack, L.K. and Zanzola, A.M. (1977) The relationship between density and crowding: some architectural modifiers. *Environment and Behavior*, 9, 3–14.

Schmidt, F.N. and Gifford, R. (1989) A dispositional approach to hazard perception: preliminary development of the Environmental Appraisal Inventory. *Journal of Environmental Psychology*, 9, 57–67.

Schmidt, D.E. and Keating, J.P. (1979) Human crowding and personality control: an integration of research. *Psychological Bulletin*, 86, 680–700.

Schmitt, R.C. (1966) Density, health and social disorganisation. *Planners*, 32, 38–40.

Schrodt, P.A. (1981) Conflict as a determinant of territory. *Behavioural Science*, 26, 37–50.

Schwartz, B. and Barsky, S.F. (1977) The home advantage. *Social Forces*, 55, 641–661.

Sears, D.O., Peplau, L.A. and Taylor, S.E. (1991) *Social Psychology* (7th edn). Englewood Cliffs, NJ: Prentice-Hall.

Seaton, R. (1968) *Miscellaneous Undergraduate Research on Spatial Behavior: A Classified and Annotated Listing*. Berkeley: Dept of Architecture, University of California.

Sebba, R. (1991) The landscapes of childhood: the reflection of childhood's environment in adult memories and in children's attitudes. *Environment and Behavior*, 23, 395–442.

Sebba, R. and Churchman, A. (1983) Territories and territoriality in the home. *Environment and Behavior*, 15, 191–210.

Segall, M.H., Campbell, D.T. and Herskovits, M.J. (1966) *The Influence of Culture on Visual Perception*. Indianapolis: Bobbs-Merrill.

Seligman, M.E.P. (1970) On the generality of the laws of learning. *Psychological Review*, 77, 406–418.

Seligman, M.E.P. (1975) *Helplessness*. San Francisco: Freeman.

Sells, S.B. and Wills, D.P. (1971) *Accidents, Police Incidents and Weather: A Further Study of the City of Fort Worth, Texas, 1968*. Technical report no. 15, Fort Worth Group Psychology Branch, Office of Naval Research and Institute of Behavioral Research, Texas Christian University, Fort Worth.

Selye, H. (1956) *The Stress of Life*. New York: McGraw-Hill.

Shaffer, D.R. and Sadowski, C. (1975) This table is mine: respect for marked barroom tables as a function of gender of spatial marker and desirability of locale. *Sociometry*, 38, 408–419

Sheets, V.L. and Manzer, C.D. (1991) Affect, cognition and urban vegetation: some effects of adding trees along city streets. *Environment and Behavior*, 23, 285–304.

Sherif, M., Harvey, O.J., White, B.J., Hood, W.R. and Sherif, C.W. (1961) Intergroup conflict and co-operation: the Robber's Cave experiment. Norman, Oklahoma: University of Oklahoma Press.

Sherrod, D.R., Hage, J., Halpern, P.L. and Moore, B.S. (1977) Effects of personal causation and perceived control on responses to an aversive environment: the more control the better. *Journal of Experimental Social Psychology*, 13, 14–27.

Shetter-Neuber, J. (1988) Second- and third-generation zoo exhibits: a comparison of visitor, staff and animal responses. *Environment and Behavior*, 20, 452–473.

Shiva, V. (1989) *Staying Alive: Women, Ecology and Development*. London: Zed Books.

Siegel, A.W. and White, S. (1975) The development of spatial representations of large-scale environments. In Reese, H.W. (ed) *Advances in Child Development and Behavior*. New York: Academic Press.

Sienkiewicz, Z. and Chadwick, P., (1996) Health Effects of EMF's. *Radiological Protection Bulletin*, 181.

Sims, J.H. and Baumann, D.D. (1972) The tornado threat: coping styles of the North and South. *Science*, 176, 1386–1391.

Sims, J.H. and Baumann, D.D. (1983) Education programs and human response to natural hazards. *Environment and Behavior*, 15, 165–189.

Sjoberg, P. and Drottz-Sjoberg, M.B. (1991) Knowledge and risk perception among nuclear power plant employees. *Risk Analysis*, 11, 607–618.

Skinner, B.F. (1938) *The Behavior of Organisms*. New York: Appleton-Century-Crofts.

Skinner, B.F. (1958) *Science and Human Behavior*. New York: Macmillan.

Sloan, A.W. (1979) *Man in Extreme Environments*. Springfield, IL: Charles C. Thomas.

Slotsky, R.J. (1973) *Wilderness Experience: a Therapeutic Modality*. San Francisco: School of Professional Psychology.

Slovic, P., Fischhoff, B. and Lichtenstein, S. (1978) Accident probabilities and seat belt usage: a psychological perspective. *Accident Analysis and Prevention*, 10, 281–285.

Smith, C.J. and Patterson, G.E. (1980) Cognitive mapping and the subjective geography of crime. In Georges-Abeyie, D.E. and Harries, K.D. (eds) *Crime: A Spatial Perspective*. New York: Columbia University Press.

Smith, H.W. (1981) Territorial spacing on a beach revisited: a cross-national exploration. *Social Psychology Quarterly*, 44, 132–137.

Socolow, R.H. (1978) *Saving Energy in the Home*. Cambridge, MA: Ballinger.

Solomon, S.D. and Canino, G.J. (1990) Appropriateness of DSM-III-R criteria for Posttraumatic Stress Disorder. *Comprehensive Psychiatry*, 31, 227–237.

Sommer, R. (1959) Studies in personal space. *Sociometry*, 22, 247–260.

Sommer, R. (1969) *Personal Space*. Englewood Cliffs, NJ: Prentice-Hall.

Sommer, R. (1972) *Design Awareness*. San Francisco: Rinehart Press.

Sommer, R. (1987) Dreams, reality and the future of environmental psychology. In Stokols, D. and Altman, I. (eds) *The Handbook of Environmental Psychology*. New York: Wiley.

Sommer, R. and Becker, F.D. (1969) Territorial defense and the good neighbour. *Journal of Personality and Social Psychology*, 11, 85–92.

Sommer, R. and Olsen, H. (1980) The soft classroom. *Environment and Behavior*, 12, 3–16.

Sommer, R. and Ross, H. (1958) Social interaction on a geriatrics ward. *International Journal of Social Psychiatry*, 4, 128–133.

Sommers, P. and Moos, R.H. (1976) The weather and human behavior. In Moos, R.H. (ed) *The Human Context: Environmental Determinants of Behavior*. New York: Wiley.

Sonnenfeld, J. (1966) Variable values in space and landscape: an enquiry into the nature of environmental necessity. *Journal of Social Issues*, 22, 71–82.

Sonnenfeld, J. (1969) Personaity and behavior in environment. *Proceedings of the Association of American Geographers*, 1, 136–140.

Spencer, C. and Darvizeh, Z. (1981) The case for developing a cognitive environmental psychology that does not underestimate the abilities of young children. *Journal of Environmental Psychology*, 1, 21–31.

Spielberger, C.D. (1972) Anxiety as an emotional state. In Spielberger, C.D. (ed)

Anxiety: Current Trends in Theory and Research (vol 1). New York: Academic Press.

Spivey, G.H., Brown, C.P., Baloh, R.W. et al. (1979) Subclinical effects of chronic increased lead absorption – a prospective study. I. Study design and analysis of symptoms. *Journal of Occupational Medicine*, 21, 423–429.

Srivastava, R.K. and Peel, T.S. (1968) *Human Movement as a Function of Color Stimulation*. Topeka, KS: Environmental Research Foundation.

Stankey, G.H. (1972) A strategy for the definition and management of wilderness quality. In Krutilla, J.V. (ed) *Natural Environments: Studies in Theoretical and Applied Analysis*. Baltimore: Johns Hopkins University Press.

Stansfield, S.A., Sharp, D.S., Gallacher, J and Babisch, W. (1993) Road traffic noise, noise sensitivty and psychological disorder. *Psychological Medicine*, 23, 977–985.

Steinglass, P. and Gerrity, E. (1990) Natural disasters and post-traumatic stress Disorder: short-term versus long-term recovery in two disaster-affected communities. *Journal of Applied Social Psychology*, 20, 1746–1765.

Stephens, R. and Spurgeon, A. (1995) Neuropsychological effects of long-term exposure to organophosphates in sheep dip. *Lancet*, 345, 1135–1138.

Stern, P.C. (1992b) What psychology knows about energy conservation. *American Psychologist*, 47, 1225–1232.

Stern, P.C. and Gardner, G. (1981) Psychological research and energy policy. *American Psychologist*, 36. 329–342.

Stevens, W., Kushler, M., Jeppesen, J. and Leedom, N. (1979) *Youth Energy Education Stategies: A Statistical Evaluation*. Lansing, MI: Energy Extension Service, Dept of Commerce.

Stewart, T.R. (1987) Developing an observer-based measure of environmental annoyance. In Koelega, H.S. (ed) *Environmental Annoyance: Characterisation, Measurement and Control*. New York: Elsevier.

Stokols, D. (1972) On the distinction between density and crowding: some implications for further research. *Psychological Review*, 79, 275–277.

Stokols, D. and Altman, I. (eds) (1987) *Handbook of Environmental Psychology*. New York: Wiley.

Stokols, D. and Novaco, R.W. (1981) Transportation and well-being. In Altman, I., Wohlwill, J.F. and Everett, P. (eds) *Transportation and Behavior*. New York: Plenum Press.

Stokols, D., Shumaker, S.A. and Martinez, J. (1983) Residential mobility and personal well-being. *Journal of Environmental Psychology*, 3, 5–19.

Stone, E.F., Gueutal, H.G., Gardner, D.G. and McClure, S. (1983) A field experiment comparing information-porivacy values, beliefs and attitudes across several types of organisations. *Journal of Applied Psychology*, 68, 459–468.

Storms, M.D. and Thomas, G.C. (1977) Reactions to physical closeness. *Journal of Personality and Social Psychology*, 35, 412–418.

Studer, R. (1970) The organisation of spatial stimuli. In Pastalan, L. and Carson, D. (eds) *The Spatial Behavior of Older People*. Ann Arbor, MI: University of Michigan Press.

Study of Critical Environmental Problems (SCEP) (1970) *Man's Impact on the Global Environment: Assessment and Recommendations for Action*. Cambridge, MA: MIT Press.

Suedfeld, P. (1987) Extreme and unusual environments. In Stokols, D. and Altman, I. (eds) *Handbook of Environmental Psychology*. New York: Wiley.

Suedfeld, P. and Mocellin, J.S.P. (1987) The 'sensed presence' in unusual environments. *Environment and Behavior*, 19, 33–52.

Suedfeld, P., Turner, J.W. and Fine, T.H. (eds) (1990) *Restricted Environmental Stimulation: Theoretical and Empirical Developments in Flotation REST*. New York: Springer.

Sundstrom, E. (1978) Crowding as a sequential process: review of research on the effects of population density on humans. In Baum, A. and Epstein, Y.M. (eds) *Human Response to Crowding*. Hillsdale, NJ: Erlbaum.

Sundstrom, E. (1986) *Work Places: The Psychology of the Physical Environment in Offices and Factories*. New York: Cambridge University Press.

Sundstrom, E., Herbert, R.K. and Brown, D.W. (1982a) Privacy and communication in an open-plan office: a case study. *Environment and Behavior*, 14, 379–392.

Sundstrom, E., Town, J.P., Brown, D.W., Forman, A. and McGee, C. (1982b) Physical enclosure, type of job and privacy in the office. *Environment and Behavior*, 14, 543–559.

Sundstrom, E., Town, J.P., Rice, R.W., Osborn, D.P. and Brill, M. (1994) Office noise, satisfaction and performance. *Environment and Behavior*, 26, 195–222.

Sussman, N.M. and Rosenfeld, H.M. (1982) Touch, justification and sex: influence on the aversiveness of spatial violations. *Journal of Social Psychology*, 106, 215–225.

Swan, J.A. (1970) Response to air pollution: a study of attitudes and coping strategies of high school youths. *Environment and Behavior*, 2, 127–152.

Tarnopolsky, A., Watkins, G. and Hand, D.J. (1980) Aircraft noise and mental health: 1. Prevalence of individual symptoms. *Psychological Medicine*, 10, 683–698.

Taylor, R.B. and Lanni, J.C. (1981) Territorial dominance: the influence of the resident advantage in triadic decision-making. *Journal of Personality and Social Psychology*, 41, 909–915.

Taylor, R.B. and Stough, R.R. (1978) Territorial cognition: assessing Altman's typology. *Journal of Personality and Social Psychology*, 36, 419–423.

Taylor, S. and Brown, J. (1988) Illusion and well-being: a social psychological perspective on mental health. *Psychological Bulletin*, 103, 193–210.

Thompson, S.C. and Stoutmeyer, K. (1991) Water use as a commons dilemma: the effects of education that focuses on long-term consequences and individual action. *Environment and Behavior*, 23, 314–333.

Thomson, G. (1986) *The Museum Environment* (2nd edn). Stoneham, MA: Butterworth.

Thrower, T. (1987) Kitchen designs lay traps for the elderly. *Geriatric Medicine*, February, 67–69.

Tinsley, H.E. and Johnson, T.L. (1984) A preliminary taxonomy of leisure activities. *Journal of Leisure Research*, 16, 234–244.

Tolchinsky, P.D., McCuddy, M.K., Adams, J., Ganster, D.C., Woodman, R.W. and Fromkin, H.C. (1981) Employee perceptions of invasion of privacy: a field

simulation experiment. *Journal of Applied Psychology*, 66, 308–313.

Tolman, E.C. (1948) Cognitive maps in rats and men. *Psychological Review*, 55, 189–208.

Tooby, J. and Cosmides, L. (1990) The past explains the present: emotional adaptations and the structure of ancestral environments. *Ethology and Sociobiology*, 11, 375–424.

Tracor (1971) *Community Reaction to Aircraft Noise* (vol 1) (NASA Report CR-1761). Washington, DC: National Aeronautics and Space Administration.

Treisman, A.M. (1964) Verbal cues, language and meaning in selective attention. *American journal of Psychology*, 77, 206–219.

Trigg, L.J., Perlman, D., Perry, R.P. and Janisse, M.P. (1976) Antipollution behavior: a function of perceived outcome and locus of control. *Environment and Behavior*, 8, 307–313.

Trites, D., Galbraith, F.D., Sturdavent, M. and Leckwart, J.F. (1970) Influence of nursing unit design on the activities and subjective feelings of nursing personnel. *Environment and Behavior*, 2, 303–334.

Tromp, S.W. (1980) *Biometeorology: The Impact of Weather and Climate on Humans and Their Environment*. Philadelphia: Heyden.

Trowbridge, C.C. (1913) On fundamental methods of orientation and 'imaginary maps'. *Science*, 88, 888–896.

Turnage, J.J. (1990) The challenge of new workplace technology for psychology. *American Psychsologist*, 45, 171–178.

Turner, C.W., Layton, J.F. and Simons, L.S. (1975) Naturalistic studies of aggressive behaviour: aggressive stimuli, victim visibility and horn honking. *Journal of Personality and social Psychology*, 31, 1098–1107.

Tversky, A. and Kahneman, D. (1973) Abailability: a heuristic for judging frequency and probability. *Cognitive Psychology*, 5, 207–232.

Tversky, B. (1981) Distortions in memory for maps. *Cognitive Psychology*, 13, 407–433.

Tye, M. (1991) *The Imagery Debate*. Cambridge, MA: MIT Press.

Tyler, T.R. (1980) Impact of directly and indirectly experienced events: the origin of crime-related judgements and behaviours. *Journal of Personality and Social Psychology*, 39(1), 13–28.

Ulrich, R.S. (1979) Visual landscapes and psychological well-being. *Landscape Research*, 4, 17–23.

Ulrich, R.S. (1981) Natural versus urban scenes: some psychophysiological effects. *Environment and Behavior*, 13, 523–556.

Ulrich, R.S. (1984) View through a window may influence recovery from surgery. *Science*, 224, 420–421.

Ulrich, R.S. (1993) Biophilia and the conservation ethic. In Kellert, S.R. and Wilson, L.O. (eds) *The Biophilis Hypothesis*. Washington, DC: Island Press.

UNESCO-MAB (1988) *Man Belongs to the Earth*. Paris: UNESCO.

US Riot Commission (1968) *Report of the National Advisory Commission on Civil Disorders*. New York: Bantam.

Valins, S. and Baum, A. (1973) Residential group size, social interaction and crowding. *Environment and Behavior*, 5, 421–439.

Vaughan, E. (1993) Individual and cultural differences in adaptation to environmental risks. *American Psychologist*, 48, 673–680.

Veitch, J.A., Gifford, R. and Hine, D.W. (1991) Demand characteristics and full-spectrum lighting effects on performance and mood. *Journal of Environmental Psychology*, 11, 87–95.

Veitch, R. and Arkkelin, D. (1995) *Environmental Psychology*. Englewood Cliffs, NJ: Prentice-Hall.

Vinsel, A., Brown, B., Altman, I. and Foss, C. (1980) Privacy regulation, territorial displays and effectiveness of individual functioning. *Journal of Personality and Social Psychology*, 39, 1580–1607.

Walden, T.A., Nelson, P.A. and Smith, D.E. (1981) Crowding, privacy and coping. *Environment and Behavior*, 13, 205–224.

Walmsley, D.J., Boskovic, R.M. and Pigram, J.J. (1983) Tourism and crime: an Australian perspective. *Journal of Leisure Research*, 15, 136–155.

Wandersman, A. (1981) A framework of participation in community organisations. *Journal of Applied Behavioral Science*, 17, 27–58.

Wang, T.H. and Katzev, R.D. (1990) Group commitment and resource conservation: two field experiments on promoting recycling. *Journal of Applied Social Psychology*, 20, 265–275.

Warren, D.H. and Scott, T.F. (1993) Map alignment in travelling multisegment routes. *Environment and Behavior*, 25, 643–666.

Warren, D.I. (1978) Exploration in neighbourhood differentiation. *Sociological Quarterly*, 19, 310–331.

Wecker, S.C. (1964) Habitat selection. *Scientific American*, 211, 109–116.

Weenig, M.W.H., Schmidt, T. and Midden, C.J.H. (1990) Social dimensions of neighborhoods and the effectiveness of information programs. *Environment and Behavior*, 22, 27–54.

Weinstein, C.S. and Pinciotti, P. (1988) Changing a schoolyard: intentions, design decisions and behavioral outcomes. *Environment and Behavior*, 20, 345–371.

Weinstein, N. (1978) Individual differences in reactions to noise: a longitudinal study in a college dormitory. *Journal of Applied Psychology*, 63, 458–466.

Weinstein, N. (1989) Effects of personal experience on self-protective behaviour. *Psychological Bulletin*, 105, 31–50.

Weiss, B. (1983) Behavioral toxicology and environmental health science. *American Psychologist*, 38, 1174–1187.

Welch, B.L. (1979) *Extra-auditory Effects of Industrial Noise: Surveys of Foreign Literature*. Dayton, OH: Aerospace Medical Research Laboratory, Wright Patterson Airforce Base.

Wener, R. and Keys, C. (1988) The effects of changes in jail population densities on crowding, sick call and spatial behavior. *Journal of Applied Social Psychology*, 18, 852–866.

Wener, R., Frazier, F.W. and Farbstein, J. (1987) Building better jails. *Psychology Today*, 21, 40–44, 48–49.

Westin, A.F. (1970) *Privacy and Freedom*. New York: Athenaeum.

Westin, A.F. (1967) *Privacy and Freedom*. New York: Athenaeum.

Wxner, L.B. (1954) The degree to which colors (hues) are associated with mood-tones. *Journal of Applied Psychology*, 38, 432–435.

Wheeler, E. (1967) Architectural considerations in planning for handicapped children. *Rehabilitation and Physical Medicine.* Section XIX, March.

White, K. (1967) The historical roots of our ecologic crisis. *Science*, 155, 1203–1207.

White, M., Kasi, S.V., Zahner, G.E.P. and Will, J.C. (1987) Perceived crime in the neighborhood and mental health of women and children. *Environment and Behavior*, 19, 588–613.

Wiggins, J.S. (1975) The relationship between personality characteristics and attitudes towards housing and related facilities in six Army posts. Unpublished manuscript, University of Illinois.

Willis, F.N. (1966) Initial speaking distance as a function of the speakers' relationship. *Psychonomic Science*, 5, 49–55.

Wilson, G.D. (1966) Arousal properties of red versus green. *Perceptual and Motor Skills*, 23, 947–949.

Wilson, O. (1984) *Biophilia: The Human Bond with Other Species.* Cambridge, MA: Harvard University Press.

Wilson, S. (1972) Intensive care delirium. *Archives of Internal Medicine*, 130. 225.

Winett, R.A. (1978) Prompting turning-out lights in unoccupied rooms. *Journal of Environmental Systems*, 6, 237–241.

Winett, R.A., Hatcher, J.W., Fort, T.R. et al. (1982) The effects of videotape modelling and daily feedback on residential electricity conservation, home temperature and humidity, perceived comfort and clothing worn: winter and summer. *Journal of Applied Behaviour Analysis*, 15, 381–402.

Winneke, G. and Kastka, J. (1987) Comparison of odor-annoyance data from different industrial sources: problems and implications. In Koelega, H.S. (ed) *Environmental Annoyance: Characterisation, Measurement and Control.* Amsterdam: Elsevier.

Wohlwill, J.F. (1966) The physical environment: a problem for a psychology of stimulation. *Journal of Social Issues*, 22, 29–38.

Wohlwill, J.F. (1974) Human response to levels of environmental stimulation. *Human Ecology*, 2, 127–147.

Wohlwill, J.F. (1976) Environmental aesthetics: the environment as a source of affect. In Altman, I. and Wohlwill, J.F. (eds) *Human Behavior and the Environment:*

Behavior and the Natural Environment (vol 1). New York: Plenum.

Wolfgang, J. and Wolfgang, A. (1971) Explanation of attitudes via physical interpersonal distance toward the obese, drug users, homosexuals, police and other marginal figures. *Journal of Clinical Psychology*, 27, 510–512.

Womble, P. and Studebaker, S. (1981) Crowding in a national park campground: Kamtai National Monument in Alaska. *Environment and Behavior*, 13, 557–573.

Woods, J.E. (1988) Recent developments for heating, cooling and ventilating buildings. *State of the Art Reviews* (Stockholm, Sweden, Swedish Council for Building Research, Healthy Buildings), 1, 99–197.

Worchel, S. and Lollis, M. (1982) Reactions to territorial contamination as a function of culture. *Personality and Social Psychology Bulletin*, 8, 370–375.

Worchel, S. and Teddlie, C. (1976) The experience of crowding: a two-factor theory. *Journal of Personality and Social Psychology*, 34, 36–40.

Worchel, S. and Yohai, S. (1979) The role of attribution in the experience of crowding. *Journal of Experiment Social Psychology*, 15, 91–104.

Wright, R. (1994) Population bomb fuse still sizzles. Los Angeles Times, reprinted in the Ann Arbor (MI) News, Aug 24, p.A-1.

Yancey, W.L. (1971) Architecture, interaction and social control: the case of a lrge-scale public housing project. *Environment and Behavior*, 3, 3–21.

Yates, S. (1982) Using prospect theory to create persuasive communications about solar water heaters and insulation. Unpublished doctoral dissertation, University of California, Santa Cruz, CA.

Yerkes, R.M. and Dodson, J.D. (1908) The relation of strength of stimulus to rapidity of habit-formation. *Journal of Comparative and Neurological Psychology*, 18, 459–482.

Yoors, J. (1967) *The Gypsies.* New York: Simon and Schuster.

Zajonc, R.B. (1965) Social facilitation. *Science*, 149, 269–274.

Zajonc, R.B. (1980) Compresence. In Paulus, P.B. (ed) *Psychology of Goup Influence.* Hillsdale, NJ: Erlbaum.

Zehner, R.B. (1972) Neighborhood and community satisfaction: a report on new towns and less planned suburbs. In Wohlwill, J.F. and Carson, D.H. (eds) *Environment and the Social Sciences: Perspectives and Applications.* Washington, DC: American Psychological Association.

Zifferblatt, S.M., Curtis, C.S. and Pinsky, J.C. (1980) Understanding food habits. *Journal of the American Dietetic Association*, 76, 9–14.

Zimbardo, P.G. (1969) The human choice: individuation, reason and order versus deindividuation, impulse and chaos. In Arnold, W.J. and Levine, D. (eds) *Nebraska Symposium on Motivation*. Lincoln, NE: University of Nebraska Press.

Zimolong, B. (1985) Hazard perception and risk estimation in accident causation. In Eberts, R.E. and Eberts, G.G. (eds) *Trends in Ergonomics/Human Factors II*. Amsterdam: Elsevier.

Zlutnik, S. and Altman, I. (1972) Crowding and human behavior. In Wohlwill, J.F. and Carson, D.H. (eds) *Environment and the Social Sciences: Perspectives and Applications.* Washington, DC: American Psychological Association.

Zube, E.H., Pitt, D.G. and Evans, G.W. (1983) A lifespan developmental study of landscape assessment. *Journal of Environmental Psychology*, 3, 115–128.

Zubeck, J. (1969) *Sensory Deprivation: 15 Years of Research*. New York: Appleton-Century-Crofts.

Zuckerman, M. (1979) *Sensation-seeking: Beyond the Optimal Level of Arousal*. Hillsdale, NJ: Erlbaum.

Zuckerman, M. (1980) To risk or not to risk. In Blankstein, K.R., Pliner, P. and Polivy, J. (eds) *Assessment and Modification of Emotional Behavior*. New York: Plenum.

INDEX

Abey-Wickrama, I. 9, 147
accommodation *see* residential environments
accretion measures 12
acid rain 188, 204
action *see* reasoned action
adaptation 26, 156
adaptation level theory 39, 167
Adler, A. 162
advocacy issue 204
aesthetics 5, **6**, 37–8, 96, 185–8
affect *see* emotion
affordances 23
age 71
   see also children; elderly persons
aggression 48, 51, 87
agrochemicals 62, 191–2, **193**
air pollution 58–61, 146, 188–90, 191
air pollution syndrome (APS) 59
air pressure 58, 146
air quality 55–61, 63–4
aircraft noise 147
Ajzen, I. 116, **117**
alpha personal space 67–8
alternative energy sources 197–8
altitude 58
Altman, I.
   environmental psychology definition 2
   place attachment 97
   population density 84, 85
   privacy 82, 83, 100
   social environment model **91**
   territory 77
altruistic behaviour 87
ambient stimulation 44
ambient stressors 142, 143, 145–55
Ames room 3, 24
analogue representations 33
anchor point hypothesis 30
Angyal, A. 122
animals, social environment 76, 85–6
anomie tourists 132
Antartica 163–4
antecedent theories of
   crowding 89
   environmental preservation 180, 182,
      186, 195–8, 200
antecedent strategies (conservation) 180,
   182, 185, 200

anthropometric standards 94
Appleton, J. 121
Appleyard, D. 28, 31
appraisal
   EAI 156
   environmental 36–43
   stress 138, 151, 167–8
approach-avoidance conflicts 74
APS *see* air pollution syndrome
Archea, J. 85
architectural determinism 94
architecture 4
   see also design
archival research 12
Ardrey 75, 79
arousal
   aesthetics 38
   cognition theory 74, **75**
   crowding 89
   performance 105–6
   personal space 73, 74
   stress 140, 165
artificial light 52–4, 101
asbestos 62
attachment, place 40, 97–8
attitudes
   behaviour 43, 115–16, 182–4
   Ecological Attitude Scale 41
   environmental appraisal 41–3
   natural environment 115–18
attraction 70, 72, 87
attribution 72
augmentation 35
autonomy 122
availability heuristic 177
Averill, J.R. 167

Bailey, J.S. 200
Baird, B.N. 174–6
Baltes, M.M. 186
Bandura, A. 42
Banzinger, G. 56
Barker, R. 4, 89
Barker, R.G. 165
barometric pressure 58, 146
Baron, R.A. 51, 57
Baron, R.M. 187, 188
Baum, A. 87–8, 95, 104, 148, 151, 156, 163

Beaufort wind scale **55**, 56
Becker, F.D. 12, 78
behavioural constraint 158, 167
behavioural geography 4
behavioural sink studies 86, 147
belief 41
Bell, P.A. 10, 51, 114, **166**, 168, 180
Bem, D.J. 41
benefits *see* costs and benefits
Benjamin, M.L. 77
Berlyne, D.E. 38, 120
beta personal space 67
Bickman, L. 157, 182
Biek, M. 182–3
biodiversity 171, 204
biophilia 118
biophobia 118
Black, J.C. 100
blind persons 31
Bochner, S. 134
body temperature 48, 49–50
Borsky, P.N. 46
bottom-up processing 19, **20**
Brennan's Law 35
Briere, J. 146
Broadbent, D.E. 165
Bromet, E. 62
Brower, S. 76, 77, 144
Brown, J. 176
Brown, L. 178
Brown, P.J. 128
Brunswik, E. 2, 23
Buell 143
building-related illness 63
built environment 4, 5, 88, 92–114
Bullinger, M. 146
Bunting, T.E. 123
Burch, W.R. 128
Burgess, R.L. 186
burglary 78–9
butterfly curve hypothesis 39
Byrne, D. 72

Calhoun, J.B. 4, **86**, 147
cancer 188, 189
Canter, D. 4
carbon dioxide 59
carbon monoxide 59, 60, 61
carpentered world hypothesis 25
Carson, R. 170
Cass, R.C. 36, **37**
cataclysmic stressors 142, 143, 155–63
CERI *see* Children's Environmental Response
   Inventory

Chadwick, P. 195
change, perception 26–7
Charry **57**
Chavis, D.M. 113
Cheek, W.H. 128
Chernobyl 1, 163
children
   CERI 123
   environmental preferences 126
   light 53
   school design 108–9
   spatial cognition 31–3
Chiras, D.D. 173, 179
Chiswick, N.R. 84
chloroflurocarbons CFC's 59, 60
Christian, J.J. 86
Christianity 117
CID *see* Comfortable Interpersonal Distance
   Scale
cities 35–6, 114, 165
classical conditioning 41–2, 115
classrooms 108, 165
closed-plan interiors 102
clothing 48, 49
cognition
   see also perception
   environmental 5–7, 18–43
cognitive abilities, task performance 12
cognitive bias 177
cognitive maps 5–7, 10, **11**, 14, 27–36
Cohen, S.A. 12, 46, 47, 141–2, 145
coherence 37, 121
Cohn, D. 200
Cohn, E.G. 56
'cold weather helping norm' 50
   collative properties
   environmental appraisal 38
natural environment 120
colour 54–5, 95–6
colour coding 35–6
comfort 73
comfort envelopes 49
Comfortable Interpersonal Distance Scale
   (CID) 68
Commons, The 177–8
communal space 111
communication 40, 74
communities 113–14, 134, 184–5
commuting 154–5
complexity 37, 38, 65, 120, 121
concept-driven processing *see* top-down
   processing
conditioning *see* classical conditioning;
   operant conditioning

confidence 128
conflict 81
confounding variables 8
consent see informed consent
consequence models, crowding 89
consequent strategies, preservation 180–1,
    186, 198, **200**
conservation
    economic issues 201
    energy 193–8, **199**
    resources 159, 204
    strategies 180–5
    water 198–200
consistency theories 43, 115
constancy 26–7
contrast 120
control
    crowding 87, 89
    environmental preference 126
    natural disasters 156–7
    noise 46
    risk 154, 176
    stress 138, 143, 151, 167
    territorial 79
convergence, natural environments 120
Coote, J.A. 159
coping strategies, stress 141, 145, 151
Cornelius, P.E. 164
correlational studies 9
costs and benefits, environmental damage
    174–6
Cousins, L.R. 123
Cox, V.C. 87, 112, 148
Cox, T. 138
Craik, K.H. 10, 36
crime 50–1, 78–9, 103, 148–9
'crisis effect' 156
Crompton, J. 132
crowding 85–9, **90**, 130–1, 147–8
cue utilisation 23–4
cultural factors
    crowding 88
    environmental perception 24–5
    personal space 72
    privacy 84
    territory 77–8
culture shock **134**
Cunningham, M.R. 50
curtailment, energy useage 195–7
Cuthbertson, B.H. 159
Cvetkovich, G. 155, 176

daily hassles 142, 143
Dann, G. 132

darkness 53
data collection techniques 10–12
data-driven processing see bottom-up
    processing
De Groot, I. 59
De Jonge, D. 35
De Joy, D. 176
death imprint 162
deep ecology 182
defence 78–9
defensible space 77
demographic variables, environmental
    preference 126
density, population 85–9, **90**, 147–8
density-intensity model 87, 89
dependent variables 8
Deregowski 24
descriptions, environmental appraisal 36, **37**
descriptive research 9
design 4, 92–114
destinations 132–3
detection, stimuli 19
determinism, architectural 94
development, spatial cognition 31–3
De Young, R. 200
difference, 'just noticeable' 19
differences see cultural differences;
    individual differences; sex differences
Dillon, H. 162
disasters 7, 142, 143, 155–63
disposition 124
    see also personality
distance perception 21, **23**
distortion, cognitive maps 35
dominance 79
dormitories 87, 104, 109, 148
Dosey, M. 73
Downs, R.M. 28, 31, 34–5
driving 154–5
Drottz-Sjoberg, M.B. 159
dust (particulates) 61

EAI *see* Environmental Appraisal Inventory
Earle, T. 155, 176
Eastlake **152**, **153**
Ebbesen, E.B. 114
ecocentrism 118
ecofeminism 182
ecological approaches
    crowding 89
    PTSD 159
Ecological Attitude Scale 41
ecological perception 21–2
ecological psychology 4, 165

ecological theory 3
ecological validity 23, 24
ecology, deep 182
economic issues, conservation 201
Edney, J.J. 25, 80
education 182–4, 198–9
EERIs *see* Environmental Emotional Reaction
    Indices
efficiency, energy conservation 197–9
ego enhancement tourists 132
Ehrlich, P. 174
elderly persons 104–5, 110–**12**
electromagnetic fields 195
Eliot 143
emotion
    attitude formation 41–2
    EERI 10, 38–9, 119
    perception of change 26
encoding, change 27
energy 193–8, **199**
enframement, natural environments 120
Environmental Appraisal Inventory (EAI)
    156
environmental damage 170–85
    see also pollution
Environmental Emotional Reaction Indices
    (EERIs) 10, 38–9, 119
environmental load 65, 165
Environmental Personality Inventory (EPI)
    123
Environmental Preference Questionnaire
    (EPQ) 123, 126
environmental possibilism 94
environmental probabilism 94
Environmental Quality Index (EQI) 36, 119
    see also Perceived Environmental Quality
      Index
Environmental Response Inventory (ERI)
    123, 124, 126
'environmental spoiling effect' 114
environmental stress approaches 168–9
environmentally disenfranchised 94
EPI *see* Environmental Personality Inventory
EPQ *see* Environmental Preference
    Questionnaire
EQI *see* Environmental Quality Index
ERI *see* Environmental Response Inventory
Erikson, K.T. 158
erosion measures 12
errors
    cognitive maps 34–5
    technological catastrophes 159–62
Esser, A.H. 79, 80
estimation 176–7

ethics 12–13, 172–3, 182
ethological models, personal space 73
evaluations, environmental 36–7
Evans, G.W. 35, 47, 141–2
Everett, P. 190
evolutionary approaches, environmental
    preservation 121
experience, perception 3
experimental method 8–9
extraindividual behaviour patterns 165
extreme environments 163–4
Exxon Valdez 195

feminism *see* ecofeminism
Festinger, L.A. 4
field studies 8–9, 14, 76
'fight or flight response' 137
Firestone, I.J. 83–4
Fishbein, M. 116, **117**
Fisher, J.D. 72, 186, 187, 188
fishing industry 178
flats 103–4
Flin, R. 9, 154
Foa, U.G. 165
formaldehyde (HCOH) 60
Forrester, J.W. 174
fossil fuels 171
Freedman, J.L. 87
Frey, J. 146
Fridgen, J.D. 131
friendship 103
Fritz, C.E. 162
'frontier mentality' 173
fuel 171
Furnham, A. 134
furniture 96, **97**, 101
future 203–5

Gaia hypothesis 173
Gardner, G. 198
Gardner, G.T. 185, 191
Gärling, T. 27, 29–30
GAS *see* General Adaptation Syndrome
Geller, E.S. 183, 185–6, 190, 198, 201
gender 31, 71, 77, 78, 83
General Adaptation Syndrome (GAS)
    139–40, 143
geography 4
Gergen, K.J. 53, 96
Gestalt theory 2, **20–22**
Giannini, A.J. 57
Gibson, J.J. 2–3, 22–3
Gifford, R. 41, 67, 99, 126, 156
Glass, D.E. 8, 45, 108, 138, 145, 151

Goffman, E. 103
good continuation **21**
'good forms' 20
Goransen, R.E. 9, 51
governments 172
'green' issues *see* conservation; pollution
greenhouse effect 171
greenlock 130–1
groups 72, 184–5
guilt 162, 163
Gulf War veterans 192
Gump, P.V. 165

habituation 26
Haley, R.W. 192
Hall, E.T. 3–4, 69, **70**, 72
halls of residence 104, 152
Halpern, D. 103, 142, 147, 150, 151, 153
Hardin, G. 174, 177–8
Hart, R.A. 32
Hartig, T. 129–30
Hasell, M.J. 100
Hawkins, L.H. 57
Hawthorne effect **105**
Hayward, D.G. 108–**9**
Hayward, S.C. 186
hazards *see* cataclysmic stressors
HCOH *see* formaldehyde
health
    crowding 147
    light 54
    noise 46–7
    pollution 60–1, 188–92
    population density 86
    sick building syndrome 63–4
    stress 143, 146–7
    temperature 49–50
Heberlein, T.A. 198
Hedge 64, 154
Heft, H. 32
Heilbroner, R.L. 172, **173**
helping behaviour 72
Herald of Free Enterprise (Zeebrugge ferry
    disaster) 157, 159–**63**
Hershberger, R.G. 36, **37**
Herzberg, F. 106
Herzog, A.W. 147
hierarchy of needs 85, 132
high-rise flats 88, 103–4, 152, 194
higher-order beliefs 41
Hildreth, A.M. 73
hippocampus 33–4
Hodgkinson, P.E. 158, 162
hodometers 11

Holahan, C.J. 87
Holmes, T.H. 98, 142, 143
'home court advantage' 79, **80**
homonomy 122
Hopper, J.R. 179
hospitals 109, **110**
host communities 134
housing *see* residential environments
Howard, G.S. 197–8
Howell **111**
Hull, R.B. 121
Hunt, R.B. 157

Ialongo, N.S. 31
immune system 47, 140, 143
impression formation 72
incongruity 38, 120
independent variables 8
individual differences
    see also personal factors
    building design 94–5
    environmental appraisal 37
    environmental perception 25
    environmental preference 122–6
    social support 149
    spatial cognition 31
individual good-collective bad traps 178
information, cognitive maps 33–4
information processing 121, 126, 165
informed consent 12–13
Inglehart, R. 182
'inside-outside problem' 2
institutions 79, 108–13
interaction *see* social interaction
interior design 100–2
intervention strategies, environmental
    damage 180–5
interviews 76
intimacy equilibrium theory 74
invasion of privacy 13
ionisation 56–7
Iso-Ahola, S.E. 134
Ittelson, W.H. 4, 26–7
Ivinskis, A. 79

Jacobs, H.E. 200
Jerkova, H. 47
Jermier, J.M. 154
jet lag 52
Johnson, T.L. 129
Joseph 157
'just noticeable difference' 19

Kahneman, D. 165, 183

Kanizsa figure 20, **21**
Kanner, A. 142
Kaplan, R. 9, 37, 95, 119, 121, 167
Kaplan, S.
  environmental appraisal 37
  environmental preference 9, 123, 126
  natural environment 118, 119, 121
  outdoor recreation 127–8
  stress 165, 167
Karl, T. 171
Karlin, R.A. 86
Kates 155, 156
Katzev, R. 200
Katzev, R.D. 183
Kaye, S.M. 37
Keys, C. 148
King, D. 9, 51
Kira 94, 100
Klitzman, S. 146
Knopf, R.C. 127
knowledge 28
Knowles, E.S. 74
Kobasa, S.C. 151
Kopp, J.T. 200
Kremorova, B. 47

La Pière, R.T. 116
laboratory stop-distance methods 68
laboratory studies 8–9
landmarks 28, 29, 32–3, **34**
Lang, J. 95
Lanius, U.F 9, 38–9
Lanni, J.C. 76
Laufer, R. 84–5
Le Corbusier 93
lead 62
learned helplessness 176
learning
  attitude formation 41–2
  biophobias 118
  social 42, 73
  spatial 33
Lebovits, A. 62
Lee, T.R. 35, 159
legal issues, conservation 181–2, 202
legibility 30, 37, 121
leisure *see* recreation
lek systems 76
lemmings 85
Lens model of perception 23–5
Leopold, R.L. 162
Lepore, S.J. 148
levee effect 156
Levine, B.L. 184–5

Levy, L. 147
Lewin, K. 3
life events 142, 143, 146
light 52–5, 96, 101, 106, 146
Link, J.M. 50
littering 26, 185–6
Little, B.R. 70
Litton, R.B. 120
load, environmental 65, 66, 165
locale system 34
locus of control 87, 126, 156
Lucas, R.C. 130
Lynch, K. 27–8, 29, 30

MAB *see* Man and Biosphere programme
McAndrew, F.T. 36
McCallum, R. 87
McCaul, K.D. 200
McClelland, G.H. 177
Macdonald, S.M. 159
McDonald, T.P. 33
McKechnie, G.E. 9
Man and Biosphere programme (MAB) 4
management
  environmental 174
  outdoor recreation 130–1
  resources 192–201
Mandell, L. 128
maps *see* cognitive maps
marking, territorial 78
Marks, E.S. 162
Marrans, R. 128
Marshall, M. 82, 83
Maslow, A. 130, 132
Mayo, C. 78
Meadows, D.H. 191
meaning, environmental appraisal 40–1
Mearns, K. 154
Mehrabian, A. 38, 54, 65, 112, 126
Meisels, M. 73
memory, cognitive maps 33, 35
mental health
  air pollution 146
  crowding 147–8
  noise pollution 47, 147
  social support 149
mental triangulation 29
Mercer, G.W. 77
methodology, research 8–13, 14, 68
microstressors 142, 143
Middlemist, R.D. 13, 73
Milgram, S. 89, 114, 165
Miller, G.T. 188
Mishima, H.R. 200

missing hero situation 178
Mitchell, M.Y. 147–8
Mitchell, R. 88
Mitchelson 99, 100
Moar, I. 10, **11**, 35
models
   conservation behaviour 174, **175**
   consequence 89
   control 89
   density-intensity 87, 89
   ethological 73
   Lens 22–5
   Neisser's cyclical model of perception
     19, **20**
   overload 89
   person–environment interaction 15–16
   preference 121
   reinforcement affect 41–2
   stress 164–7
Moore, G.T. 32
Moos, R.H. 56, 90
Morris, P.A. 133
motivation 127–9, 131, 132–3, 187
moving house 97–8
Müller-Lyer illusion 3
Murray, M.A. 37
museums 112
mystery 37, 121

Nadel, L. 33
Naess, A. 182
Nasar, J.L. 37
national parks 127, 130–1
natural disasters 143, 155–9
natural environment 5, 115–36
naturalistic observation 69, 76
needs, hierarchy 85, 132
Neely, J. 194
neighbourhoods 113–14
neighbours 149–50
Neisser's cyclical model of perception 19,
  20
Nesbitt, P.D. 74
networks, social support 149–50, 151, 157
Newman, O. 77, 103, 150
Nielsen, J.M. 179
Nigg, J.M. 159
nitrogen cycle 171–2
nitrogen dioxides 60
noise 8, 9, 19, 44–8, 146–7
   perceived control 46
   predictability 46
   volume 46
non-purists 127

norms, social 116
norms of uninvolvement 165
novelty 38, 65, 120
nuclear disasters 159, 162–3
nurseries 108

observation 11, 42, 69, 76
occupational noise 45
O'Keefe, J. 33
OP *see* organophosphates
open-plan interiors 83, 102, 108
operant conditioning 42, 115, 180–1
Ophuls, W. 181
optic arrays 22
organophosphates (OP) 62, 191–**2**
O'Riordan, T. 116
Orleans, P. 31
Ornstein, R. 174
Osmond, H. 96
outdoor recreation 127–31
outer space 164, 204
overload models, crowding 89
Owens, K. 56
Oxley, D. 95
ozone 60, 61, 171

Page, R.A. 8
Pandey, J. 148
Pardini, A.U. 183
Parron, T. 192
part-whole relations **21**
particulates (dust) 61
Paslawskyj, L. 79
Passini, R. 30, 31
Patri, P. 93
Patterson, A.H. 84, 87
Paulus, P.B. 148
peace 127–8, 204
Pearce, P.L. 31, 132, 133, 134, 135
Pearson, J.L. 31
Peatross, F.D. 100
Peel, T.S. 54–5
Pellegrino, J.W. 33
Pepler, R.D. 50
PEQI *see* Perceived Environmental Quality
  Index
perceived control 46, 151, 176
Perceived Environmental Quality Index
  (PEQI) 10, 36, 119
perception
  see also appraisal
  environmental 18–27
  environmental damage 174–7
  introduction 2–3

natural disasters 156–7
pollution 59
risks 7, 159
temperature 48, 51
wind 56
performance *see* task performance
person–environment interaction models
    15–16
person–thing orientation scales 122, 126
personal factors
    see also individual differences
    crowding 87–8
    environmental preference 126
    privacy 83
    residential satisfaction 100
    territory 77
personal projects analysis 124
personal space 3–4, 67–75
personalisation 78, **98**
personality
    see also disposition
    environmental 122, 123
    Environmental Personality Inventory 123
    natural disasters 156–7
    personal space 72
    stress 151
pesticides 191–2, **193**
Phifer, J.F. 151
physical environment 44–66
    see also built environment; natural
        environment
    cognition 5–7
    crowding 88
    personal space 71
    privacy 83–4, 85
    stress 142, 143, 145–7, 155–63
    territory 77
physiological responses
    organophosphates 192
    stress 139–40, 143, 165, 167–8
Piaget, J. 31–2
Pitt, D.G. 9, 130–1
place attachment 40, 97–8
place identity 124
planfulness 36
planning, urban 35–6
Platt, J. 178–9
playgrounds 108–**9**
pleasure–arousal hypothesis 38
political issues
    conservation 201
    environmental problems 172
pollution
    air 58–61, 146, 188–90, 191

commons dilemma 178
environmental toxins 62–4
future 204
health 188–92
radiation 159, 162–3
Weber's Law 26
Ponomarenko, I.J. 47
population
    density 85–9, **90**, 147–8
    growth 170, 204
    limitation mechanisms 85–6
Porteus 94
possibilism, environmental 94
post occupancy evaluation 95
post-traumatic stress disorder (PTSD) 157–8
postmaterialism 182
Poulton, E.C. 50
preferences
    EPQ 123, 126
    leisure 130
    natural environment 119–26
    residential 99–100
preparedness 118
preservation strategies 180–5
    see also conservation
preservationism 118
President's Commission on Americans
    Outdoors 128, 129
pressure
    air 58, 146
    social 128, 179
primary territories 77, 78, 79
primitive beliefs 41
prior residence effect 76
prisoner-of-experience phenomenon 177
prisons 112, 148
privacy 13, 82–5, 95, 100, 110
probabilism, environmental 94
propositional storage 33
protection 73
proxemics 67–91
proximity **21**
Pruitt-Igoe project 103
psychic numbing 162
psychological ecology 3
psychological responses
    natural disasters 157–9
    organophosphates 192
    stress 140–1, 145, 167–8
psychophysics 2, 19
PTSD *see* post-traumatic stress disorder
public territories 77, 78, 79
public transport 190–1
punishment 179, 181, 199

purists 127
purpose 41

radiation 159, 162–3, 188–9
radon gas 62, **63**, 188–**9**, **190**
Rahe, R.H. 142, 143
rate of time preference 201
Reason, J. 159–61
reasoned action, theory of 116, 117
recognition 19
recreation 127–31
recycling 180, 183, **200–1**
re-entry shock 164
reinforcement affect model 41–2
relationships, residential 103
religion 117
renewable energy 197–8
research
    major areas 5–8
    methods 8–13, 14, 68
residential environments 97–105
    energy conservation 193, 194, **196**, **197**
    institutions 108–13
    neighbourhoods 113–14
    population density 147–8
    stress 152–3
residential homes 110–12
resources
    community management 184–5
    conflict 170–1, 172
    conservation 204
    management 192–201
resourcism 118
REST *see* restricted environment stimulation
    therapy
restoration 127–8
restricted environment stimulation therapy
    (REST) 167
retirement homes 104–5
Revell, G.R.B. 121
reward 179, 180–2, 199
Rice, B. 105
Rim, Y. 56
risk 7, 154, 159, 174–7
road rage 155
Rodin, J. 86, 168
Rohe, W. 87
rooms 95–7, 100–2, 103
Rosen, S. 47
Ross, H. 96
Rossman, B.B. 128
Rotton, J. 61, 146
Ruback, R.B. 148
Rubonis, A.V. 157

Russell, J.A. 10, 38–9, 54, 96, 119

Saarinen, T.F. 28
SAD *see* seasonal affective disorder
Sadalla, E.K. 95, 96, 103
Saegert, S. 86
Samuelson, C.D. 182–3
satisfaction
    leisure 130
    residential 99–100
    travelling 133–4
Schmidt, F.N. 156
Schmidt, S. 31
schools 108, 165
Schrodt, P.A. 80
Sears, D.O. 114
seasonal affective disorder (SAD) 52, 146
Sebba, R. 115, 119
secondary territories 77, 78, 79
Segall, M.H. 3, 24
self-report techniques 10, **11**
self-traps 178
Seligman, M.E.P. 118, 138, 176
Sellafield 159
Selye, H. 139
Sensation Seeking Scale 123, **125**, 126
sequential maps 28
serotonin irritation syndrome 57
sex differences
    personal space 71
    privacy 83
    spatial cognition 31
    territory 77, 78
Sheets, V.S. 96
shift work 52
shipping disasters 157, 159–62
Shiva, V. 182
sick building syndrome 63–4, 66, 154
Siegel, W.A. 32
Sienkiewicz, Z. 195
simulations 9, 68
Singer, J.E. 8, 45, 145, 151
single-family houses 102–3
Sitka deer 86
situational factors
    crowding 88
    personal space 70–1
    privacy 83–4
    territory 77
size, classrooms 108
size constancy 21, **23**
Sjoberg, P. 159
sketch map technique 27–9
skin temperature 48

Skinner 42
Slotsky, R.J. 129
Slovic, P. 176
smells 61
Smith, H.W. 76, 77–8
smoking 61
social behaviour
    darkness/light 53
    extreme environments 164
    noise 48
    temperature 50
social environment 7, 67–91, 70–1, 84,
    147–50
social facilitation effect 88
social interaction, population density 87
social learning 42, 73, 115
social norms 116
social penetration, personal space 74
social physics approach, crowding 89
social pressure 128, 179
social psychology 3–4
Social Readjustment Rating Scale 143, **144**
social support networks **149**–50, 151, 157
social traps 178–9, 181
sociofugal environments 96, **97**
sociopetal environments 96, **97**
solar energy 197–8
Sommer, R. 4, 12, 67, 73, 96, 108, 204–5
Sommers, P. 56
Sonnenfeld, J. 36
sound 44
Southgate **152**, **153**
space
    see also proxemics
    communal 111
    interior design 100–2
    outer 164, 204
    personal 3–4, 67–75
    room design 95
    schools 108
    work environments 107–8
space adaptation syndrome 164
spatial cognition 27–36, 43
spatial maps 28
Spivey, G.H. 62
'spoiling effect', environmental 114
Srivastava, R.K. 54–5
Stankey, G.H. 127
Stansfield, S.A. 47
status 70–1
Stea, D. 28, 34–5
Stellman, J.M. 146
Stephens, R. 192
Stern, P.C. 185, 191, 193, 198

Steven, G. 74
Stevens, W. 198
Stewart, M. 158, 162
Stewart, T.R. 24
stimulation, ambient 44
stimulation seeking 128
stimulus detection 19
stimulus screening 123, 126
Stokols, D. 2, 85, 100, 154
Stone, E.F. 84
Stough, R.R. 79
street gangs 81
stress 7, 19, 100, 137–69, 176
stress response 137, 142, 143–5
stress theory 176
stressors
    ambient 142, 143, 145–55
    cataclysmic 142, 143, 155–63
    environmental 141–2
    nature 137–8
Studebaker, S. 88
student accommodation 104, 148
subjects, ethical problems 12–13
Suedfeld, P. 167
suicide rates 192
sulphur dioxide 60
Sundstrom, E. 47, 83, 85, 95, 106, 107,
    108, 126
superordinate scale bias 35
support spaces 101
support systems 101
surprisingness 38, 120
survey knowledge 28
survivor guilt 162, 163

Tarnopolsky, A. 147
task performance
    air pollution 61
    colour 54
    definition 12
    noise 47
    population density 86
    stress 145
    temperature 50
taxon system 34
Taylor, R.B. 76, 79
Taylor, S. 176
technological catastrophes 159–63
Teddlie, C. 89
temperature 48–51, 146
territory 75–81
three-factor theory, environmental
    appraisal 38
Three Mile Island 62, 159, 162, 163

threshold 19
Thrower, T. 11
Tinsley, H.E. 129
tobacco smoke 61
Tolman, E.C. 27
top-down processing 19, **20**
tourism 131–4, **135**
toxins, environmental 62–4
trace measures 12
transactional model of stress 138
transactionalists 3
transport 45, 147, 154–5, 190–1, 193–4
traps *see* social traps
travel 131–4, **135**
Trites 109, **110**
Turner, C.W. 155
Tversky, A. 183

Ulehla, Z.J. 128
Ulrich, R.S. 109, 118
understimulation approaches, stress 165–7
United Nations Educational, Scientific and
    Cultural Organization (UNESCO) 4
urban planning 35–6
US Riot Commission (1968) 51

Valins, S. 87
values
    attitudes 41
    goals 179, **180**
    outdoor recreation 128
    postmaterialistic 182
vandalism 152, 167, 186–8
variables 8
Vaughan, E. 176
VDUs *see* video display units
Veitch, J.A. 53
vicarious learning 42
video display units (VDUs) 106
Vinsel, A. 95

Wang, T.H. 200
war 204

Warren, D.I. 113–14
waste disposal 180, 200
    see also littering
water 178, 198–200
Watson, B. 190
wayfinding 5–6, 29–30, 31
weather 50, 58, 146
Weber, M. 2
Weber's Law 19, 26
Welch, B.L. 146–7
Wener, R. 148
Westin, A.F. 82, **84**
Wexner, L.B. 55
White, K. 117
White, M. 148–9
White, S. 32
wind 55–6
Wohlwill, J.F. 32, 38, 39, 120, 167
Wolfe, M. 84–5
Womble, P. 88
women 31, 71
Worchel, S. 89
work
    environment 105–8
    noise exposure 45, 47, 146–7
    shifts 52
    stress 153–5
Wright, H. 4

Yancey 103, 150
Yates, S. 183
Yerkes-Dodson Law 105–6, 120, 165
Yoors, J. 84
you-are-here maps 35

Zajonc 57, 88
Zeitgebers 52
Zimolong, B. 154
Zlutnik, S. 85
zoos 112–13
Zube, E.H. 9, 36, 126, 130–1
Zubek, J. 167

PICTURE CREDITS

The author and publisher would like to thank the following copyright holders for their permission to use material in this book:

Academic Press for Figure 4.2 (p.68) from M.P. Duke and S. Nowicki (1972) 'A new measure and social learning model for interpersonal distance' *Journal of Experimental Research in Personality*, 6, 119–132; **AKG Photo** for Figure 2.11 (p.40); **Allyn & Bacon** for Figures 4.6 (p.80), 4.7 (p.81) and Box 6.2 (p.124); **American Psychological Association** for Figure 5.10 (p.111) from S.C. Howell (1980) 'Environments as hypotheses in human aging research' in L. Poon (ed.) *Aging in the 1980's*, copyright © 1980 by the American Psychological Association. Adapted with permission, Table 8.2 (p.194) and 8.3 (p.196) from C.P. Stern and G. Gardner (1981) Psychological research and energy policy, *American Psychologist*, 36, 329–342, copyright © 1981 by the American Psychological Association, reprinted by permission; **Architectural Association** for Figure 5.6 (p.104); **Steve Bell** for Figure 9.1 (p.205); **Brooks/Cole Publishing Company** for Figure 4.5 (p.75), 4.9 (p.91), Table 2.1 (p.32), Box 3.5 (p.53) and Figure 7.1 (p.138), from *Environmental Psychology* by F.T. McAndrew. Copyright © 1993 Brooks/Cole Publishing Company, Pacific Grove, CA 93950, a division of International Thomson Publishing Inc. By permission of the publisher; **Cambridge University Press** for Box 7.6 (p.161) from J. Reason (1990) *Human Error*; **J Allan Cash** for Figure 5.1 (p.93, right); **Eastern Counties Newspapers** for Figure 1.1(a) (p.3); **Baruch Fischoff** for Figure 8.8 (p.193) from 'Handling Hazards', *Environment*, 20, 16–20, published by Heldref Publications; **Greenpeace** for Figure 8.5 (p.187); **Holt, Rinehart and Winston** for Figure 2.4 (p.24) from *An Introduction to Environmental Psychology* by W.H. Ittelson and H.M. Proshanky, copyright © 1974 by Holt, Rinehart and Winston, Figures 2.5 (p.28) and 2.6 (p.34) from *Environmental Psychology*, Fourth Edition by P.A. Bell, A. Baum, J.D. Fischer and T.C. Greene, copyright © 1996 by Holt, Rinehart and Winson, and Figure 7.3 (p.141) from *Introduction to Psychology*, Eleventh Edition by R.L. Atkinson, R.C. Atkinson, E.E. Smith and D.J. Bem, copyright © 1993 by Harcourt Brace & Company, reproduced by permission of the publisher; **Hulton Getty** for Figure 5.11 (p.113); **Life File** for Figures 1.2 (p.6), 1.4 (p.15), 5.1 (p.93, left), 5.3 (p.98) and 6.3 (p.122); **National Radiological Protection Board** for Figures 3.5 (p.63), 8.6 (p.189) and 8.7 (p.190); **Prentice Hall** for Figure 6.1 (p.117) from *Understanding Attitudes and Predicting Social Behavior* by Azjen/Fishbein, © 1980. Adapted by permission of Prentice-Hall, Inc., Upper Saddle River, NJ; **Routledge** for Box 7.6 (p.161) from P. Hodgkinson and M. Stewart (1991) *Coping with Catastrophe*; **Taylor and Francis** for Figures 7.4 (p.148) and 7.7 (p.153) from D. Halpern (1995) *Mental Health and the built environment*; **John Wiley & Sons, Inc.** for Figures 3.2 (p.49) and 4.8 (p.90).

Further titles in the *Applying Psychology to...* series are available from Hodder & Stoughton.

0340 64756 6 **Applying Psychology to Health** by Philip Banyard £7.99 ☐

0340 64392 7 **Applying Psychology to Early Child Development** £7.99 ☐

0340 64758 2 **Applying Psychology to Organisations** by Sheila Heyward £7.99 ☐

0340 64329 3 **Applying Psychology to Crime** by Julie Harrower £8.99 ☐

0340 64757 4 **Applying Psychology to the Environment** by Susan Cave £8.99 ☐

For full details of this series, please call Kerry Grieves at Hodder & Stoughton on 0171 873 6246. Look out for the forthcoming *Applying Psychology to Sport*.

All Hodder & Stoughton *Educational* books are available at your local bookshop, or can be ordered direct from the publisher. Just tick the titles you would like and complete the details below. Prices and availability are subject to change without prior notice.

Please enclose a cheque or postal order made payable to *Bookpoint Limited*, and send to: Hodder & Stoughton *Educational*, 39 Milton Park, Abingdon, Oxon OX14 4TD, UK. EMail address: orders@bookpoint.co.uk

Buy four books from the selection above and get free postage and packaging. Just send a cheque or postal order to the value of the total cover price of four books. Alternatively, if you wish to buy fewer than four books the following postage and packaging applies:

UK & BFPO £4.30 for one book; £6.30 for two books; £8.30 for three books

Overseas and Eire: £4.80 for one book; £7.10 for two or three books (surface mail)

If you would like to pay by credit card, our centre team would be delighted to take your order by telephone. Our direct line (44) 01235 400414 (lines open 9.00 am–6.00 pm, Monday to Saturday, with a 24 hour answering service). Alternatively you can send a fax to (44) 01235 400454.

Title_____ First name_____ Surname_____

Address _____

_____

_____

Postcode _____ Daytime telephone no. _____

If you would prefer to pay by credit card, please complete:

Please debit my Master Card / Access / Diner's Card / American Express (delete as applicable)

Card number ☐☐☐☐☐ ☐☐☐☐☐ ☐☐☐☐☐ ☐☐☐☐☐

Expiry date _____ Signature _____

If you would not like to receive further information on our products, please tick the box ☐.